Where Faith Meets Culture

Where Faith Meets Culture

A *Radix* Magazine Anthology

Margaret G. **Alter**, Kurt **Armstrong**, Robert **Bellah**, Bob **Buford**, Krista **Faries**, David **Fetcho**, Susan English **Fetcho**, Sharon **Gallagher**, David W. **Gill**, Joel B. **Green**, Os **Guinness**, Virginia **Hearn**, Walter R. **Hearn**, Donald **Heinz**, Margaret McBride **Horwitz**, Mark **Labberton**, Henri **Nouwen**, Earl F. **Palmer**, Susan S. **Phillips**, Dan **Ouellette**, Steve **Scott**, *and* Luci **Shaw**

EDITED BY **SHARON GALLAGHER**

CASCADE *Books* • Eugene, Oregon

WHERE FAITH MEETS CULTURE
A *Radix* Magazine Anthology

Copyright © 2010 Wipf and Stock Publishers. All rights reserved. Except for brief quotations in critical publications or reviews, no part of this book may be reproduced in any manner without prior written permission from the publisher. Write: Permissions, Wipf and Stock Publishers, 199 W. 8th Ave., Suite 3, Eugene, OR 97401.

Cascade Books
An Imprint of Wipf and Stock Publishers
199 W. 8th Ave., Suite 3
Eugene, OR 97401

www.wipfandstock.com

ISBN 13: 978-1-60899-144-0

Cataloging-in-Publication data:

    Where faith meets culture: a *Radix* magazine anthology / edited by Sharon Gallagher.

    xii + 228 p. ; 23 cm. Includes bibliographical references.

    ISBN 13: 978-1-60899-144-0

    1. Christianity and culture. 2. Spiritual life—Christianity. 3. Christian life. I. Gallagher, Sharon. II. Title.

BR115 .C8 w58 2010

Manufactured in the U.S.A.

With gratitude to the *Radix* writers

How beautiful on the mountains

are the feet of those who bring good news,

who proclaim peace, who bring good tidings,

who proclaim salvation,

who say to Zion, your God reigns!

Isaiah 52:7 (NIV)

Contents

Acknowledgments • xi

I The Good Life: Wholeness and Meaning

1 Intimacy, Fecundity, and Ecstasy • 3
   by Henri Nouwen
   Because we have a home and belong to the Lord, we can be in the midst of the network of wounds and needs without being pulled apart.

2 Reflections on a Meaning-Filled Life • 16
   by Bob Buford
   For me prayer is not separate from daily life. It's a way of being. It's like being with my wife for a weekend at the farm. We're there with one another.

3 Wounds of Childhood and the Grace of God • 26
   by Margaret G. Alter
   We seem desperately to believe in a pain-free world where life is simple and problems are manageable, but we find ourselves repeatedly called by God into a complex demanding life.

II Discipleship: Call and Response

4 The Constellation of God's Call • 35
   by Mark Labberton
   God's call on our lives enables us to see a constellation where before we had seen only stars.

5 Knowing Means Doing: A Challenge to Think Christianly • 40
   by Os Guinness
   What does it mean to be part of the world's educated elite, and be responsible to the Lord for that knowledge?

6 The Earth Is the Lord's: Stewardship in an Age of Crisis • 48
by Sharon Gallagher
As a matter of discipleship, Christians should be in the forefront of the environmental movement. Scripture reveals a God who delights in Creation.

III Contemporary Challenges

7 Modern Technology: Servant and Master • 57
by David W. Gill
What has been lost is the value of the inefficient, the non-rational, the aesthetic, the spiritual, the traditional.

8 Finding Your Way in Science and Faith • 68
by Walter R. Hearn
If science gives us maps, faith gives us a compass. We need both.

9 Why Love Will Always Be a Poor Investment • 82
by Kurt Armstrong
It is the relationship-as-commodity mentality and not fear of the abuses of traditional marriage that has fostered today's mood of suspicion toward making a lifelong commitment.

IV The Word Speaks to Life

10 Guess Who's Coming to Dinner: Sitting at the Table with the Prodigal Son • 91
by Joel B. Green
How could Jesus turn a question, about whether we will be invited, into an examination of the lists of those whom we invite?

11 Theological Themes in the Fiction of C. S. Lewis: Good and Evil in the Chronicles of Narnia • 102
by Earl F. Palmer
In Prince Caspian the meeting with Aslan takes time. Lewis saw discipleship as a thousand single steps.

12 Care of Souls in Today's America • 114
by Robert Bellah
The faith we proclaim comes alive when it is lived in community, above all when it is lived in worship, in the word and sacrament that heal us, and transform us, and that reaffirm our membership in one body.

V Art and Soul

13 The Need to Pay Attention: Darkness, Light, and the Visionary Eye • 127
by Luci Shaw
Missing our cues, we fail to notice the fingerprints of the Creator in the ordinary textures and phenomena of living because we are distracted by daily urgencies.

14 The Rich Legacy of Christian Music • 140
   by Donald Heinz
   Angels sang Gloria in excelsis over Bethlehem. The New Testament set Christ's birth to music. Christ was music: the early church called him God's song.

15 The Art of Worship: Breaking Our Tools to Receive God's Gifts • 150
   by David and Susan Fetcho
   What does it take to allow the arts their rightful place at the table of our worship? . . . Art depends for its life on discovery and risk, surprise, gift, and grace.

VI Spiritual Formation

16 Sabbath Living • 159
   by Susan S. Phillips
   The Sabbath sanctifies time. So often we think of space as sanctified. We create a temple or church in which to contemplate God. The Sabbath is a "temple in time."

17 East Meets West: The Distinctives of Christian Meditation • 170
   by Steve Scott
   A Christian grounding must be the testing area for the truth-claims of any spiritual technique . . . Jesus shifts our attention from the void of our own emptiness to the inexhaustible depths of his grace.

18 Journal-Keeping: The Poor Person's Art • 179
   by Virginia Hearn
   A personal journal can be a remarkable aid to spiritual growth. In the Bible, God's people were frequently told to remember what the Lord had done for them.

VII Media

19 It's a Wonderful Life: Charles Dickens's *A Christmas Carol* and Frank Capra's Film • 189
   by Margaret Horwitz
   "A Christmas Carol" is a story of salvation, and "It's a Wonderful Life" is a story of answered prayer. Both of them demonstrate the consequences of selfish, as opposed to compassionate, behavior in relation to community.

20 The Gospel Songs of Bob Dylan and Mavis Staples • 201
   by Dan Ouellette
   Two dynamic albums give witness to the power of Gospel music.

21 Why Harry Potter Is Not the Chronicles of Narnia • 206
   by Krista Faries
   There are two things that set the Chronicles of Narnia apart from the Harry Potter books. The first is that the Chronicles of Narnia are transformational. The characters grow and change, and so do we. The second is, in a word, Aslan.

List of Contributors • 215

Permissions • 218

Bibliography • 221

Praise for *Radix* Magazine • 227

Acknowledgments

THANK YOU TO THE authors for the articles published in this anthology and for all the articles they've written for *Radix* over the years. We're grateful for the work of these and the other authors, artists, and poets whose work has filled the pages of *Radix* with wisdom and beauty and just the right turn of phrase.

The magazine is produced by a multitalented and much-appreciated team. Thank you to copy editor Virginia Hearn, poetry editor Luci Shaw, music editor Dan Ouellette, subscription manager Joyce Li, and editorial assistants Bill Colbert and Matt Horwitz.

We're also grateful for the faithful direction and encouragement of the board of trustees: Cully Anderson, Susan Fetcho, Maj-Britt Hilstrom, Susan Phillips, and Raymond Yee.

All these people are part of the community that has created and sustained *Radix* over the years. It continues to be a rich and rewarding collaboration.

Sharon Gallagher, *Radix* editor

I

The Good Life
Wholeness and Meaning

1

Intimacy, Fecundity, and Ecstasy

Henri Nouwen

IN JOHN'S GOSPEL JESUS speaks about the vine and the branches. He says, "Make your home in me as I have made mine in you. When you remain in me, with me in you, you will bear ample fruit. And I told you so, so that my joy can be in you and your joy can be complete." I would like to reflect on those words.

About a year or two ago I met a man named Jean Vanier. Jean was a professor of philosophy in Toronto. He came from an aristocratic family and studied in Paris. His father, a man with great prestige, was governor-general in Canada and had been Canadian ambassador to France. Jean, his son, was a man who might have followed in his father's footsteps. But one day Jean met a priest who worked with severely handicapped people. He was so impressed by the intimate contact this priest had with those people that he, too, decided he wanted to live his life with severely mentally handicapped people. He formed a small community called L'Arche (The Ark) and invited nonhandicapped people to live in households with handicapped people.

Something very deep happened there to Jean and to the others. They began to discover more fully what it means to live a life in Christ, a spiritual life. That one L'Arche community became many communities and they are now all over in France, the United States, Africa, Haiti, and other places. One community is in Mobile, Alabama, and another in Erie, Pennsylvania. They are being organized in Boston and Washington, D.C.

Out of that experience of living with severely handicapped people, Jean Vanier came to a conclusion, a kind of vision, that all human beings have three rights, or three privileges. They are the right and privilege of intimacy, the right and privilege of fecundity, and the right and privilege of ecstasy. He told me this when we were having a retreat together and I really liked the words: *intimacy, fecundity, ecstasy*. I sort of carried them around with me, not deliberately thinking much about them, until I was reading the text from John which I just mentioned. There, when Jesus said, "Make your home in me as I have made mine in you," I realized he was speaking about *intimacy*. "And when you remain in me, with me in you, you will bear ample fruit." There he was speaking about *fecundity*. "And I told you this so that my joy can be in you and your joy can be complete." That is *ecstasy*.

I was very moved that Jean Vanier had discovered these qualities through living with people who are weak, vulnerable, and broken. In their brokenness they revealed what the spiritual life is all about. With those broken people Jean had a real encounter with the Lord.

INTIMACY

I am going to talk first about intimacy. I invite you to struggle with me, because what I want to do first is describe to you how I have been experiencing life here in the U.S., particularly in the schools in which I've been teaching, and see if we can make some inner connection.

First I would like to share some of my impressions. One thing that has struck me is that the people with whom I live as well as I myself are struggling with strong needs. We have real neediness for affection, for attention, for having some influence, for power, for being recognized and acknowledged. I am overwhelmed by those needs at times. I keep realizing how intense they are. Sometimes those needs keep me, and others, wondering if we are really loved, if we are really accepted, if we are really cared for.

One tragedy is that when those needs are satisfied, often it's for a very short time. People keep looking for more affirmation. It is frightening that those who have received a lot of praise and acknowledgment sometimes are the most fearful people. They are afraid that maybe tomorrow it won't be so good. "Oh yes, you praised me yesterday, but what about today?" "Oh yes, that show went well, but having to do the next show makes me nervous again." Sometimes you see people, who are famous and highly acclaimed, killing themselves out of fear of not being able to hold on to that acknowledgment.

I see that need not only in people who have secular professions, but also in the ministry and in myself. When I give a wonderful sermon about humility, I want to know what everybody thinks about it. Did you like my sermon? What did you think about it? So that need is always there.

So I've been asking myself, "Where do those needs come from?" When I started identifying them, I realized that quite often needs are born out of wounds, out of an experience of not being fully accepted, not being really loved, not being fully cared for. A lot of our attention and searching is trying to identify those wounds. What happened somewhere in the past that made me so needy? In counseling or psychoanalysis sometimes a lot of energy is invested in identifying the culprit. "Yes, mother didn't really love me fully, or the church didn't, or the people I was living with didn't."

Something went wrong that gives a person that sense of not being fully welcomed in life. That feeling keeps us going around and around to find that sense of belonging that we still don't really have. Sometimes we think that even when we have identified the culprit the explanation becomes an excuse. We explain where the needs come from and then excuse ourselves with "Well, that's who I am. Something went wrong, and that's why I'm still doing all this."

Looking at this network of wounds and needs, you realize that it can reach far back into history as well as extend far into the future. If you wonder why you were wounded, you realize that those who wounded you also had needs. Their needs were born out of their wounds—and on and on it goes. You can say to yourself, "I'm not going to hurt anybody." But just wait awhile. Somebody will accuse you of not understanding them, not really caring for them, or not really loving them. Against our best desire to be a really good person we still find that we hurt people. And so there is that interlocking network of wounds and needs that stretches out. It is what Jesus called the *world*.

Jesus said, "If you love those who love you, what thanks can you expect? If you loan to those who are going to give you back the same amount, what is special about that? If you care for those who care for you, what news is that?"

How do we live in this world, entangled in that network? Is there another way of living? Jesus said, "Make your home in me, as I have made mine in you."

Now that is an incredible statement; it means that we have a *home*. God has given us a home. The problem may be that we are never there. The tragedy of life is that although we have a home, we always question it and are looking for one in the world, in that network of wounds and needs, hoping to come to a sense of home. But we don't have to look for it, because it's there. "Make your home in me as I have made my home in you."

That image of home is very central in the Old and New Testaments. There are many words about home, house, tent, dwelling place, temple, refuge. The Lord often speaks about his home: "Come to my home; see where I live; in the house of my Father are many dwelling places." There are also many references to home in the Psalms.

Jesus said, "I have made my home in you, I have decided that *you* are going to be my home. Are you willing to claim that home as yours? Are you willing to make your home there too? Are you willing to live there, where I have made my dwelling place?" Jesus spoke about home as the place of love, the first love. "I have made my home in you so that you can hear the voice of the first love." We can receive and give love only because we have been loved first. We can receive acceptance and give acceptance only because we have been accepted, because Jesus has built a home for us, a home of love, a home of full, unconditional, unlimited acceptance. That is the home we have to claim as ours, so that we don't have to stay in that network of needs and wounds, but can realize that there is a home where we belong.

To claim our home where the Lord has built his is an essential quality of the spiritual life. Jesus said to the disciples, "You do not belong to the world, just as I do not belong to the world. Therefore, I am sending you into the world as my Father sends me into the world." The great paradox of the spiritual life is that precisely because we have a home and belong to the Lord, we can be in the midst of the network of wounds and needs without being pulled apart and destroyed. We are firmly anchored in the house of God.

The contemplative life and the prayerful life are both lives in which you slowly descend with the mind into the heart. The idea that God has made his home in us so that we can make our home in him should be more than just a nice idea. It sounds good, but can we start to experience that at-homeness and make it a personal truth? Or is it just a wonderful idea that in fact does not motivate us? Prayer is to descend with the mind into the heart, so the idea that we have a home in God becomes a spiritual knowledge, a knowledge of the heart (*heart* meaning the center of the whole person).

Prayer and silence and Scripture reading and meditation are all part of that movement from the head into the heart, so that the Word, the knowledge of God, can become flesh in us, in an ongoing incarnation. The idea that God has built his home in us becomes so real that when we preach or teach or minister or help "in the name of the Lord" it means something. That name has become our dwelling place, our home. If I say something to you "in the name of the Lord," it means that the *name* is the *place*. It is the home. "Where are you?" "I am in the name." "Where are you living?" "In the name." So whatever you do—speak, eat, drink, play, work, or teach—do it in the name. That is the space where it's happening, and that has to become a spiritual truth.

To the degree that this truth becomes true spiritual knowledge for us, we will come to experience that the Lord whom we encounter in the center of our heart is the Lord who embraces all human beings in his love. The closer we come to encounter the Lord who became flesh, the more we realize that the Word who became flesh took on all human flesh, all humanity, in time and space. The mystery is that the closer we come to the heart of God, the closer we come to the heart of the people of God. We will discover that precisely when we are in the most intimate corner of our being, we find ourselves most intimately connected with the people of the world. That is the mystery of the Incarnation.

It is a profound experience to realize that what is most intimate is most universal, that what is most personal is most all-embracing, and that the intimacy of prayer leads to an intimacy of solidarity with the people of the world. When we pray to the Lord it is not Henri Nouwen or Mary or John or any one individual who prays, but the Spirit of God prays in you, and the Spirit is the spirit of all people. In the instant of encounter with the Lord, it's not just you who prays, but in you all humanity prays, and if God hears your prayer he touches not just you individually, but you who stand there in the name of all people.

The great mystical truth of the spiritual life is that the more intimately connected you are with the Lord, the more in solidarity you are with all the suffering people of the world. And that solidarity, that intimacy with God's people, leads you to all sorts of places you have never dreamed of. Suddenly you find yourself moving to inner places and outer places depending on where the Voice sounds. That's an incredible experience. You aren't going around out of need anymore but out of the freedom of being so deeply loved and so deeply accepted that it doesn't matter it you are in Nicaragua or Norway or Holland, because you are always in the house of the Lord. The house of the Lord is the most intimate place and it is also the widest. All humanity is part of that household.

It is not possible for you to see God in the world, but God in you can see God in the world. If you have God in your heart, you see God in the world; if you have a demon in your heart, you see the demonic in the world. Heart speaks to heart, solitude speaks to solitude, God speaks to God. The spiritual life is a participation in the divine life in which you've been lifted up to the Trinitarian mystery of God's inner life, where God speaks to God. If you see God in the eyes of the people, it is God in you who opens your eyes to see God in those people. That's a mysterious spiritual mutuality that comes to you through intimacy.

FECUNDITY

Now, let me say something about fecundity. Jesus said, "When you remain in me, with me in you, then you will bear ample fruit." That's fecundity. And that fruit is born out of intimacy. I am slowly discovering that the Lord asks us to be fruitful but he does not ask us to be productive. There is a distinction between fruitfulness and productivity or successfulness or effectiveness. We western pragmatic people haven't always fully understood that distinction.

A Product is something you make. You do this, and this and this, and you have a product. And if you do it again, you have the same product. And if you do it again and again and again you have a lot of products and people say you are quite productive. Every time I call my brother in Holland, he asks, "Henri, did you write another book?" I say, "Yes, I wrote another book." "How many copies did you sell?" "Did you read it?" I ask. "No, no; how many copies did you sell?" He wants to know because he wants to have a brother who is productive and successful. But if he wants me to sell a lot of copies, I might have to write another type of book.

People are admired for their productivity. "How many members are in your church? Oh, that's a lot! You're doing well." Or "How many votes did you collect?" or "How many houses did you call on?" We are people of statistics. We believe that numbers tell us who we are. The mentality of productivity is seductive. We fall into the trap of thinking that people who produce a lot—whether material things or ideological things or even spiritual things—are people worth admiring.

But the Lord is not talking about that. He is not asking us to produce a lot so we can feel good about ourselves. He is asking us to be fruitful. And we don't *make* fruit. We receive fruit as a gift and say, "That is very beautiful." We don't say, "I always thought it would look exactly like this." What we don't make, we cannot predict or define. The most beautiful example of this is the child. You don't make love to "make a child"; it's awful to use that language. A child is not a product, it is a gift. When you look at a child and say it is the most beautiful child that has ever been, you are always right. Because it is unique, it has never been before. It is a gift born out of love and out of mutual vulnerability.

If I make something, I have to be in control of the situation. I know that I put *this* there and *that* there. I follow the rules, and there it is. But if I want fruit, I enter into a place of vulnerability. People who love one another become extremely vulnerable. They take off their armor, their weapons, their defenses. They love one another because they love one another. Love has no other goal than love itself. They don't look beyond each other. But out of that, fruit is born and fruit is received in gratitude as a gift, as something beyond our expectation. That is true of all the fruits of the Spirit. Joy, gentleness, compassion, and care are fruits.

If you have a little community and you ask, "Are we feeling joyful?" and somebody says, "Listen, I don't feel fruitful; tell me how I get there," you cannot say, "Do *one*, *two*, and *three* and you will be joyful." Joy is not made, peace is not made, compassion is not made. They are fruits.

Probably the most important quality of fruit is that we have to leave it alone in order for it to grow. We cannot take the seed out and check it every two minutes to see if it is growing. We have to leave it alone or it won't grow. What we can do is take the weeds around it away and be sure that it is safe for it to grow.

That is one of the main qualities of the spiritual life. We set very gentle boundaries within which the fruit can grow. That is what worship is all about. That is what the Eucharist is all about. That is what preaching and teaching are all about. That is what healing and medical care and good law practice are really all about: allowing people to receive the fruit of their life without fear.

Take the Eucharist. A little bit of bread, not enough to take your hunger away. A little bit of wine, not enough to take your thirst away. A few readings, not enough to take your ignorance away. You stand there in a circle and you are poor people. And then you say, "The Lord is in our midst." Precisely when we discover our vulnerability in that circle, in the community of the faithful, we say, "Here is the Lord. This is the day that the Lord has made. He is among us." That is the spiritual fruit that comes among us when we join hands in mutual vulnerability.

That is what counseling is about. You are very careful to say a few things to create a climate in which God's healing power can manifest itself and heal that person. That is what medical care is about—letting the healing forces come freely into the sick person.

But we are so terribly manipulative that we always want to fill up empty spaces. We want more songs, more hymns, more sermons, more words, more projects to fill up our time. We fear empty space.

Most people are afraid of silence. If someone says, "Let's be silent," the only question is, when are we going to stop this and talk again? Silence is something we have to learn. It takes a lot of time to feel silence as a space where the fruit can grow. And fruitfulness takes place in the most unexpected places.

When I was in Nicaragua recently I saw some of those unexpected fruits. I went to Latin America to be productive, to do something good for the people, to help them take care of their problems and clean up the mess. But as soon as I got there I realized that, if anything, I had to learn to receive the gift of the people. People wanted to give me something. Could I receive it?

There was a 17-year-old boy who was shot and killed in Lima. I went to pray with the boy's family. A little later there was a Eucharist in the church and I celebrated it. I told myself I had to say something to the boy's mother because, imagine a 17-year-old son killed—what agony, what pain. I was a little nervous as you always are when you have to go into a situation that is painful.

After the mass, I thought, now I have to go to the mother and her family and tell them that I have some understanding of what is going on. I thought I should know what to say, with all my education and psychological training, but I was really struggling with trying to say words. I came close to the family and said, "I want to say how much I really feel with you." But I didn't even look at the people. I was just struggling with saying it. And I looked up and I saw a woman in front of me and two sons, and an aunt and an uncle, and a grandparent, all standing there. And they said, "*Gracias, Padre, gracias. Muchas gracias. Muchas gracias. Muchísimas gracias.*" I said, "I just want to say . . . "*Gracias, Padre, muchísimas gracias.*" I said, "I just wanted to let you know how much . . ." "*Gracias, Padre, muchas gracias.* You said mass and it was so wonderful and so beautiful and you prayed for Tony." I said, "Yes, but I just want you to know that . . ."

Finally the mother came up to me and said, "Father, don't be so depressed!" And she pulled me up, and said, "Don't you know that the Lord loves us? He took Tony away and we loved Tony, but to love the Lord is much greater. And here are my sons, and here is my aunt and uncle. Come have food with us, come to our house. We can stand the pain of Tony's loss because God is with us."

Suddenly I realized that I was receiving the fruit that had come out of brokenness and poverty, out of the incredible vulnerability of those people. They simply asked, "Can you take the fruit of our sorrow? Can you take the deeper understanding of God's love with you, maybe to your own people? Are you willing to receive the gift so that we also can experience your love in your receiving?" That was very important for me. Suddenly my whole experience of Latin America became an experience of receiving the gift of the people—gifts for me as gifts for us, and maybe for the First World.

ECSTASY

Finally, I want to say something about Jesus' words, "My joy can be in you and your joy can be complete." Joy is one of the most important, if not the most important, visible quality of the spiritual life. A spiritual life leads to joy. We are people who have mostly lost that joyfulness. Look around at people's faces. Are they joyful? A lot of people look bored to me, very bored.

Boredom is one of the illnesses of the First World. Many people are bored stiff. Boredom does not mean having nothing to do, it means having a lot to do but wondering if anything is happening. It's being busy and hardly able to keep it up, but wondering if you are really doing anything meaningful.

I was in the Senate a few weeks ago, and, my goodness, everybody is so busy. They are busy at knowing how busy it is. Everything is extremely urgent, and everybody is always on their toes and almost hyperventilating. I was there to talk about Nicaragua. I talked to several senators about putting their name on a resolution. I was trying to get to know them and before I knew it I was running from one place to another, sort of being the messenger from one senator to another. Then I went away and came back three weeks later and everybody had forgotten about the emergency I was concerned about. Now they were talking about totally different things that were just as urgent.

I wonder what it means when people are so caught up in one emergency after another that they don't even remember last week's emergency. Nothing is at a deep level. As you come closer to those people you encounter an incredible sense of questioning, "Is anything happening? Am I part of any real spiritual event that is worth living for? Do I have a vision of life that is in any way significant?" The same busyness happens at universities. There's one more paper, one more exam, and we pray, "Oh, God, how do I do it all? There's so much to do, and I've no time for you. I'm on my way to something else."

I say, wait a minute. Are we doing anything? Are we growing? Are we developing? Or are we only preparing ourselves for the next thing? When that thing comes around, it's not even worth it. To move out of the static place—that is what *ecstatic* means. Static is what is the same, fixed, unchanging. It's unbelievable how we, for all our running around, in some mysterious, strange, morbid way, keep hovering around the static place. It's the place that is familiar. We become *so* familiar with being busy that we don't live anymore. The static place, where things are no longer moving, is the place of death. There is an incredible fascination with death in this world.

I see more and more that somehow we are pulled toward places that are static. They give us a sense of sameness, and a lot of us live out of that place. In interpersonal relationships, you might say, "Oh, I know that guy—he is a typical obsessive neurotic." When you say that, you see how he stiffens up. There he sits in the box, "obsessive neurotic." That solves your problem. Labels that we give to others can be death decrees. They show you don't expect anything new of the person, because they are a typical type.

Jesus condemns those judgments. When we judge, it's like a declaration of fixation. That person is no longer there to surprise us. If we explain a person, we don't have to deal with him or her anymore.

We think about ourselves, too, in a death-oriented way. For instance, we say, "I know myself. I went through counseling and talked about my problems and found out that I'm a little bit obnoxious at times, and have a hard time with certain people. I am 50 years old and I've seen all that and I feel that my character is pretty clear, and I just ask you to be so good as to listen to me. Don't expect anything new—my goodness, I'm 50. I'm not going to change."

A lot of people settle in their character and say, "I know myself." That is a declaration of death. "I am not going to be anything new. Don't think that anything new is going to happen to me. I've studied myself long enough. I've had years to think about myself and I pretty well have an idea what it's all about, and could you please hang around me and not expect anything new? Try to live with me." Healing is difficult, because we don't know what to do without our problems. Somehow our problems become our channels of communication. Even our painful symptoms become things we get attached to. "How are you doing?" "Fine, but I still have this pain in my back—so pay attention to me." Imagine if you didn't have pain any more. What would you do? Something in us clings to our pain because it has become a way to identify ourselves. We hang onto it because we are afraid of relating to people in ways that are unfamiliar. How would it be to be without all those symptoms?

We spend so much energy organizing the world around our problems—our visual problems, communal problems, city problems, national problems. We deal with reality in terms of problems. It's how we think, even about national and international policies. We have decided that most of the problems in the world are East-West problems; communism/capitalism. We have big words for it, and we don't want that to change. We make decisions, in that context.

It is very hard to think imaginatively in new ways. It's hard because we are caught in certain ways of thinking and feeling. Jesus keeps saying, "Move out of that static place." But in the world of today, where there is so much fear and anxiety over the nuclear threat, that fear goes right into the bodies of individuals and into the community. We just take it for granted that we are all scared.

A survey of young people found that most of them didn't expect to live until the year 2000. Imagine a child who is nine not expecting to become 25. That's an incredible way of growing up. Fear has become so familiar that we don't even know how it would be without it. "Security" has become the central word in our life—personal, social, national security. We prefer to be secure and miserable rather than insecure and happy. We want to know what is going to happen next. And next. And next. We don't want to leave it open. It's very frightening.

Jesus said, "Live ecstatically. Move out of that place of death and toward life because I am the God who is living. Wherever I am, there is life, there is change, there is growth, there is increase and blossoming and something new. I am going to make everything new."

For us to dare to live a life in which we continue to move out of the static places and take trusting steps in new directions—that is what faith is about. The Greek word for *faith* means "to trust"—to trust that the ground before you that you never walked on is safe ground, God's ground, holy ground.

Walk and don't be afraid. Don't want to have it all charted out for you. Let it happen. Let something new grow. That is the walk of faith—walking with the Lord, always walking away from the familiar places. "Leave your father, leave your mother, leave your brother, leave your sister. Follow me. I am the Lord of love." And wherever there is love, fear will be wiped out. "Perfect love casts out all fear."

You can go out and you will live. You will live eternally because Jesus is the Lord of life. That is the ecstasy. You can start participating in it every time you step out of your fear and out of the sameness. It doesn't require big jumps, but simply small steps.

Do you choose life? Or are you choosing death, that fearful place where you hang onto what you are most familiar with? Ecstatic living, real joy, is precisely connected with stepping onto unknown ground, trusting that you are in safe hands.

Joy is always new. There is a lot of old sadness, but there is never old joy. Joy is always a surprise, and that's ecstasy.

I hope you realize that intimacy, fecundity, and ecstasy are intimately connected. Intimate life with the Lord and the people brings joy, fruitfulness, and leads to the ecstatic life. Every time you experience that ecstasy of living, intimacy gets deeper and the fruit gets richer.

I am very glad that Jean Vanier told me what he learned from those very broken people. I'd love to touch them and be with them and embrace them, wash them and help them. I would feel that I was touching the flesh of God. Even though they are childless, they are fruitful. When they touch other people I see something new happening in other people's lives. I went with those so-called retarded people to a Trappist community and the monks were changed just by meeting them. Isn't that fruitful? I went with them to a family, and the family loved them and touched them, and they were changed—and that's a fruit they hadn't expected.

Wherever we live, we can live celebrating ecstatically, always having a party. There's something new, a smile, because God is with us and we want to live. When Jean Vanier told me what he had learned from handicapped people, I suddenly realized that he had been speaking about the most intimate spiritual life and also about what real service is. It is intimacy. It is fruitfulness. And it is ecstasy.

Ubi caritas et amor, Deus ibi est. (Where there is charity and love, God is there.)

2

Reflections on a Meaning-Filled Life

Bob Buford

M Y FRIEND PEB JACKSON probably knows more influential Christians in business, politics, and entertainment than almost anyone I know. He is one of the great networkers of all time. I once asked him why more successful people can't seem to break the addiction to success and go on to the next season of their lives, to what I call *significance*. He thought for a minute and then answered, "They can't measure significance. They are so used to measuring their lives in terms of money, with the lines going upward and to the right. They just can't stand to see the line going downward even if they are very rich."

HOW DO YOU MEASURE SIGNIFICANCE?

Life for most of us is built on a constellation of habits, and for successful people the need for measurable results is one of the habits most deeply ingrained. Writer and analyst George Gilder made this observation:

"Men lust, but they know not what for. They fight and compete, but they forget the prize; they spread seed, but spurn the seasons of growth; they chase power and glory, but miss the meaning of life."

Hmmm, missing the meaning of life. That's important. But how does one measure the meaning of life? My friend Jim Collins spent three years thinking about this question. When we had dinner last October, he told me that business-oriented people confuse money with mission. The good becomes the enemy of the great. Here's the way Collins put it in *Good to Great and the Social Sectors*, which he handed me that night.

> The confusion between inputs and outputs stems from one of the primary differences between business and the social sectors. In business, money is both an input (a resource for achieving greatness) and an output (a measure of greatness). In the social sectors, money is only an input, and not a measure of greatness.
>
> A great organization is one that delivers superior performance and makes a distinctive impact over a long period of time. For a business, financial returns are a perfectly legitimate measure of performance. For a social sector organization, however, performance must be assessed relative to mission, not only to financial returns. In the social sectors, the critical question is not "How much money do we make per dollar of invested capital?" but "How effectively do we deliver on our mission and make a distinctive impact, relative to our resources?"

As I have thought about my own life, in retrospect I can see pretty clearly what happened: In the season I call Halftime, mission became, for me, more important than money. It didn't happen overnight, but it happened. I knew there was something more and I began to seek it. The more I focused on mission, the more it drew me forward.

Peter Drucker, the manager guru of all time, whom I met with two to four times a year in those Halftime years, always drew me back to a single question: "Yes, but to what end?" He taught me over and over that "mission comes first," then comes measurement. For a business, Peter always told me, "Profit is a requirement, not the objective of a business." Think about it.

Bob Klitgaard, the president of Claremont Graduate University, where Drucker taught and where the Drucker Institute resides, wrote this as part of a tribute to Peter:

> On my desk, I keep the last two pages of a 12-page letter Peter Drucker wrote to Bob Buford some 15 years ago. The letter's first 10 pages gave advice related to the institution Bob was initiating. Its last two pages contained advice about Bob's role as leader. Peter wrote about Bob's being "the maker of policy and the designer." He also mentioned quality control. "But as I tried to stress, your first role—or perhaps one of the two first ones—is the personal one. It is the relationship with people, the development of mutual

confidence, the identification of people, the creation of a community. This is something only you can do." "It is not something that can be measured or can be easily defined. But it is not only a key function. It is one only you can perform."

ORDER AND THE BOOK OF DAYS

The difficulty of measuring significance keeps many people frozen in one stage of their life. Peter Drucker's advice clarified my own mission and pretty much set the DNA for the 15 years since—and for my life's work. He was right: building relationships with people is the most important thing I do. But is there any way to measure or evaluate what has now become my priority?

As addicted as I always have been to measuring both performance and contribution, I struggled for years to find a way to add it all up, especially as I became less and less active in running up the score in business (performance or achievement) and more and more involved in what I mean when I say, "The fruit of my work grows on other people's trees" (contribution).

In the second stage of my life, it's all about relationships. All that will remain when I'm gone will be those parts of me that I have invested in the lives of others. But how do I make that concrete enough to satisfy my compulsive need to measure results? What's the human side of my enterprise in this second stage of my life (which I call Life II)?

I think I have found a way. I call it my *Book of Days*. If I were to make a picture of my life of relationships, it would be a mosaic. A mosaic consists of fragments, little bits and pieces. Individually, they seem like random sizes and colors, but assembled as they are, for example, as in the ceiling of St. Peter's in Rome, they make a coherent picture. You have to step back a bit to see the pattern, but when you do, it snaps into focus.

Relationships and encounters are the fragments of our lives. They come at us from all directions: an e-mail, a cell phone call, a planned meeting, a random hallway encounter. Clarity about calling and mission is what fits them together to make a picture.

The New Testament describes 47 encounters of Jesus with individual people. Each one is personal. No two are treated alike (think of Mary, Martha, Judas, Pilate). Most of my life now is spent in encounters with individuals. Some lead to big outcomes, others don't. Some are long projects (writing books, convening meetings, speaking to large groups), but quite a few are "just conversations."

My Book of Days is my way of making a mosaic out of the fragments of my life. Here's how it came about. A few years ago, my wife, Linda, and I went to see an art exhibit for Robert Longo at Metro Pictures in New York. As we entered Metro's cavernous Tribeca Gallery, what we saw took our breath away. There were 365 pictures, all the same size (about 2 feet by 3 feet), all framed exactly the same, all done in the same medium (black and white—pen, ink, paint, and charcoal on vellum).

Longo, a gifted artist, lives and works in New York, where he is impacted each day by a barrage of images from the media. For this exhibit he had painted and drawn a memorable image for each day of his life for a year, 365 images for 365 days. To see them all at once required this enormous mosaic representing a year of what got through Longo's filter, of what remained. They were all strong forceful images.

The gallery was selling these pictures in patterns of 10 selected by the artist. I said, "Great!" Linda said, "No way. I'm not letting Robert Longo take over my home!" I reasoned this way and that way with her over a long, civilized lunch at Union Square Café, but it was no deal.

Well, rats. But as the afternoon of other gallery visits wore on, an idea gradually dawned on me. "I can do this," my mind said. "I can collect the fragmentary encounters of my life—and it's worth doing." That afternoon I went to Borders and bought my first *Book of Days*, blank pages large enough to hold an 8-1/2-inch-by-11-inch letter. That day I pasted an artifact to bring that day back to mind. And I've done that every day since for almost three years now: a mosaic of the little pieces of my life.

Since most of my life is now (I hope) devoted to contribution and significance, that's most of what shows up in my Book of Days. It's a kind of treasure chest of what I've attempted to do and of how people have responded. Individual lives, one at a time: very human, much warmer, and more alive than numbers. It's my "gift from heaven," right there in an alive, human format.

It's a reminder that my life has pattern and meaning. I usually look over several pages each week, six to nine months after the fact, and there is always a coherence to it, a sense of direction. It's encouraging.

All the time people ask, "How do I discover my mission in life?" I always say, "It's right there in your life and it has been there a long, long time. You just need to back up and see the pattern."

The mission is in the mosaic, and the mosaic is made up of the fragmentary encounters of your life. It takes some thought, but the pattern is right there, waiting to be discovered. Try it. You'll see.

> 1 Corinthians 13:12–13 (21st Century King James Version)
>
> 12: For now we see through a glass, darkly, but then face to face. Now I know in part; but then shall I know, even as also I am known.
>
> 13: And now abideth faith, hope, charity, these three; but the greatest of these is charity.

DISORDER AND THE BOOK OF PSALMS

Does it ever seem that life just won't fall into place the way you planned? I keep calendars, I make appointments, I have daily plans, weekly plans, plans for my whole life. I want to take charge of life, to be proactive. But, much of the time, perhaps most of my time, my life, and the life of most of those I know, is much more spontaneous than our linear plans would describe.

I make all sorts of plans, but what is useful for my life and for my "musings" *just happens*. Perhaps I am reacting to events like having lunch with a guy who thought he might die and had made a list of 50 specific things he wanted to tidy up in order to "leave well." Then there are the (smarter-than-mine) reactions of friends responding from their experiences to this idea of "finishing well."

I try to make an orderly, linear book out of my musings. But it's frustrating. Stuff happens and I react to it.

Peter Drucker once shocked me by saying, "People who plan are the unhappiest people in the world. Opportunity is unpredictable. Most of the time, opportunity comes in over the transom. And opportunity doesn't stay long. If you don't respond to an opportunity, it moves on."

The same is true for problems. If you don't change plans and react, they get worse. As Shakespeare said, "Readiness is all." Readiness and reaction.

So the nature of my musings, as I call them, is both spontaneous and reactive. They can't really be put in order. I tried, and it didn't work because my life, like yours I expect, just won't conform to my plans. It's messy. It's disorderly. It's one surprise after another.

Linda has watched with bemused sympathy as I have twisted and turned in the breeze, trying to solve my "making order out of chaos" issue. This past weekend she told me she's taking a course on the Psalms. She said, "Your musings don't have any order. They are like Psalms. They are reactions along the road of life. The Psalms aren't theology. They are more about how people relate to change." Then she read me this (from course material prepared by her friend, Verdell Krisher):

PSALMS

Are they poems, Are they conflicting?

Are they prayers, Are they experiential?

Are they praises, Are they majestic?

Are they songs, Are they dark?

Are they laments, Are they intense?

Are they personal, Are they accusing?

Are they communal, Are they comforting?

The answer is "Yes."

The Psalms are collected into five books, but as Philip Yancey says, "The 150 psalms are as difficult, disordered, and messy as life itself."

So, looking back on my "musings for friends," I find them to be like life in the Second Half—disordered and surprising—but often wonderful. Only occasionally is the Second Half as I plan it.

Here we see David when he had fled from Saul into a cave (Psalm 57).

Have mercy on me, O God, have mercy on me,
    for in you my soul takes refuge.
I will take refuge in the shadow of your wings
    until the disaster has passed.
I cry out to God Most High, to God,
    who fulfills his purpose for me.
He sends from heaven and saves me,
    rebuking those who hotly pursue me.
God sends his love and his faithfulness.
I am in the midst of lions: I lie among ravenous beasts—
    men whose teeth are spears and arrows,
    whose tongues are sharp swords.
Be exalted, O God, above the heavens;
    let your glory be over all the earth.

PRAYER AS A STATE OF BEING

Recently I've been thinking about prayer, which is a big part of my life. Let me begin with a parable by Leo Tolstoy that for me gets to the heart of it. It's from Henri Nouwen's book titled *Spiritual Direction*.

> **Three Monks on an Island**
>
> Three Russian monks lived on a faraway island. Nobody ever went there, but one day their bishop decided to make a pastoral visit. When he arrived, he discovered that the monks didn't even know the Lord's Prayer. So he spent all his time and energy teaching them the "Our Father" and then left, satisfied with his pastoral work. But when his ship had left the island and was back in the open sea, he suddenly noticed the three hermits walking on the water—in fact, they were running after the ship! When they reached it, they cried, "Dear Father, we have forgotten the prayer you taught us." The bishop overwhelmed by what he was seeing and hearing, said, "But, dear brothers, how then do you pray?" They answered, "Well, we just say, 'Dear God, there are three of us and there are three of you, have mercy on us!'" The bishop, awestruck by their sanctity and simplicity, said, "Go back to your land and be at peace."[1]

Nouwen follows this parable by saying, "There's a difference between learning prayers and prayerfulness."

For me, prayer is not separate from daily life. It's a way of being. It's like being with Linda for a weekend at the farm. We're there with one another. We talk over lunch and dinner, but it doesn't particularly matter what we say. It's more about who we are. It's about being together. Sharing lives, with someone you love and trust.

Prayer is like that for me. It's a state of being together with God. It's not usually triggered by liturgy or special needs. It's more like what the Bible instructs us to do: Pray without ceasing.

I may pray the Lord's Prayer, repeat the words of the Doxology or of liturgical prayers occasionally in the day, often at night. There's no such thing as a mental void. When I wake up from sleep, I have a tendency to role-play my coming day in imagination, especially if I'm anxious about the day ahead: giving a speech, confronting something that's not going especially well. Once I get that kind of thought going, it's difficult to get back to sleep. So I fill the void with ritual prayer.

---

1. Quoted in Nouwen, *Spiritual Direction*, 55–56.

If I've been with an especially stimulating, emotionally engaging group of people the day before, I find that they stay in my head at night. They're there. If they have strong personalities, they leave emotional impressions. I'm still doing business with them, saying things we didn't say, finishing conversations we didn't complete, wondering if there's more to say or do.

Knowing that there's only so much room in my mental box, I may "sing" the Doxology silently. I say the 23rd Psalm or the Lord's Prayer, often drifting back into sleep knowing that I am loved by God, a love that fills the God-shaped void within me.

Often when I pray, I use a framework that has come echoing down century after century. It's easy to remember using the acronym A.C.T.S., which stands for Adoration, Confession, Thanksgiving, Supplication.

First, *Adoration*: Simply bringing God to mind, sometimes using a remembered song, often a Psalm like this one:

> O Lord, You have searched me and known me.
> You know my sitting down and my rising up;
> You understand my thought afar off.
> You comprehend my path and my lying down,
> And are acquainted with all my ways.
> (Psalm 139:1–3)

Next comes *Confession*: Usually for me that's a matter of my own childish and natural self-absorption. I ask and receive forgiveness.

Thanksgiving is the largest part of my prayers these days. I often use a mechanism for gratitude that I learned from psychologist Larry Crabb in his book, *Inside Out*.

I begin in gratitude for my inner life with Christ now, and for my eternal life to come when I'm done here. I move on to the relationships I'm grateful for. Then I recall projects I've had the privilege to work on with others. Last, I'm thankful for the material treasures that are a platform for my life and work.

Finally, I get around to my wish list, *Supplication*, which is always the shortest part, often just the phrase, "Thy will be done on earth (and in my life) as it is in heaven."

Sometimes, particularly when I'm driving (eyes open) or walking alone for exercise, I use my hands as artifacts for prayer: holding a hand upward for praise; palm forward for confession, imagining that my palm rests on the chest of Christ on the cross, my sins passing on to him; palm up for thanksgiving, an attitude of receiving; and palm down for supplication, leaving my concerns in the lap of God.

I always, always feel renewed and refreshed in the knowledge that although things seldom turn out as I've planned and imagined them, they always eventually do turn out. Is this me? Is it God intervening? Is it the interaction of my prayers with those of hundreds of other people who pray their own prayers? I don't know and I don't have to know.

We live in mystery. Each of us experiences a reality that others can't see. We mustn't presume to know too much.

I do know this. There is a God. He is not distant, but close at hand. He's part of me, braided into who I am. I'm never alone. God loves me. I trust him. That's about it.

SOME QUESTIONS TO CONSIDER

How Do You Measure Significance?

1. Can you in a phrase clearly state your mission in life?
2. Who or what helped you clarify your mission in life: a writer, a motion picture, your parents, a mentor?
3. What is the downside of not having a clear mission?

Order and a Book of Days

1. Could you make a Book of Days? Sure you could. All it takes is a blank book, scissors, a glue stick, five minutes a day, and the raw material of your life.
2. What is the "mission in the mosaic" in your life: the good things and the hard things? What is the pattern?
3. Looking at the pattern, what does it indicate that life probably has in store for you next?

Disorder and the Book of Psalms

1. If you were to write a psalm expressing your current state of mind, what would it say?
2. What movie, song, poem, or quote would you pick to say "This is my situation now"?
3. Look over your calendar of the past two weeks. Describe an unpredicted happening, something that was not according to plan.

Prayer as a State of Being

1. If you had only three words, how would you describe your relationship with God? Is it personal, intimate, distant, trusting, suspicious?
2. When do you feel closest to God? Is it a special time or place? Or any place?
3. Does God speak to you? When you "ring," does he answer? How? Through the Word? Through intuition? Imagination—where you "just know"? Through people? Through circumstances?

3

Wounds of Childhood and the Grace of God

Margaret G. Alter

IN RECENT YEARS, WE have heard a great deal from the media about dysfunctional families. In his much rebroadcast PBS series, popular spokesman John Bradshaw suggested that 97 percent of American families are dysfunctional.

Much has been said about child abuse and toxic parenting. Formerly accepted forms of correction, like spanking, have fallen into disrepute. Many adults report struggling with guilt and shame cycles associated with particular family stresses—Adult Children of Alcoholics, for example.

Some voices from within the Christian community and some from without assert ominously that the sins of the fathers are visited on the children: innocent children are being irreparably damaged. Others look longingly back to earlier times in American life as a golden age for families.

The word *dysfunction* has begun to carry the emotional baggage once associated with the word *sin*. The mere mention of it makes people begin to feel guilty and anxious. Young adults worry about becoming "a dysfunctional family." They put off having children until "we straighten our lives out." Parents in the midst of the ever immediate demands of child-rearing tremble lest they also should make a mistake. Many search for some path of parenting that is "the right way" to do it.

Church people sometimes talk to me of their hopes for constructing a "perfect Christian family." If I were to piece together the meaning of the word "perfect" implied by eager Christians over many years, I would conclude that we must at least be kind, cheerful, helpful, happy, decisive, well-organized, peaceful, and certainly prayerful. Under the best of circumstances, this is accomplished in a setting where the kids are fighting over a job nobody wants to do, bills to be paid, (junk mail mixed with bills and school notices) piled up on the hall table, dinner needing preparing, and a neighbor calling with an emergency errand because their car is in the shop.

Rebecca Pippert has said that we are created for Paradise,[1] and perhaps she is right. We seem desperately to believe in a pain-free world where life is simple and problems are manageable, but we find ourselves repeatedly called by God into a complex, demanding life where we must make on-the-spot decisions never having sufficient information.

God continually, relentlessly places before us intense demands of ordinary life. And we carry into our relationships and decision-making our childhood experiences and wounds.

A few voices bring the grace of reality to this oppressive idealism. Murray Bowen, one of the great pioneers of family therapy, noted the early vestiges of such anxious perfectionism around family systems theory. He concluded that family therapists become a dysfunctional group because they are so eager to distance themselves from "those families" whose cases they report that they become unable to tolerate differing opinions. With much humor and aplomb, Bowen described stresses found in all families, indeed in all groups, using his relationship to his own family as an example.[2] Having made famous the dangers of the "family ego mass"—that is, our inability to separate our own emotional life from those of our family—he quipped that within five miles of the family home, he couldn't think differently from his family.

Sociologist Stephanie Coontz adds historical perspective to the search for pain-free family life. She challenges the "myths" of the ideal American family of the past in her book *The Way We Never Were*, sub-

---

1. Pippert, *Hope Has Its Reasons*.
2. Bowen, "On the Differentiation of Self."

titled *American Families and the Nostalgia Trap*.[3] In an article based on the book, Coontz enumerates the variety of family forms that have appeared, disappeared, and coexisted throughout our history, asserting that families have always been "vulnerable to rapid economic change and have always needed economic and emotional support from beyond their own small boundaries." "Raising a family is hard enough without having to live up to myths. In fact, the American family is as strong—and as fragile—as it ever was."[4]

Another sociologist, University of California professor Robert Bellah, returns our discussion to basic Christian doctrine. He cites Bradshaw's assertion and suggests that Bradshaw had discovered original sin. Bellah goes on to question that 3 percent of American families are "functional."

There is an immense graciousness in the doctrine of sin. It assures us that life is not going to be perfect. The kingdom of God is here and is yet to come. We have hope in Christ and yet we are fallen.

We will live with evidence of that fallen state throughout our lives. No family is without stress; no child has an easy, pain-free childhood. No adult reaches a place in his or her life's journey where virtue flows and decision-making is easy.[5] We will very likely experience evidences of hurt collected in childhood. These are the unbendable conditions of being finite. Our God, through becoming human in Jesus, invites us to embrace this finitude, our humanness with its limits and failings, its wounds and ensuing feelings.

Some of the tensions that therapists note in families that are not working well appear in all families some of the time or even much of the time. Therefore, as any of us reflects on our childhoods in depth, we will recognize a trail of pain. We are born into a fallen world, and part of our life process will be sorting through what our psyches have made of that pain.

As we consider the wounds of childhood, perhaps we can place it against finitude itself. That is, we can look directly at what we are as human beings and how we go about collecting wounds to begin with.

Perhaps the initial human problem is that we are all born premature, a fact of life for us large-brained bipeds. Were our brains fully developed

---

3. Coontz, *Way We Never Were*.
4. Coontz, "Where Are the Good Old Days?"
5. Lewis, "Pilgrim's Problem."

and our protective skulls complete, our heads would be too big for us to be born at all. Therefore, we come into the world vulnerable, sensitive, and completely dependent. Without significant care, we would die, and without mother's ministrations we experience intense feelings of helplessness and hopelessness. Our gradual journey from complete helplessness to adult competence is fraught with stresses, real and imagined.

Child psychologist Selma Fraiberg elaborates for parents the complex "meaning-making" of children: "When [Roger] was four, he worried about his 'bad thoughts.' He thought of killing people, of being a robber, of setting fires . . . [Finally] he has learned at last that thoughts and actions are not the same, that his thoughts could not magically produce effects!"[6]

What meaning we make of our internal and external experiences—helplessness and mastery, parental love, stresses, sorrow or anger, conflict with siblings and friends—this is a great mystery that psychology is only beginning to understand. When we talk of healing childhood's wounds, this is the dilemma we seek to solve.

As we were growing up, no one knew exactly what meaning we were making of our experience. One characteristic is extremely common: we spontaneously manage our helplessness by assuming responsibility for family suffering. One mother reported a terrible fight with her husband, concluding, "Worst was how Davey [her five-year-old son] took it. He looked stricken. When I said, 'Davey, it's not your fault,' he replied, 'Well, maybe just a little.'"

The story repeats over and over. A man in his forties says of his deeply depressed father, "He would have been more responsive if I had been a different son." An eight-year-old girl tells her aunt how she "is keeping her father from drinking." Her aunt wisely asserts that her dad's drinking has nothing to do with her, but will the child believe her? An eleven-year-old boy repeatedly gets into trouble because that keeps his depressed mother too anxious about him to sleep all day. With his father working in another town, he assumes that only he can help the situation. "If I didn't do it," he weeps, "you would think I didn't love you."

This terrible imagined omnipotence through which we assume control of the suffering of others is our built-in human empathy[7] gone astray in a fallen world. The burden we assume makes the journey back

6. Fraiberg, *The Magic Years*.
7. Hoffman, "Is Altruism Part of Human Nature?"

into our wounds treacherous because we appropriate for ourselves so many imaginary crimes.

People share with me the deep suffering of some early memory. "I felt like such a bad person. Why should any child feel that way?" The truth is that most of us experience feeling irredeemably bad at times in childhood, frightened sometimes like "Roger" in Fraiberg's book by our own "bad thoughts." Our complete dependence as small children made us vulnerable to our mother's anxiety, our father's drinking, our childcare worker's sadness.

The sympathetic vibrations within us sought an answer for their distress lest they and we, we imagined, be destroyed. If we were unable to attract their attention to our concerns at least some of the time, we began to lose ourselves. Our concentration focused on rescuing them. If to this vulnerability were added sharp reprimands, spankings, harsh punishments, or real cruelty, we may indeed live with ghostly memories of our own badness.

Some indeed have remembered profound neglect and abuse. Emotional representations of these experiences have cemented themselves into our psyches. God, who in Jesus, insisted on offering us freedom, continues to prod us to uncover the woundedness which binds us. We are called to face these shadowy interpretations of our past, right in the midst of the insistent demands of daily life.

Feelings of shame and badness from childhood are common if not normal. Children are not born perfect and do not lead happy innocent lives before adolescence. They have a great deal to learn in order to survive in this complex world, and much of that learning process is very hard. They must master not only the family and the culture but also the workings of their imaginations and emotions.

Emotional stress in our parents or real harshness from them are taken in as appropriate punishment for profound badness in ourselves. When we seek out our childhood wounds, we will unearth those places where we have taken to heart much over which we had no control. The residue may well be an ominous sense of being bad. Paradoxically, the badness is an attempt to be in control when we feel helpless: "Well, if Mom's depression is my fault then at least I can do something about it." This brings us to the greatest issue that any of us face as human beings: managing our own feelings of helplessness, the core experience of being finite. In fact, if assuming responsibility for family problems is common among children, spontaneous repression of bad feelings is universal.

It is this that God addresses directly in the Incarnation. God entered into humanness in all its aspects from infancy to death. We observe Jesus living a full range of finitude. In the process we see him acknowledging a wide range of feelings and acknowledging the loving companionship of God. In the worst of times, Jesus responds intensely from his feelings. In Gethsemane, for example, he is desperately alone; in fact, he is doomed. He prays psalm-like from his pain, crying out for release from his mission. Jesus lived the depth of human suffering, and therefore, through Jesus, we can approach God with trust. Because God knows our experience, we can endure our own suffering, see our own memories with honesty, and can have confidence that we will not be destroyed.

Exploring childhood memories is not a place to go alone. It is important to seek out a pastor or a trained counselor to accompany you. Like Lazarus, raised from the dead by Jesus in John 11, we need others to untangle our bonds. Jesus did not expect Lazarus to unbind himself and we cannot unbind ourselves either. Although all of us have happy memories of childhood, the ones that cause us the most trouble will be sad ones: sharp words, rejection on the playground, failure in school, domination from an older sibling, supplanting by a younger sibling, a parent's drinking binges. All these forces beyond our control bring us face to face with profound feelings of helplessness and ensuing feelings of shame and guilt. As memories emerge, our counselor companion can embody for us the accompanying love of God, assisting us in facing our fearful feelings and coming to terms with the helplessness of our finitude. We can borrow our counselor's calm in the face of terrifying anxiety.

We are created for Paradise, Pippert writes, and because we easily focus our whole hearts on being rescued and protected by an omnipotent Father God, we may well miss the enormous gift of the Incarnation. We may miss that we can live joyfully in the real world, to the East of Eden.

We seem naturally inclined to try to be God, to be in control, to resist our frightening feelings that speak to us of our finitude. From infancy we take on ourselves the impossible demand of rescuing our parents from their anxiety and consequently we blame ourselves for our failure. We meet our God, who often fails to rescue. Instead he enters with us into the entire human experience, a faithful companion.

II

Discipleship
Call and Response

4

The Constellation of God's Call

Mark Labberton

CONSTELLATIONS HAVE ALWAYS SEEMED a little bewildering to me. As a child, I remember sitting under the clear night sky while some adult tried to explain that three particular stars formed a belt. Not only that, the belt hung around Orion's waist, they said.

What are they seeing, I wondered. Who was Orion? Why or how are they seeing him? Orion and his friends were a little more visible when I eventually "saw" them through the technology of the planetarium. Their outlines were sketched as the white arrow traced their forms. But when all that disappeared and it was just the stars again, I wondered what we had seen. Was it anything at all? What was meant when someone exclaimed, "There's Orion!"? I knew that the stars were there, but in what sense was Orion "there"?

Sometimes, the phrase, the "call of God," raises the same questions as Orion and his belt. The "stars" we gaze upon by faith shine forth: Scripture/tradition/community experience. God's call appears in the constellation that these and other "stars" form for us. Some of us stand under this vast sweep and point joyfully and confidently toward the constellations of God's call and design. Meanwhile, others of us look and look, straining to discern the patterns that are truly there, acknowledging our problematic eyesight, trying to use all of the corrective lenses God seems to have provided to restore and illumine our vision. After all, what constitutes our sense of call? Is God's call "there" like the Big Dipper? Or is it "there" like the North Star?

WHY DO YOU STAND LOOKING UP TOWARD HEAVEN?

The "two men in white robes" asked the disciples that question after Jesus' ascension. Why, indeed? In that context, why was any constellation of God's call still needed or sought?

If in Jesus Christ, God's will has been spoken and seen, don't we already have the only voice, the only image, we need? His first and second commands, for example, give us our guidance—and the model of Jesus' early ministry shows us how to live them out. The stars and their relation are already fixed. On any given night, you either see Orion or you don't. The stars that comprise his belt don't change. Are we then just killing time with our questions about God's call, when what God is asking is that we "do justice, love kindness, and walk humbly with our God"? What we have seen and heard, and touched in Jesus Christ, trust and do.

It might seem we are pointlessly star-gazing, were it not for the fact that the predominant images of God's call for people in Scripture are more intimate and personal than even this sense of God's will. For Israel, God's will was evident in the Torah, but God still called Moses to lead the people in the wilderness. All of us are meant to worship God in spirit and in truth, yet Saul met the risen Christ and was called "as one untimely born" to be an apostle to the Gentiles. God's will and God's call can be identical but are not always synonymous. They both center in Jesus Christ. They are consistent with one another, but a call seems to be a more particular expression or purpose within the wider sweep of God's design.

The galaxies are there. Truth, goodness, and beauty are always God's agenda. It's the burning bush, the whirlwind, the angel chorus, that rivets our attention, that sharpens our vision. It is God's call on our lives that enables us to see a constellation where before we had seen only stars. Our call is recognized as that special context in which truth, goodness, and beauty become our own particular work.

LET THE ONE WHO HAS EARS ... SEE?

What all this helps us recognize is that seeing is no small feat. But maybe part of the problem lies here: we are trying to see, when what we are to do is to hear. "Call," after all, implies the sound of a voice more than the appearance of a map. Our attempts to discern constellations may be pure distraction. Noah, Abraham, and Moses, for example, didn't see some pattern and follow it. They heard God's voice-and obeyed. It was a process of hearing, not of seeing. In fact, it was despite what could be seen, in contradiction to what circumstances would indicate, that each nonetheless heard the voice of God's call and responded. They walked by faith and not by sight.

Yet, we would be hard pressed, of course, to be able to explain the nature of such hearing. What are the distinctive, distinguishable qualities of God's voice? Scripture assumes these realities and events rather than explaining, defending, or analyzing them. For the "great cloud of witnesses," God's call was personal, specific, directive, purposeful. Jonah, for example, would have appreciated a little more interpretive freedom than the words "Go to Nineveh" allowed! No interpretation was necessary. In fact, to want more details would seem an impertinence. The call was clear. The issue was obedience.

Perhaps, then, our quest to discern God's call is frustrated by our efforts to find visual clues or signs, when we should be listening for the Word of God. We are being controlled by an inappropriate metaphor! Maybe trying to "see" reveals an insistence that God "show me," with its implicit corollary, "prove it." By contrast, "Speak, your servant listens" and "Here am I, send me" express an openness to God's call that presents far more risk and far less control.

The relationship of seeing to hearing is not so simple, however. For when "the Word became flesh," God spoke in person. God's personal, self-revealing, oratory took human form. The One who had only been heard could now be seen. Never before or since was the call of God more tangible. Looking at Jesus, the crowd was told, "Let the one who has ears, hear." As they looked, they heard. Seeing enhanced their hearing. Even so, some saw but still did not hear.

In discerning the constellation of God's call we are trying to see better in order to hear better. But like the risen Christ's admonition to Thomas, "Blessed are those who have not seen and yet have come to believe," Scripture suggests that when seeing supplants or replaces hearing, we have the cart before the horse. To put it in the priority order of the Kingdom, we seek to discern the constellation of God's call on our lives so that through what we see we will be better able to hear. This is part of what Augustine meant by faith seeking understanding. It's part of what Calvin defended as the interdependence of Word and Spirit. Discerning God's call is strongest when done with our ears and our eyes.

THE HEAVENS ARE TELLING THE GLORY OF GOD

When by faith we affirm that we see in the constellation of Scripture/tradition/community experience a pattern that seems to spell our name, in what sense is this a discovery of what is "there" and in what ways is it just a confession of a faithful hope? We are told, "The firmament proclaims God's handiwork . . . there is no speech, nor are there words; their voice is not heard; yet their voice goes out through all the earth, and their words to the end of the world."

The firmament contains the "stars" that shine in the pages of the Bible, in the living traditions of faith, in the Christian community around us, in our experiences of life and faith. But is God's call "there" like the Big Dipper? Or is it "there" like the North Star?

Either way we answer this, we implicitly acknowledge that what we see and hear has a very great deal to do with how we have been trained to look and listen. I would not have seen the belt of stars or known it was Orion's unless it had been pointed out. Nor would the phrase "North Star," a sure, fixed point, have sounded like helpful news. How does such seeing help us to hear God's call?

The most amateur astronomer knows that the constellations anyone sees depends on where one stands. In what hemisphere? In what season? In what weather? At what time? With what instruments? Even in what culture? All of these and other factors will directly and profoundly influence what the astronomer finds. But what is not up for grabs is whether there are stars, or whether many of them can be seen. It is in the constellations we see that we make connections and discern patterns with meaning and implications. Is the difference between astronomy and astrology the difference between an interest in stars and an interest in constellations? If so, is theology parallel with astrology and, therefore, with the suspect, the frivolous, the unsubstantiated?

Certainly the act of seeing constellations is a process of interpretation. So is hearing God's call. The discernment of patterns is always interpretive. No reality, patterned or otherwise, is ever discerned in an uninterpreted way, with absolute neutrality and clarity. But our everyday experience of apparently discrete realities, like tables, telephone poles, and stars, leads us to believe that they are "there" in ways that are different from realities like friendship, joy, or love. In seeing patterns, discerning relationships, making connections, we actively interpret. Does admitting this mean surrendering any sure relationship to reality that is more than mere interpretation?

Some postmodern voices argue that what we end up with in any act of interpretation is all we had to begin with: interpretation. That is, there are stars in the sky, black marks on a page, but the way they are seen, constellations discerned, significance or meaning found, is a result only of our conventions of interpretation, which tenaciously cling to false expectations of objective reality. What we find is really just a statement of how we see. The constellation exists only in stargazers' minds. What we may term the call of God is, in fact, simply an expression of what is found in believers' hearts.

It is one thing to question claims of divine revelations. Doing this questioning can be defended for many reasons, not least if you're going to stake your life on it. It is quite another thing, however, to assert that any claims of revelation can by definition be nothing other than interpretation. Yet this is the postmodernist climate in which Christians stand and profess to hear the call of God. To make any such claim ought to be done with humility, acknowledging the inherent, permeating subjectivity involved. It will always be a confession of faith. But in the end, for Christian theology, it matters enormously whether the "call of God" is truly "of God" or whether the constellation is merely in the eye of the beholder. What the Christian wants to confess is having seen and having heard far more. Naïve realism, with its assumption that stars or constellations are simply as they appear, clearly proves inadequate.

"We see through a glass darkly." But we can see, and what we see is not simply ourselves in galactic relief. It is God's call "there" and "here." That makes all the difference.

5

Knowing Means Doing
A Challenge to Think Christianly

Os Guinness

Raymond Aron, the great French thinker, once remarked that very few people are contemporaries of their own generation. That sounds a little odd, but if you think about it, most people live considerably behind the times, understanding their own day second hand at best. And curiously, living in the "information society" only makes our problems worse.

Most people are clustered toward the two poles of an enormous continuum. At one end is the "happiness is a small circle" philosophy. Know as little as you need, care as little as you can (preferably with a hot tub at the center of things) and you can get by comfortably. At the other end is the idea of instant total information and the phenomenon that Daniel Boorstin calls "Homo-up-to-datum": the drive to know everything in order to predict everything in order to control everything.

How do we as followers of Christ line up on the continuum? Clearly the first extreme is irresponsible, but the other is at best illusory, and at worst, idolatrous. God only knows that total information which is necessary for true wisdom. The rest of us quite simply don't and never will.

Our task is to live responsibly between these extremes. And the real problem is not just knowing as much as you can or even making sense of what you know. The deepest problem of all is to know what to do with knowing so much in today's world, especially since many of the ways we're taught to know discourage us from doing anything responsible with what we know.

For instance, Malcolm Muggeridge tells the story of an incident in the Biafran war. An execution was just about to take place when a European camera crew arrived. To his dismay, the cameraman discovered he had no battery and shouted, "Stop." So they stopped the execution while he hurried off, fetched a battery, and replaced it. The cameraman then shouted, "Shoot"—and they did, in both senses. Muggeridge asked, "Which of the two was more barbaric?" The rough justice in the Biafran backwoods, or the civilized world with its evening news, conveyed with that sort of detached knowledge behind it?

There was a similar incident two years ago in Alabama. A local television crew came upon a man who had covered himself with gasoline and was burning himself to death. They filmed him for 45 seconds before they turned the cameras off and rescued him so that he wouldn't burn himself more. Again, which was worse? The tragic incident or the fact that to the television crew the human person was less important than the story?

Far from aberrations, those two stories are typical of the way knowledge is treated in our world. Sometimes such attitudes are even stated explicitly, such as in Christopher Isherwood's famous statement, "I am a camera with its shutter open; quite passive, recording, not thinking."

Examples such as these raise a crucial challenge to us as followers of Christ. We must be critical not only of the substance of ideas that we encounter but of the very style in which knowledge is purveyed to us, whether at university or in business, for the Scriptures show us repeatedly, both in what is taught and what is modeled, that the style of knowing is a true indication of the substance known.

We could examine many truths in Scripture about which the style is as important as the substance, but let me develop one particularly difficult example. We are living in an age which knows more than ever before, yet less is done about what is known than ever before. Perhaps 90 percent of modern knowledge elicits from us an unconscious shrug of the shoulders and a "So what?" In England we have a phrase, "I don't want to know about it." It simply means, "I don't care, and don't tell me because I don't want to care." Similarly the French have a very expressive shrug of the shoulders which dismisses the entire situation. So whether it's the reaction to a math formula or global starvation, the gap today between knowing and doing is as great as it has ever been in Western history.

Why is that so? Clearly there are several roots to the problem. One is a sense of ethical confusion that underlies the crisis. Another factor is psychological. With today's range of choice, pace of change, intensity of need, and urgency of appeals, many people become so overloaded that they become uncaring as a way of handling the overload. Their psychological thermostats are switched off.

Another factor is the influence of modern philosophers, whose attitudes toward knowing wash down like rain from the university departments to the streets. Written into the common Western attitude toward knowledge is the idea that knowing and doing are quite unrelated.

Another factor behind the lack of caring is institutional. The rise of modern bureaucracy brings with it the omnipresence of the specialist and the expert. The price of such narrowing is an inevitable loss of the sense of the wider whole, and a loss of the sense of the long term consequences of the expert's actions. The net result in all these examples is a break in the link between knowing and doing.

FACING UP TO THE BIBLICAL DEMAND

How do we live in today's world both faithful to Christ and consistent with a Christian thought-style? What we find in Scripture is a style of being responsible for knowing which is so different from our world's that we are almost overwhelmed. Responsibility is inherent in knowing.

In Scripture God addresses us as the one who has the first word, as creator, and the last word, as judge. We therefore live out our lives between the first word and the last great word and thus are created able to respond. In short, we are responsible.

The responsibility of knowledge can be seen at several important points in the Bible. First, it is the silent component in many basic doctrines. The heart of the notion of the fall, for example, involves what Paul calls "holding the truth in unrighteousness." The break between knowing and doing originated in disobedience. Our epistemology is only a sophisticated version of what goes right back to Genesis 3.

Or again, why is Biblical repentance not simply an easy regret, or turning over a new leaf, or a New Year's resolution? Simply because knowing means doing. We repent because a knowledge of God's truth and a knowledge of our sin comes home with such a double force of conviction, that for the first time we do what we have to about what we know. Knowledge and responsibility are thus joined properly for the first time since we were born.

The same effect is true also of faith. Biblical faith is not cheap grace or nominal assent because knowing means doing and obedience means faith. You can't divide them. Remove obedience from faith and you have cheap grace. Remove faith from obedience and you have legalism. Only where they are inseparable do you have true faith.

The point can be seen most soberly in judgment. Why is God's judgment not arbitrary, not cruel? Because God's judgment is his leaving us, or sometimes driving us, to the consequences of our own choices. Sin is the right to the claim to ourselves, but the link between knowing and doing cannot be broken brazenly forever. God's judgment is the act that links the two together again.

Second, the responsibility of knowledge is present in the root meanings of the words. The clearest example is the Hebrew for "to know" itself. Everyone knows that the Hebrew word "to know" is also the same word that is used for intercourse. But what many forget is that it is also the word for caring. In the Hebrew understanding, to know something is to have power over it, and to have power over it is to have responsibility to it. Thus to know something is to care for it.

A fascinating example is Proverbs 12:10, which reads, "A righteous man cares for his beast, but the wicked man is cruel at heart." In Hebrew it is "the righteous man 'knows' his beast." When the righteous man sees his horse (or donkey or whatever) he sees it as it is under God. It is not just there for him. His beast is not a human being made in the image of God, as he is. But it is a fellow creature with its own integrity which must be treated true to the truth of what it is.

The wicked man, by contrast, is cruel at heart. To him the beast was merely "objectified." It was there, but only as an object for him. Perhaps he wanted his daughter to ride it the next day, and therefore looked after it. Perhaps he wanted it to carry his bricks for another ten years, and therefore looked after it well. Or perhaps he didn't and treated it cruelly. But either way the beast was merely an object to him. It had no integrity in itself. Its value was only instrumental, not intrinsic.

If the truth of that single verse alone had been practiced, the history of the West would have been different—for example, over environmental problems and industrial relations. An entire ethic is wrapped up in the etymology of the words.

Third, the responsibility of knowledge can be found in specific teaching about knowing and doing. In the Old Testament, for instance, if you come across your neighbor's cloak and know whose it is, but do not return it, you are as guilty as if you had stolen it. Knowing equals responsibility. If a husband hears his wife make a vow and says nothing, his silence is complicity and he is liable for the vow. (The reverse in the New Testament is when Peter gave Sapphira a chance to show that she knew what Ananias had vowed. Only when she showed that she knew was she judged also.) Similarly, a witness who fails to testify is as guilty as the person who committed the crime. The person who saw the crime being committed is asked to cast the first stone, because the witness is the link between the criminal who committed the crime and the community which judges the crime.

This notion of the responsibility of knowledge is woven into the social fabric of the entire Old Testament and it is the same truth that can be found throughout the New Testament—for example, in the book of James, "The man who knows the good he ought to do, but does not do it, is a sinner."

Fourth, the responsibility of knowledge can be seen most profoundly of all in the life of our Lord. It stands to reason that if the first Adam broke the link between knowing and doing, the Evil One had to try to break that link again when the second Adam came. His temptations in the desert all bear down exactly on that link. The devil wanted Jesus to make claims but not to follow through on their consequences, to know who he was but not to be responsible to follow through on the logic of who he was.

Another example is Peter calling Jesus to sidestep the cross, or our Lord knowing he could have called down 12 legions of angels, but refusing to do it. Supremely the temptation is there in the taunt on the cross, "If you are the Christ, show it by coming down." Being the Christ, he could. Being the Christ, he couldn't. Knowing who he was kept Jesus riveted to that cross more securely than any Roman nails ever could.

Adam and Eve broke the link between knowing and doing, but our Lord maintained it unbroken to the end. His responsibility of knowledge marked his footsteps to Jerusalem and held him to the cross. No one can read Scripture carefully and fail to see the striking ways in which knowledge and responsibility have been linked so inseparably.

BETWEEN TWO WORLDS

But of course, we are modern people, caught between Christ's demands and our world. How do we live out the tension? There are no easy answers, but let me mention two examples of how we ought to think through some of these questions to find a more faithful way of living.

First, think through the challenge in terms of education and careers. E. F. Schumacher, author of *Small is Beautiful*, used to quote the Chinese calculation that it took 30 peasants 90 worker years to put a liberal arts student through school. They then raised the question, what did the student owe the peasants at the end? That question may seem irrelevant to us, since we are not dependent on peasants or even on the State or on our parents. But we are Christians, and our primary responsibility is not to peasants or governments, or even parents. Our responsibility for our knowledge is to the Lord.

What does it mean to be part of the world's educated elite, and to be responsible to the Lord for that knowledge? There tends to be a great divide at this point. Most students use their education as a passport to status, security, success, privilege, and affluence. Only a minority use their educations in an almost monastic sense for stewardship and service. Archbishop William Temple used to warn that young people who go out and exercise their freedom to choose careers with no sense of calling and service, commit the greatest sin of their lives. The greatest amount of their time, energy, and working hours go toward something that has no relation to God's service because there is no responsibility of knowledge.

Or what about the responsibility of knowledge and teaching? Today, most schools, colleges, and universities are structured in a way that is far from being Biblical, or even classical. This is true of many Christian colleges. I always find it curious, having been through Oxford, which is thoroughly secular in many ways, that a secular, modern university can be closer to the Scriptures than many Christian colleges today, at least in its approach to understanding of learning.

There was a point at which the Greeks and the Scriptures were very close: the deepest knowing cannot be put into words. Both understood that at the heart of knowing there is more to knowing than knowing will ever know. So the deepest knowledge cannot be spelled out adequately or specified in words. It cannot be expressed adequately in books, lectures, or seminars. Many profound truths can be told, but the deepest cannot. They have to be learned, as Plato and the Greeks understood, by experience, under an authority, from a master. Only then will people learn to know what even a master could never spell out or specify in words.

This means that at the heart of the deepest knowing is the need for an apprenticeship relationship. The Greek word for "disciple" is not so much *learner* as *apprentice*. "Jesus chose twelve to be *with him* and to be sent out to preach." Many people consider that being with Jesus was just a special privilege which the disciples had. But it was the heart of their learning, their discipleship. Probably the reason Jesus never wrote a book or founded a seminary or did many of the things that we would think would be absolutely essential for a master teacher, was because he was doing things far deeper and far more essential.

So it is that Oxford, founded in Christian origins, retains its almost Biblical tutorial system even though it is highly secularized today, whereas many Christian colleges that consider themselves consistently Christian have almost no element of apprenticeship in their learning.

Let me add one observation by way of relief as I close. There are many answers to the problem of handling the responsibility of knowledge in a day of overload. But the best, I believe, is to know your calling and, above all, its limits and your finiteness. People who try to gain a Renaissance knowledge today and then act on it are likely to suffer burnout. The only way we can handle today's knowledge is to know our callings and their limits.

The different spheres of our callings are like a series of concentric circles. We all live at the bull's eye. Now we can go where we don't live, and we can do things even beyond where we can afford to go, such as vote, write letters, or send money. And if we extend our influence to the furthest limits, the last limit of all is prayer. We can pray for countries which we will never be able to visit and so on.

But at the end of the day, when we reach the limits of the last concentric circle, those limits are not simply a curse. They provide a point of rest and a reminder of our finiteness. And in a fallen world, knowing our finiteness is not only a consequence of sin, but a matter of deep rest. "Sufficient unto the day is the evil thereof." The Lord alone is sovereign, and we are not. So when we've done all we can, anything beyond that is neither our calling nor our responsibility.

Ecclesiastes says that the more a person knows the more he has to suffer. Our generation probably knows the truth of that as much as any generation in history. But it's not just the substance of what we know that matters, it's also the way we handle what we know. For what we do with what we know is what Christian knowing is all about.

6

The Earth Is the Lord's
Stewardship in an Age of Crisis

Sharon Gallagher

The Earth is the Lord's and all that is in it,
The world, and those who live in it. (Psalm 24:1)

IN PICTURES TAKEN FROM space, earth, the blue planet, is incredibly beautiful, with its delicate atmosphere that keeps us alive. But this beauty and life are very fragile. The balance is intricate, a little more or a little less of certain chemicals and it would be another place entirely, arid, and without life, like the surrounding planets.

Those of us who believe in a Creator believe that all this was done deliberately. The Earth was "without form and void" and, out of that void, God created a place where we could live. God created the earth, the seas, trees, plants, sea creatures, and animals, and called them all good. And then God created human beings and called them good, at least initially.

This beautiful place, carefully and lovingly made, is now in jeopardy. Ancient forests and jungles that create the earth's oxygen are being destroyed, major rivers that provide life for millions of people are now polluted and toxic, and global warming threatens the whole planet with extinction.

Psalm 24 tells us that the earth is the Lord's. We don't own it, we were told to care for it and instead we've almost destroyed it.

STEWARDSHIP

I recently visited a church where a worship team led an unfamiliar song. One stanza, projected in big letters on the screen, derided those who "save the whales and kill babies." Environmentalists, who hold a wide range of attitudes on the abortion issue, were all labeled baby-hating tree huggers, leaving the impression that concern for the environment is antithetical to Christian morality. In truth, as a matter of discipleship, Christians should be in the forefront of the environmental movement.

In Genesis we're told that God entrusted stewardship of the earth to the first couple, with a blessing and an injunction to "be fruitful and multiply." In the New Testament, Jesus tells a parable about good and bad stewards to let his disciples know how we're to use God's gifts (Matthew 25). The good stewards made the most of what the master had given them, the bad steward buried what the master had given him and was chastised. What would have happened to stewards who trampled and destroyed what God gave them?

The earth is a gift to all its inhabitants. But we humans are the ones who can make reasonable choices about its future, and we're the ones causing its degradation.

We should be cultivating the earth and guarding its fecundity. Instead, species of animals and plants are going extinct at an increasingly alarming rate. Honeybees have started dying off from a mystery disease that many believe is caused by pesticides. Bees are tiny creatures but their extinction would cause a huge environmental crisis. Their pollination is essential for over 130 thousand kinds of plants.

APOCALYPSE

Unless we change our patterns of consumption, we're heading for a future of floods, draughts, famines and plagues. These possible ecological disasters may sound like end of the world scenarios. But we aren't meant to cause this destruction and suffering or stand by and watch it happen. The horrors described in the book of Revelation are a result of sin.

The U.S. once had an evangelical Christian called James Watt as secretary of the interior. Watt's attitude toward the parklands and other natural resources that were in his charge was that ultimately they really didn't matter. Since the earth was going to be destroyed anyway, preservation efforts were a waste of time.

Human beings, one could argue, are also all going to die, but we don't accept murdering them or hastening their demise. When people are ill, we pray for their healing and hope for their recovery. When we hear about people whose lives are shortened because of inadequate care, we're outraged. We need to have this same outrage, this same sense of care, and this same prayerful attitude toward the future of the earth.

If someone we loved was ill or dying would we stop feeding and caring for them? No, our care for them would increase. The Lord told us that "no man knows the day or the hour" of his return. We're not called to engage in endless speculation about when that hour will be. We're called to live as faithful disciples while we're here.

Martin Luther once famously said that if you believe that the world will end tomorrow, you should plant a tree. That is an argument for hope and for faithful stewardship of the earth.

BODY AND SOUL

There's a region of Appalachia where the tops of mountains are being blown off in an intensive new coal mining procedure. The process is degrading to the environment—ruining fishing streams, water supplies, and the area's natural beauty. Some Christians who organized to protest the mining were told by a critic "Christians should just care about saving people's souls."

The reality is that here on earth, where we are now dwelling, souls come in bodies. Scripture tells us that God cares about how we treat people—body and soul. Jesus cared about the physical well-being of the people around him. As he urged people to repent and believe and be reborn, he also healed them physically. Scriptures tell us that we'll be judged by how we treat the most vulnerable among us, visiting those who are sick or imprisoned. If we give a cup of cold water in His name, surely it's not meant to be poisoned.

PRO-LIFE

In recent years, American Protestants and Catholics have united to express concern about the beginning and end of life. Now, ecological damage threatens to destroy all life. As unpolluted water sources become scarce, children, the poor, and the elderly will be most at risk. The infant mortality rate, already high in the developing world, will increase dramatically worldwide. With increasing scarcity, competition for resources will lead to wars and deaths, not only of military personnel, but of civilian men, women and children.

In Sunday school we used to sing, "Jesus loves the little children / all the children of the world. / Red and yellow, black and white, / all are precious in his sight." If we believe that Jesus loves all the children of the world, we need to make the world a safer place for them.

The concern for the sanctity of life should lead Christians to the forefront of the environmental battle.

THE LEAST OF THESE

When I first became concerned about environmental issues I sensed that some social justice friends thought this was a "yuppie" issue. Privileged, educated, Westerners like me wanted to vacation in pristine beauty spots. The important issues were poverty, injustice, and peace.

But environmental issues are inextricably bound together with issues of social injustice, poverty, and war. Although environmental degradation impacts all of us, it is the poor who suffer most. In the U.S., major toxic dumps are located in poor communities, people who can't move to safer areas.

Poor countries have few resources to allocate for waste clean-up. In China 400,000 people die prematurely from air pollution every year. More than 70 percent of lakes and rivers (including the Yangtze) are polluted and unsafe to drink. The earth is groaning under this load of waste and pollution.

Pollution in one country harms all countries; the earth has one ecosystem. We really are the world. We learned this early on when airborne pollutants from U.S. factories caused acid rain in Canada. Some countries have signed pacts that limit fishing rights but countries who don't comply are rapidly depleting the world's supplies. Species that aren't fished into extinction may die off because of the oceans' rising temperature.

Since we in the U.S. represent 5 percent of the world's population and use 26 percent of its energy, our attempts to get developing nations like China and India to cut back sound hollow. They watch our movies and see how we live—they want to live that way too. How can we tell them not to take the steps that we've taken toward our own prosperity? But the earth simply can't sustain other countries consuming resources and creating waste at the levels that we in the U.S. are doing now. And it can't sustain the increasing rate of our consumption.

The U.S. deforested most of its land long ago, and after depleting our own resources, we depend on oxygen from countries who still have forests. Throughout the Bible we see that God has a heart for the poor. The Bible says that if we loan to the poor, God will count it as a loan to himself. Ecologically speaking, we've been doing the opposite, borrowing from the poor with no intention of repayment.

GOD'S GLORY

The Amazon rainforest produces 20 percent of the world's oxygen and has been called the lungs of the world. But these forests are being cut down at the rate of 7,500 square miles a year. The Amazon contains about 15–20% of earth's species, thousands of which have yet to be classified. Many rain forest plants have medicinal value, and many more may have. But the value is not only utilitarian. When Charles Darwin first saw the Amazon he tried to describe "the sensation of delight which the mind experiences" and concluded, "the land is one great, wild, untidy, luxuriant hothouse, made by nature for herself." (It's interesting that while Darwin can't bring himself to mention God, he feels emotion as well as pattern in the created order.)

We would say that the Creator found joy in the creation. Scripture reveals a God who delights in the beauty of creation. Jesus tells the disciples, "Consider the lilies of the field . . . even Solomon in all his glory was not arrayed as one of these." In other passages we learn that creation praises God: "Let the field exalt, and everything in it. Then shall the trees of the forest sing for joy." (1 Chronicles 16:33). Scripture also tells us that nature is a powerful witness to God's character. People who've rejected God will be under judgment because God's character is revealed in nature. We shouldn't allow this reflection of God's character to be defaced.

The Bible tells the story of God's boundless love for humanity, ultimately shown in giving His son, to live among us and die for us. But Scripture also reveals a God who cares for all creation. We know He cares for us, because "His eye is on the sparrow," but he also cares about the sparrow.

In the book of Job, God asks: "Do you observe the calving of the deer? Can you number the months that they fulfill. And do you know the time when they give birth?" (Job 39:1–4). Clearly, God does observe these things.

After Job's testing and insults from his friends, he questions God, asking why the righteous suffer. God answers his question: "I am the creator God and you are a creature and can't expect to understand my ways." But first Job is taken on a whirlwind tour of the universe, ending with a description of Leviathan (thought by most translators to be a whale).

This tour of creation ends with a long description of the whale, including these lines:

> It leaves a shining wake behind it;
> One would think the deep to be white-haired.
> On earth it has no equal,
> A creature without fear.
> It surveys everything that is lofty;
> It is king over all that are proud.
> (Job 41:32–34)

When Job hears this he repents saying, "I have uttered what I did not understand, things too wonderful for me, which I did not know." The whale is a testament to God's glory. The whale is God's concluding argument.

God created sparrows and whales and trees that clap their hands and stones that will cry out if God's word is not preached. God also created humanity with the capacity to care for the rest of creation and the expectation that they would do so.

Let's protect the future of this wonderful, good place that God created for us—for ourselves, for our children, for all the meek of the earth, and for all God's creatures great and small.

III

Contemporary Challenges

7

Modern Technology
Servant and Master

David W. Gill

IN THE POPULAR MIND "technology" usually means things like machines. Technology is what engineers and techies give us: telephones, fax machines, automobiles, electric lights, water purification plants, compact disc players, jet planes, and so on. It may seem odd to question whether technology is our master or our servant. All the tools and gadgets available today are presented as things that will serve us and make our lives better (or at least more interesting). Nobody is forcing you to buy and use a car or cell phone or power saw. Of course, we might say that somebody is becoming a "slave" to "Joe Millionaire" or to e-mail or to CNN's endless stream of "infotainment," but we are still using the term fairly loosely and freedom from such "slavery" seems just a touch of a button away.

HOW TECHNOLOGY SERVES US

For most of us, most of the time, technology is a good thing. It has served us, and even liberated us, in two ways. First, technology has served us by creating *tools* that vastly extend our human powers. By this I mean *construction tools* like hammers instead of rocks, then jack hammers instead of sledge hammers ... *medical tools* like x-ray machines, prostheses, and pharmaceuticals ... *transportation tools* like planes, trains, and automobiles ... *communication tools* such as television, compact disc players, computers, and fax machines. The list of technological tools is awesome. The ways these tools have served us is spectacular. Technology helps us fulfill our basic survival needs. It has often made our lives healthier and safer and our work more productive.

Equally important, but noted less often, technology has served us by its methods. Technology is not just tools, it is a method—the way of rational analysis, of quantification and measurement, of empirical testing, of innovation of new ways of approaching problems. In the material world of things, technology is the method of rationally analyzing how to move things from one place to another, how to multiply, divide, simplify or combine various elements and factors. As such, technology helps us break down a production and distribution process into its constituent parts and then restructure the process toward greater efficiency.

And the method that works with automobile assembly lines and other material processes has also been applied to human relations as in the conduct of business meetings, the creation of effective advertising, and the development of psychotherapy. Technology is the creation of better *means*, in fact, of the "one best means, "in every field of human activity. Modern bureaucracy, for example, operates under the rule of technological method—even if in practice it often is far less efficient than we would like.

So don't get me wrong: what follows is not intended as a call back to the jungle and to irrationality, or to just give up and submit to nature, as though nature itself were God. Technology is often a good thing and a valued servant of human life and purpose.

TECHNOLOGY'S TRADE-OFFS

But the services rendered by technology come at a price. We must be careful not to deny or ignore the price we pay for technology. We should always try to identify and consider its full, real costs. Specific technologies always have *both positive and negative aspects*. It is not helpful to say that technology is neutral (or to say that it is exclusively evil or good); it is *both* good and bad. It is often said that technology is neutral and only its use or its users are good or bad. The users carry all the moral responsibility in this view.

Now certainly you can say that, for example, a gun in the hands of a crook will be put to bad use, and a gun in the hands of a good person can be put to good use. But it is the technology itself that makes possible these uses; one should not simply invent guns without weighing these outcomes and deciding whether to proceed. Guns "suggest" shooting—just like hammers suggest pounding and calculators suggest counting. If you invent, sell, or buy a gun you bear some responsibility for what is done with it.

So too, the development of automobiles not only results in freedom to travel but also in pollution, in serious injuries to people, and in the kind of glass and steel encased anonymity that facilitates social breakdown. The good possibilities of television are accompanied by the loss of human conversation and a diminishing capacity to entertain oneself in a spectator era.

Technology often functions as an *amplifier*. The scope and impact of our actions can be vastly amplified by technology. But is this neutral? Or all good? Is it good that more people are able to get good information about Jesus Christ, or hear great music, or personally visit other cultures because of technology? Sure. But remember that these same technologies enable the broadcast of both truth and lies. Furthermore, the human need is often less about quantity than it is about quality (of information, music, travel, etc.). "Infoglut" can be as big a problem as "infofamine."

Technology often brings economies of scale and efficiency. But technology's true cost is rarely appreciated. New technologies require trained technical support to be hired and available. They require time for learning by users. Technologies don't last forever; new upgrades come along; old things break down. Did we remember to factor in these costs when we asked "how much?" Old computers and automobiles need to be disposed of. Is it cost-free to recycle them? Not very often. Did General Electric factor in the cost of cleaning up the Hudson River after their PCB dumping killed it? Was this cost factored into the evaluation of how much to pay GE CEO Jack Welch? No, this cost was dumped on the community, the fishing businesses, and the next generations (fortunately, it looks like GE is now being forced to pay for the cleanup). Is the cost of repetitive motion injury (e.g., carpal tunnel syndrome) to data-entry people factored in to computerization costs?

There is also a huge trade-off in human skill when technologies come in. For example, medical personnel acquire sophisticated expertise in reading MRI and bone-scan analyses—but they lose expertise in touching and in listening to patients. Patients themselves, e.g., pregnant women, gain some things, e.g., fetal monitoring readings—but gradually lose the ability to know or care for their own bodies and health. I am not saying we should go back to the old days, mind you, but when patients become totally dependent on technology and technological experts, something has been lost.

As cell-phone usage grows, people are losing the ability to listen attentively to one another. Why? Because you don't need to pay attention to what, for example, someone asks you to buy at the store. You grunt "yes" but weren't listening much. Then as you walk the aisles of the store you get out your cell phone and call home to ask what it was that you were supposed to buy. Maybe this is not a huge loss to our grocery shopping lives but it symbolizes a general phenomenon: when you can always make a quick call on your cell phone you lose the need and then the capacity to pay attention, focus, and remember.

Similarly, when you can always fire off more follow-up e-mails to someone, you are less careful to be sure how you express yourself to that person. If you had to type or hand-write a letter, address an envelope, and take it to the post office, you would be more careful in your expression. When I receive a personally typed or handwritten letter, I read it over thoughtfully and appreciatively. When it is one of twenty e-mails from my colleague, I have no idea if he meant them all as equally (un?) important. I relax and focus my attention elsewhere, knowing we can always swap a few more messages to clarify things.

But what is the cost of all these e-mails and phone calls in money and in time? Is the gain worth the price? I use e-mail a lot and experience both its benefits and costs. I have resisted getting a cell phone, though I may yet break down. The point is to be aware of technological costs as well as benefits and take aggressive steps to control and deploy it in an appropriate way.

Edward Tenner's great study *Why Things Bite Back: Technology and the Revenge of Unintended Consequences* provides almost three hundred pages of historical evidence of such hidden costs of technology. For example, computers were supposed to lead to the "paperless office." In fact the use of paper in computerized offices doubles. Why? Nobody saw it coming but it is so easy to print out multiple versions of a document as you improve it. I think my PhD dissertation might have been typed (with pain and care) all the way through three times on my typewriter in the late 70s. My more recent books have been printed at least five times because of the ease of computerized changes (I think they are better books because of this process, by the way, but we need to face up to the cost).

As technologies for football equipment (e.g., helmets) have improved on safety, football injuries have increased. Why? Because players play more recklessly, relying on the improved safety of the equipment. Improved safety regulations for small children on airplanes (each child over two must have his or her own seat and seat belt) has led to more injury and death for children. Why? Because the safety requirements on planes meant that parents had to buy tickets for their small children and strap them in rather than let them sit on their laps—and as a result more families travel by cars, which, even with seatbelts, have higher injury and death statistics than airplanes. In agriculture, the introduction of pesticides and herbicides has often killed off one problem only to make way for much worse problems that used to be held in check by that first "problem."

Technology (transportation, communication) has enabled globalization. While this has brought great blessings—better intercultural understanding, jobs and trade to depressed areas—it has also brought great problems and challenges. Global terrorists operate alongside corporate developers, global peacemakers, and environmental activists. The blessing of American democratic ideas is exported alongside the curse of Hollywood's offensive images and idiotic messages and the bullying presence of today's corporate robber barons. The overpowering of local color and cultural particularity by a homogeneous "McWorld" culture is a terrible price to pay for the ostensible blessings distributed by McWorld. It has all of the dangers present in the replacement of local agricultural biodiversity by agribusiness monoculture.

Inventors, manufacturers, sellers, and users of technologies all need to get serious about this matter of technology "trade-off. " Technology is often a great choice—but it is sometimes a terrible thing. In our present world crisis, should the inventors, manufacturers, and sellers of advanced military technologies to Saddam Hussein, Osama bin Laden, and others of their ilk, be given a free pass morally (or legally)? What they have done is not neutral. It is predominantly bad—and their technology business profits have come at a huge cost to all the rest of us. Why are they not being held accountable? If you give a loaded gun to a child, are you not responsible when it is used? When you give the car keys to a drunk, do you have no responsibility? On a personal level, when you put a television set at the center of your family life, have you no responsibility when a subsequent lack of family communication and cohesion results in disaster?

It is time to press this issue. Technologies amplify existing potential for both good and evil. Technologies produce serious and far-reaching impacts that are often unanticipated. Those who invent them, manufacture them, sell them, buy them, and use them are all responsible when damage results—just as they deserve some credit when good results.

HOW TECHNOLOGY MASTERS US

So we live in a fundamentally *technological milieu* or environment, not a natural or social one. Technology often serves us by providing us with a wide and growing range of *tools* that greatly extend our human capabilities as well as a powerful *method* of approaching all human problems and possibilities, the method of rational, quantitative analysis, the search for measurable effective means. It is utterly critical however to examine the trade-offs, the costs and benefits, of particular technologies we bring into our lives.

But I want to step back from the issues raised by particular technologies and look at three aspects of the technological phenomenon as a whole. First, technology in the modern world displays the character of a *necessary, almost deterministic force*. Technological developments create technological problems which require further technological responses *ad infinitum*. There has been a qualitative shift from earlier eras in which specific tools and techniques were developed through the freely chosen creativity of human beings to meet specific, limited objectives. Technology now obeys its inner logic of development as rigorously as we used to think that nature obeyed its own laws. This necessity is especially visible in a larger view of the technological complex as a whole. "If it can be done, it will be done; indeed, it must be done." Technology carries its own imperative to further development. At this point technology is no longer a simple servant of humankind but its master. This apparent inevitability of technological expansion must be challenged. We must assert our freedom and learn to say "no" once in a while.

Second, technology today is *universalistic*, in two senses: it invades every area of the world and every aspect of human existence. This is what Neil Postman calls "technopoly," technology as a monopoly over all human affairs. Part of what this means is the *geographic universalization* of technology. Every corner of the world is affected by technological intervention. Global development means technological development. Traditional ways of agriculture are replaced by technological ways. Traditional forms of governance must be replaced by bureaucracies. Or else! Or else those who resist are condemned to live at best as an underclass, at worst as the refuse dump of the globally dominant technological complex.

But technological universalism or technopoly also refers to the *invasion of technology into every aspect of our lives*. *Politics* and campaigning is technicized; *sport* and entertainment; *public relations* and fund-raising obey technological laws; *churches* employ public relations techniques to build their memberships; even *prayer* and spirituality are analyzed and taught as a set of rational techniques for manipulating God and the self; even *sexuality*, the last domain of the truly wild and mysterious, has never been so technicized—not just in terms of reproductive or prophylactic technologies but the technical analysis of the sex act itself. *Our physical space* is dominated by technological instruments; *our psychic space* is dominated by the method and values of technology: rationality, effectiveness, measurable success. We need to resist this universalist pressure and guard times and places in our lives that are free of technology.

Third, technology now serves virtually as *the sacred* in our lives. The sacred, the divine, the god, is whatever occupies the very center of our existence, giving our lives unity, direction, and meaning. The traditional gods have mostly been toppled and replaced by technology, at least in the West. Traditional gods may receive lip service in church or in private conversation but in practice, on Monday morning if not before, it is Technology which we serve. It is in Technology that we hope for our future and even for our present day salvation.

Another way to express this is by saying we have moved from technology to *technologism*. Adding that "ism" is a way of saying that technological thinking and values have become the foundation, the worldview, the criterion of all judgment. Just as race and sex are good in service of a healthy, holistic human mission but bad when they become *racism* or *sexism*, so we could say that the goodness of technology is radically put in question when it is developed into technologism as an all-embracing intellectual, moral, cultural and spiritual identity.

Our values are a direct spin-off from our isms and our gods. "Technogod" commands us "Thou shalt love technology with all thy heart, mind, soul and strength." "Thou shalt measure success always in quantitative terms." "Thou shalt not allow inefficiency in any operation." "Thou shalt not permit anything irrational, nonrational, or suprarational to live outside my rule."

When something or someone is omnipresent, omnipotent, and not subject to criticism, when it inspires and compels our sacrifices and praise, it sounds like a god to me. The question is: is Technology an adequate god, or is it a bogus pretender to divinity that needs to be demythologized and desacralized? Is the Technogod ultimately a liberating, redeeming god or an enslaving one?

FINDING OUR WAY FORWARD IN A TECHNOLOGICAL ERA

The question is "who or what is in control of our lives?" Have we become mere "tools of our tools" as Thoreau asked? Have we in effect made Technology the god of our civilization? Gods always demand some kind of worship in return for the salvation, meaning and direction they offer. If this is so, is this covenant with Technogod one we really wish to make? The worship demanded by Technology has meant lives of frantic absorption into the latest technological thing. Our lives are dominated by the products and the problems of technology. Our learning is dominated by the acquisition of technological literacy and competence.

Perhaps we can best evaluate this covenant with technology by asking what has been necessarily excluded. And I would argue that what has been lost is the value of the inefficient, the nonrational, the aesthetic, the spiritual, the traditional. Love and beauty, for example, are prostituted and lost when they are made to serve a technological calculus. Relationships with family members and colleagues are seriously distorted when rationality and efficiency are the criteria of value.

But how will we, how can we, respond? Let's quickly dispose of three popular responses: First, some will *deny* that technology is a problem and protest that modern technology is more or less desirable and under control. Denial is the characteristic problem addressed by Aldous Huxley's *Brave New World*. This first response is partly a product of *exhaustion*. We simply don't have the time or energy to stop and take a critical look at the broader dimensions of what is happening to our human life. We are too busy. It is also true that our technological society provides innumerable distractions and opiates to its members.

But it is also a product of a *lack of perspective*. Most of our technologically trained population at large have little significant background in history, not much more in philosophy or theology, and little significant non-Western cultural exposure. Yet these are precisely what we need for a critical perspective. We have much knowledge of a certain type; but little *wisdom*. Hence we tend to take our western technological perspective for the only one, though it is by no means the only perspective in the Western tradition, to say nothing of the rest of the world.

A second response allows that, while we have some serious dysfunctionality in our technological civilization, we only need more and better technology to resolve these problems. This is the *technophile* response, the reaction of lovers of technology, of *true believers* in technology. The priests and evangelists of technology want to get everyone on the information superhighway—with an integrated office system, linked to our home entertainment and work centers, and to our portable cellular phone and notebook computer. Thus the technological environment becomes essentially airtight and everyone is technologically linked to everything at every moment. But *where is this superhighway going*? We have started off at a vast and accelerating pace, but where are we headed? That's the question.

Opposite the technophiles are the third group, the *technophobes*. In the Industrial Revolution these were the Luddites, the band of anti-industry types who wished to smash the machine and return to a more pastoral existence. In our own era, the Hippies of the Sixties made a somewhat similar call to stop the machine and get back to the garden. But romanticism and adolescent anger make a flimsy foundation for resistance, as the subsequent absorption of the Sixties generation into the Yuppies demonstrated. Technological reactionaries are doomed to be the colorful feather in the cap of the technological giant: a dash of color on a giant who moves forward unimpeded.

A fourth response, the one I promote, is *resistance and revolution*. This calls first for a profound *awareness and critical analysis of our reality*: the *reality of the technological maincurrents* under the surface of the ocean of our existence, and the *reality of our flesh-and-blood neighbors*. For such awareness we must stop relying on *USA Today*- and CNN-type newsbytes—and invest our time in broader, deeper works of cultural criticism, including historical and multicultural perspectives which will give depth and breadth to our own analysis of social and cultural reality. Along with this we will need to turn off the TV, take off the Walkman, turn off the distractions, and carve out time to develop human relationships with a few people around our living and working areas. This means learning how to listen, how to be quiet, how to reflect deeply, how to care.

With this growing awareness, then, we need to *resist*, indeed, to *refuse* the necessity, universality, and divinity of Technology in our life and work. We need to "just say no" to technology at decisive points.

But gods don't easily vacate their thrones. To dethrone the old, we need to install a more appropriate one. To begin with, we can resist in the name of Humanity. We need a truer, more robust humanism than technologism can allow. Our thinking, living, working and playing can revolve around the *sacredness of human life* and of the earth and universe in which, and with which, we flourish or come to grief. Concretely this means that for humanists people are not reducible to statistics . . . that intelligence is not reducible to IQ numbers or degrees held or genetic maps . . . that this living student or friend before me is sacred, and is more important in his or her living wholeness and mystery than any rational calculation could ever account for. To say this is to replace technologism with a robust humanism.

Some of us in the modern West, and most people in the rest of the world as well as the older traditions of the West, would suggest that the strongest foundation on which to base such a humanism, and from which to resist Technologism or any other false gods, is a *theological* one in which the transcendent God who created the universe and humanity is invited back into our sacred space. We theological types would say that humanism is true and good because God has created humans in his own image. Technological civilization tends to promote uniformity and reduce individuals to faceless atoms in a mass society. To mistreat or undervalue a person is to mistreat an irreplaceable child of God. To exploit and abuse the earth and the universe is not merely a technological dysfunction but a serious sin against God and his creation.

In an authentically biblical philosophy of technology, technological creativity and innovation are fundamentally rooted in our being made in the image of a creative, innovative Maker. It is embedded in our nature to want to create and make good, useful tools and artifacts. Resisting technology as a Master and a pretender to the god place in our lives must thus proceed from resistance (saying no to a Technogod) to a *positive revolution in values* that rebuilds a life in which we celebrate good, life-affirming technology. As consumers of technology, our calling is not to smash the machine but to question it, appraise it in reference to our core mission and values, and then sometimes say yes to its deployment as servant in our life and work . . . and sometimes, to say no.

8

Finding Your Way in Science and Faith

Walter R. Hearn

IT'S HARD FOR ME to believe that over half a century has passed since I "made my bones" as a research scientist. By then I was already a Christian, so doing science was neither my whole life nor my deepest commitment. It was fun, it put me in contact with bright people, and it paid the rent. Doing science kept me busy, but I found time to think about how science fit together with my life in Christ. I've been thinking about that ever since.

Offering a seminar at New College Berkeley prompted me to reconnoiter once again the territory where science and faith meet, maybe to serve as a kind of tour guide for a new generation. I called my seminar, "Compass, Map, and Guidebook," thinking of equipment we find useful when exploring places new to us.

MAP AND COMPASS

Scientists often think of their work as "modeling" or "mapping" everything in the natural world. Each scientist explores only a limited range of phenomena, but all those studies eventually get melded into an overall picture. The better the model, the better scientists understand how things work. The more comprehensive our map, the more details we know about the universe we inhabit.

The map-making metaphor has always helped me relate science to my experience of Christian faith. Like Pilgrim in John Bunyan's allegory of the Christian life, I see myself as on a journey. When we travel through unfamiliar territory, it's a big help to have a map. Today our impression of the world is so strongly influenced by science and technology that we may need to remind ourselves that "a map is not the territory itself." Even the most comprehensive scientific description of, say, a living person could not determine that person's destiny. We human beings are agents. We make choices—like my decision to do scientific work, for example.

A mature religious faith makes us aware of those distinctions. In contrast to science, faith is about where we're headed, or *should* be headed. Faith provides us with an ultimate destination. Faith orients us as we check our actual position against the maps. By faith we "get our bearings" so we can alter our course if necessary, to keep heading in the right direction. If science gives us maps, faith gives us a compass. We need both.

Recently I received a copy of a topographic map of Tibet and part of China, with the Yellow River and several villages highlighted. The friend who made the copy is a Chinese American geologist who "knows the territory." He wanted to clarify for me an account I had read of a journalist's trip to Tibet. My friend's map, however, included no indication of which way was up—and every word on it was in Chinese characters. Eventually I noted in the margin a single Arabic numeral (a page number from the atlas). Aha! A symbol I knew how to read. Before finding that clue I had been holding the map upside down. Even with an accurate map, I needed something else to orient myself.

Maps are always abstractions of reality. No one map can contain all the facts that can be known about a real territory, so we choose the kind of map that fits our specific needs. For convenience we use flat maps of areas of the surface of a spherical Earth, despite inevitable distortions. For example, the Mercator projection used for neat rectangular maps of the whole world makes features near the poles appear much larger relative to those near the equator.

III • CONTEMPORARY CHALLENGES

CONTOURS OF SCIENCE AND RELIGION

The claim of religious people has always been that a spiritual realm exists, which, though unmappable by scientific methods, is as real as the "real world" of physical phenomena. What happens when the two realms meet? Do they simply coexist? Abut? Overlap? Merge into each other? Surveying their intersection, some observers note profound differences between science and religious faith. Others stress equally important similarities. At various times I have argued both ways.

It would be nice to have an aerial view of the science/religion interface, if we had a "viewpoint" from which to observe its complex contours. For this mapping exercise, science fails us because its observations are restricted to the physical realm. Of course religious *behavior* can be analyzed scientifically. Any human activity, including *scientific* behavior, can be studied scientifically—up to a point. Thus, if we were to examine the scientific enterprise through scientific eyes, any spiritual motivations for doing science would prove elusive. To those who do not accept spiritual reality, of course, *everything* has to be attributable to strictly physical causes, known or "yet to be discovered." The scientific approach pervades Western culture precisely because so many observable phenomena have been satisfactorily accounted for by physical cause-and-effect chains.

Actually, many scientists seem to resent efforts to map the scientific enterprise itself. They are likely to dismiss such "science studies" (usually published by historians, sociologists, or philosophers of science) as lying outside proper scientific bounds. With its boundaries still being debated, "science" is hard for an outsider to talk about, let alone to compare with religion. Both are complex ways of life, with a theoretical side and an empirical or experiential side. The theoretical aspect of religious life is called theology.

When we try to picture the "topology" of the scientific enterprise, physics seems to rise like a mountain, with each experimentally tested theory resting firmly atop others. Climbers to the lofty heights are rewarded by a clear view of the surrounding landscape. Meanwhile, down in the flatlands, psychologists, sociologists, and other scholars slog through jungles and swamps, seldom gaining a vantage point, often isolated from fellow explorers. Observations that might gain them recognition as "real scientists" are only weakly connected by interlocking theories.

Fifty years ago, when I was doing biochemical work, I pictured my efforts as somewhere in between. Each researcher in my field seemed to be scaling a small hill of accomplishment. If we made it to the top we could glimpse a landscape of many such knolls rising from a vast forest of scientific ignorance. Each experimentally established high point became a solid feature of the territory but still at some distance from the others.

In those heady days of molecular biology's rapid expansion, I probably operated in a rather reductionist mode. From my prior commitment to Christ, I knew that science wasn't everything ("the map is *not* the territory"). I also knew that physics wasn't the only science. Yet, as a chemist, I could easily envision chemistry eventually taking over biology and, as biochemistry became more quantitative and mathematical, everything being more or less reduced to physics.

In the 1950s and '60s I cheered the discovery of many metabolic pathways shared by living things as diverse as yeasts and human beings. Someday, I thought, exploring biochemical *differences* between species would be even more challenging. Already we knew the complete structure of a few functional proteins, unraveled with great effort. In 1953, when DNA's basic structural pattern was deciphered, the genetic significance of that pattern immediately became obvious. I doubted, however, that the total chemical structure of any specific DNA molecule would be known in my lifetime. DNA molecules were huge. Their reactive groups were out of reach, tucked inside that tightly coiled double helix. The task would be monumental.

What I did not foresee was the automation of DNA sequencing, nor the use of computers to handle the vast amount of information recoverable from each DNA molecule. If I had seen that coming, I might have been even *more* convinced that biology would be subsumed under chemistry and physics. I would have been wrong about that, too—or so it seems at the moment. Structural data on specific DNA molecules is pouring out of labs all over the world, yet much of that information seems to complicate our understanding of how living things work, rather than simplifying or unifying it.

I have begun to think differently about biology. Suppose we say that physics studies *what is always the same*—principles that remain unchanged over all time and space. I've come to see biology as studying *what is seldom if ever the same* from one time and place to another.

Organisms and species can indeed be studied by physico-chemical methods, but unless their *histories* and *environments* are taken into account, we're doing physics and chemistry, not biology. It is no longer clear to me that physics "as we know it" can ever fully absorb biology. Think of the difference this way: results of physical research are best expressed as equations; results of biological research are best expressed as case histories.

Further, before our rock-solid mountain of physics could be capped off with a climactic "Theory of Everything," it has developed a few cracks. In the ranges of very small phenomena (the quantum world) and very large phenomena (the large-scale structure of the universe), apparently irreconcilable theories have popped up. After hearing a cosmologist present evidence that a mysterious "dark matter" makes up perhaps 90 percent of the mass of the universe, I asked how that matter relates to the periodic table of elements. He replied, "Nobody knows." So much for the universality of chemistry "as we know it."

Does the steady accumulation of knowledge guarantee that we're making progress? Well, yes, if we're headed toward a goal we actually want to achieve. Christians should never fear a buildup of scientific understanding nor, for that matter, of scientific confusion. As the hymn puts it, "Our anchor holds." Maps can go out of date, so hang on to your compass.

AN ALTERED LANDSCAPE

With the sciences in a state of flux, we might expect any reconnaissance flight over the area where science and religion meet to encounter some turbulence. Two new factors have been changing the landscape at that boundary. One is the effect of John M. Templeton's largesse in legitimizing a (hyphenated) "science-and-religion" discipline as an academic field of study.

John Templeton is a highly successful international investor who wants to promote in religion the kind of innovation that has been characteristic of science. Born in 1912 in a small Tennessee town, he was raised in a Cumberland Presbyterian family. A former Rhodes scholar, "Sir John" (knighted in 1987 by Queen Elizabeth II) is now a naturalized British citizen living in the Bahamas. Since 1973, the Templeton Foundation he established has awarded an annual Templeton Prize for

Progress in Religion. The first award went to Mother Teresa of Calcutta, but awardees have also included scientists who have written about religion. The amount of the award, approximately a million U.S. dollars, was deliberately set a little higher than the amount of the Nobel Prizes to make the point that religion is just as important as science.

Each year (at least until the recent stock market decline) the Templeton Foundation has given away some 40 times that amount on imaginative projects in science-and-religion. These have included lectureships, conferences, publications, prizes for essays and books, and substantial awards for the design of new courses on science-and-religion at colleges, universities, and seminaries. Templeton's generosity and strategic thinking in targeting projects have put science-and-religion on the academic map as never before.

In addition to science-and-religion, the Templeton Foundation, headquartered in Radnor, Pennsylvania, funds initiatives in spirituality and health, character development, and free enterprise education, all interests of its founder. Publications of the Templeton Foundation Press include a number of books and collections put together by John Templeton himself, for example *Evidence of Purpose: Scientists Discover the Creator*. A reference work copyrighted by the Foundation, *Who's Who in Theology and Science*, is still very useful.

A second factor changing the lay of the land in recent decades has been the challenge of Intelligent Design (ID) to the legitimacy of the dominant neo-Darwinist influence on biology, other sciences, and culture in general. Progenitor and guiding spirit of the ID movement has been Phillip E. Johnson, Jefferson E. Peyser Professor of Law (now emeritus) at the University of California. On sabbatical leave in London in 1988, Johnson was attracted to books by prestigious scientists presenting evolution to the public and defending it from attack by creationists. Seeing weaknesses in those arguments, Johnson (born in 1940 and, like Templeton, now a Presbyterian) concluded that Darwinism goes far beyond science. For Johnson, Darwinism serves as a modern "creation myth" rooted in a naturalistic philosophy. That philosophy essentially deifies Nature by assigning to it alone the power to create.

With *Darwin on Trial*, legal scholar Johnson began turning out a series of books attacking belief in Darwinism and arguing that Darwinian theory is grossly underdetermined by experimental evidence. His recent books include *The Wedge of Truth* and *The Right Questions*.

Phillip Johnson's books attracted a number of bright young scholars, mostly Christians already skeptical of both Darwinism and "scientific creationism." Thus was born a movement promoting Intelligent Design (ID) as a viable alternative. The movement's strategy is to drive a wedge between legitimate science and the scientism of metaphysical naturalism. To most members of the ID community, even *methodological* naturalism (which most scientists would defend) boils down to an atheistic religious stance. Prominent among young ID scientists have been mathematician William A. Dembski (author of *The Design Inference, No Free Lunch,* and *The Design Revolution*), biochemist Michael Behe (*Darwin's Black Box*), and developmental biologist Jonathan Wells (*Icons of Evolution*). Philosopher of science Stephen C. Meyer directs the Center for Science and Culture of the Discovery Institute in Seattle, which has become an institutional home for ID investigations.

Do these two movements reinforce each other or are they completely at odds? Templeton and his foundation "work on the premise that scientific principles of evolution and the idea of God as Creator are compatible." Johnson and his followers agree—but admit only microevolution (at the species level) as fitting the definition of an empirically determined scientific principle. IDers see the grand story of macroevolution (accounting for all changes from non-life to human beings by random mutation and natural selection) as an unwarranted extrapolation, a kind of wishful thinking on the part of evolutionists.

I take a guardedly positive attitude toward both developments. I welcome the peacemaking approach of the Templetonians and applaud most of their efforts, though it is not clear to me that elevating science-and-religion to a level of academic prestige will do much to help ordinary believers. I think the inclusiveness inherent in some Templeton projects tends to blur or erase distinctions. In contrast, the Johnsonians see themselves as warriors, as Davids taking on establishment Goliaths, frequently insisting that there is no middle ground. They regard "theistic evolution" (a position held by many evangelical scientists) as an inconsistent and indefensible compromise. Although at present I don't consider ID a viable scientific alternative to evolutionary theory, I welcome its challenge to evolutionary speculations that go beyond the warrant of empirical evidence.

In debates over science and religion, protagonists have frequently gone too far, claimed too much. For fruitful discussion, peacemaker-types must avoid ignoring real distinctions, and warrior-types must avoid countering exaggerated claims by hurling overstatements in the opposite direction. Another caution: Intellectual movements are likely to be judged for the company they keep as well as for the ideas they promote. John Templeton has admitted being influenced by such esoteric New Thought movements as Unity and Religious Science. Among Phillip Johnson's followers are creationists insistent on a young-earth interpretation of Genesis and geology; that is not Johnson's own position, but he tries not to exclude or offend such allies.

GUIDEBOOKS GALORE

For my seminar I wanted to suggest books to help newcomers enter into the ongoing science/faith discussion. Figuring out which books to recommend was a problem I never had fifty years ago. Then, I could count less than a handful of useful books on science and faith. Today, science-and-religion books gush forth almost as steadily as the DNA-data stream. Forced to choose, I stuck with a few authors with whom I was personally acquainted, favoring books written by scientists over books about science written by others.

Many authors of exemplary books I know through the American Scientific Affiliation (ASA), which was founded in 1941 as a fellowship of evangelical Christians doing scientific work. I joined as a grad student and have remained active in ASA long after I hung up my lab coat. For some 23 years I edited its newsletter. My newsletter stories of what ASA members were doing in the lab and in their churches became the basis for my own (highly recommended!) *Being a Christian in Science*. That book is advertised at www.asa3.org/, which also contains a growing archive of articles and book reviews from ASA's quarterly journal, *Perspectives on Science and Christian Faith*.

TO START YOU ON YOUR WAY

A handy little handbook (at 205 pages) to orient you in the field is *When Science Meets Religion*, by Ian G. Barbour, who won the 1999 Templeton Prize for Progress in Religion. Since the 1960s, Barbour has produced book after book clarifying the interaction of science and religion. His *Issues in Science and Religion* (1966) brought talk of science into the broader Christian world, as Bernard Ramm's *The Christian View of Science and Scripture* (1954) had done for evangelicals. Barbour's *Issues* served as a widely used textbook in courses on science and religion, superseded by Barbour's *Religion in an Age of Science*, one of two books based on his 1989–91 Gifford Lectures in Aberdeen. (The Gifford Lectures were endowed in 1885 to bring the latest in "natural theology" to the four universities in Scotland.)

Ian Barbour is emeritus Professor of Science, Technology, and Society at Carleton College in Minnesota, where he has taught since 1955. He earned a PhD in nuclear physics at the University of Chicago, then studied theology and ethics at Yale Divinity School. In October 2003, Berkeley's Center for Theology and the Natural Sciences celebrated his 80th birthday with a symposium; in 2004, CTNS has published a *Festschrift* from that occasion, *Fifty Years in Science and Religion: Ian G. Barbour and His Legacy*.

Barbour's four categories of ways to relate science and religion (conflict, independence, dialogue, integration) have been used or acknowledged by almost every writer on the subject. *When Science Meets Religion* is organized around that framework, almost to the point of excess. In each chapter ("On the Four Views"; "Astronomy and Creation"; "Implications of Quantum Physics"; "Evolution and Continuing Creation"; "Genetics, Neuroscience, and Human Nature"; "God and Nature"), he gives an up-to-date assessment of the scientific situation, then shows how representatives of each of the four categories relate it to religion.

Barbour's own writing is informed, lucid, and fair to the positions of others. He never hesitates to acknowledge his own religious commitment, which some readers may feel pushes the limits of a theistic position too far. Barbour leans toward a universalist understanding of salvation and essentially embraces a "process metaphysics" in his theology (sometimes called "panentheism" to distinguish it from classical theism).

☙

The shortest book on my seminar list is *Belief in God in an Age of Science* by John C. Polkinghorne. At 133 pages, it's the only one I could read in one evening. It is the latest work by a mathematical physicist who is also an Anglican priest and prolific writer of excellent books on science and faith for the general public. I've never read a book by Polkinghorne that I didn't enjoy. That includes his theological heavyweight, *The Faith of a Physicist*, published in England as *Science and Christian Belief*), based on his 1993–94 Gifford Lectures in Edinburgh. Polkinghorne frequently cites the larger volume in this new book, based on his 1996 Terry Lectures. (Like the Gifford Lectures, the Terry Lectureship at Yale Divinity School has sought for almost a hundred years to build "the truths of science and philosophy into the structure of a broadened and purified religion.")

John Polkinghorne earned a PhD in quantum field theory and a DSc for research on elementary particle physics at Cambridge. After teaching mathematical physics at Edinburgh he returned to Cambridge, becoming in 1968 the university's Professor of Mathematical Physics. In 1972 he resigned that post to pursue theological studies and in 1982 was ordained a priest in the Church of England. After several years as a parish priest and vicar, he returned to Cambridge as Dean of Trinity Hall, finally as president of Queen's College, a post from which he retired in 1996. Another "Sir John" (knighted in 1997), Polkinghorne has been a Fellow of the Royal Society since 1974. In 2002 he won the Templeton Prize for Progress in Religion.

The subtitle of Polkinghorne's Gifford Lectures was "Reflections of a Bottom-Up Thinker." I suspect that I resonate so well with what he writes because I also tend to start with what is proximate and work my way toward the ultimate. (Top-down thinkers go the other way, beginning with axioms, philosophical propositions, or fundamental doctrines.) Among other Gifford lecturers and other Templeton awardees, Polkinghorne may stand out as being more at home with traditional Christian interpretations of the Bible. He built the framework of his Gifford lectures around the phrases of the Nicene Creed, for example, perhaps startling his hearers with his affirmation of the bodily resurrection of Christ.

To me, the high point of this latest book is a chapter on "Finding Truth: Science and Religion Compared." After defining five distinct phases in the construction of scientific theories and showing how they featured in turning questions about the nature of light into modern quantum theory, Polkinghorne shows how theologians went through very similar steps to work out a satisfactory "theory" of the human/divine nature of Jesus Christ. "Does God Act in the Physical World?" is another pithy chapter. In it he seems to regard chaos theory as more likely to be fruitful than quantum theory (in which he is an expert) in trying to make sense of God's agency in the world. Expect to be intellectually challenged by *Belief in God in an Age of Science*.

⁕

The authors of *Species of Origins: America's Search for a Creation Story*, Karl W. Giberson and Donald A. Yerxa, have come on the scene more recently than Barbour or Polkinghorne with this useful book. Both are at Eastern Nazarene College (ENC) in Massachusetts, where Yerxa teaches history and Giberson (pronounced GUY-berson), teaches physics, and the history and philosophy of science.

I chose this book even before reading it because I had been favorably impressed by an earlier book by Giberson, *Worlds Apart: The Unholy War between Religion and Science*. Addressed to college students brought up in the author's Wesleyan tradition, it included a section called "I Was a Teenage Fundamentalist" about the author's gradual disenchantment with "creation science" as his faith matured. Karl Giberson represents a new generation of Christian scholars trained in science and able to write convincingly for younger readers.

After earning a PhD in atomic physics at Rice University, Giberson returned to ENC, his alma mater, to teach in 1984. In 1996 his course on "Issues in Science and Religion" won a Templeton award, and he has recently participated in the Templeton Oxford Seminars on Science and Christianity. That program was initiated by the Council of Christian Colleges and Universities to give promising young scholars opportunities for research and writing over three consecutive summers at Oxford. Giberson may be an "ink-oholic," since he edits both ENC's journal *The Christian Scholar* and the ambitious Templeton-supported monthly tabloid *Science and Theology News*. Since 2003 Giberson has also been editor-in-chief of *Science & Spirit*, which seemed to lose its way after morphing in 1998 from a small Templeton-supported newsletter to a slick bimonthly magazine.

Despite its tricky title, *Species of Origins* is a scholarly effort to clear up misunderstandings and errors in "basically unresolvable" disagreements between creationists and evolutionists—a landscape that for many seems "shrouded in an impenetrable fog." Beneath the book's academically acceptable prose I detect the authors' sympathy for a confused churchgoing population, perhaps occasionally the intensity of Giberson's own face-off with creationism as a student. The creation/evolution issue is, after all, what most people associate with the subject of science and religion. This extensively documented account of rival "creation stories" culminates in the authors' assessment of Design arguments.

❦

So far my selections have all been by physicists, but here's an exception: *Rebuilding the Matrix*, by Denis Alexander. I was eager to read this one, subtitled *Science and Faith in the 21st Century*, because I greatly appreciated the author's earlier book, *Beyond Science*. With the Cold War and the possibility of nuclear holocaust on people's minds at that time, Alexander defended science while showing that the Christian gospel offers meaning to life that science cannot deliver. Thirty years later, he is still trying to humanize science. To do so, he argues, requires "rebuilding the matrix," by which he means restoring the theistic convictions that led to modern science in the first place.

Denis Alexander is a fellow of St. Edmund's College, Cambridge, England, and leader of a molecular immunology research group at the Babraham Institute. He also edits the journal *Science and Christian Belief* for Christians in Science (CiS), an evangelical fellowship in the UK, like ASA in the U.S.). He mentions having served at the American University Hospital in Beirut when it was taking in casualties from the Muslim west side during the Lebanese civil war.

Rebuilding the Matrix is the heaviest book on my list, both in size (510 pages) and in writing style. Alexander wrote his 1972 book for a general audience interested in science but perhaps intimidated by it. This new book seems directed primarily toward fellow scientists and other academics. A third of it recounts the history of modern science in considerable detail, ending with an informative chapter on how "The Warfare Merchants" pounded in a wedge between science and its theistic roots (thus "shattering the matrix"). In other chapters, Alexander takes on hard philosophical questions raised by prominent thinkers from materialistic rationalists to postmodernists. This book has the feel of a carefully laid out argument, maybe too comprehensive to follow easily but worthy of sustained study. I read the hardback but a less expensive paperback version should be forthcoming.

Now for a book by a journalist rather than a scientist, *By Design: Science and the Search for God* by Larry Witham. Its enjoyable journalistic style may make it the best book on my list for casual onlookers who want to know what's going on. For such readable writing I can tolerate a few shortcuts, though I know Witham worked hard to get the facts right. A bibliographic essay at the end credits his published sources and many personal interviews. At one ID event he interviewed me for hours (for "deep background," as the journalists say) about events with which I was familiar. From his book I learned details I hadn't known about those and other events.

Larry Witham is a reporter assigned to the national desk at the *Washington Times*, where he specializes in religion and its interaction with social issues. Covering school board debates over teaching evolution drew him into scientific questions and into writing an earlier book about those controversies. He was born in California, raised a Lutheran, and as a student was more interested in art than in science. He has been a newspaperman for some twenty-one years.

In *By Design*, Witham uses two centennials as bookends. He begins with the 1959 Darwin Centennial at the University of Chicago, one hundred years after publication of *Origin of Species*. That five-day festival celebrated the triumph of evolutionary thinking and included a Thanksgiving Day "secular sermon" by Sir Julian Huxley from the pulpit of Rockefeller Chapel. Witham brings his story to a close in 2002, one hundred years after the first Gifford Lectures by William James (which became *The Varieties of Religious Experience*). Witham reprises the psychologist's ideas of tough-mindedness and tender-mindedness in our choices of skepticism or belief, pondering changes in public attitudes toward science and faith since 1959.

While I was preparing for the seminar, a friend sent me an autographed copy of his book, *Doubts about Darwin: A History of Intelligent Design*. The author, Thomas Woodward, has been an enthusiastic "participant observer" of the ID movement. This book, based on his PhD dissertation, relies heavily on his contacts with Phillip Johnson, who says in the foreword that "Tom Woodward knows as much about the history of Intelligent Design as any person could." Woodward teaches communication, theology, and the history of science at Trinity College in Florida. Since his student days at Princeton he has been active in Christian apologetics, and founded the C. S. Lewis Society at Trinity College.

I added this one to my seminar list. Although it parallels Witham's appreciative assessment of the ID movement, it has a different twist. The doctoral studies Woodward began mid-career were in the field of rhetoric, a term that has been undermined by pejorative political use of the phrase "*mere* rhetoric." Rhetoric (paired with logic in classical curricula) is the art of framing an argument to make it convincing, especially to hearers with no initial inclination to accept it—in other words, the art of persuasion. A presenter of an argument is called a "rhetor" (a word new to me) and a scholar who analyzes the argument, a "rhetorician."

Woodward's book is a rhetorical history of ID's campaign of persuasion. An appendix discusses the "rhetoric of science" and some of its scholars. I hadn't heard of that field before, so from the appendices, text, and extensive endnotes I learned more than I expected to about a story with which I was already familiar. The rise of ID's influence may not be a story "of Biblical proportions" but it has overtones of that shepherd boy armed with only a slingshot. Why worry about a few pebbles? Ask the defenders of evolution at the National Center for Science Education about that!

***

Good books keep coming out to get you started on your journey into science and Christian faith. A guidebook is like a traveling companion, so choose one you will enjoy along the way. You'll find plenty more to choose from later on.

Have a pleasant trip. And don't forget your compass.

9

Why Love Will Always Be a Poor Investment

Kurt Armstrong

Contemporary Western culture is so thoroughly saturated with the values and assumptions of the corporate world that it comes as no surprise that we now construct even our understanding of romantic relationships in economic terms:

1. Where once a person had a boyfriend or girlfriend, husband or wife, we now refer to one's significant other as a "partner." As with the corporation partner in the business world, the "partner" in a relationship is presumably always on the lookout for the best deal, the "partnership" that will maximize his or her interests.

2. Only a fool would consider marching down the aisle without first signing a pre-nuptial agreement drawn up by a lawyer. It is a meticulously organized contract that carefully delineates the divvying up of the material possessions and guardianship of children should the marriage—excuse me, "partnership"—ever be "dissolved."

3. These "contracts" are recognized by the courts, and are designed to make the "termination" of a "partnership" very efficient. No more messy divorces; just follow the step-by-step details of the mutually agreed upon terms of the binding contract.

4. Time spent with a "partner" is thought of as "investing in the relationship." Never mind things like love or commitment or responsibility; it's about making an "investment."

5. A good investment ought to provide the investor with calculable and escalating returns.

6. In our progressive, open-market "partnerships," we pride ourselves for having moved beyond encumbering, old-fashioned marriage, so any "partnership" can be abandoned if the current one is too demanding, if the returns are too low, or if a better option happens to present itself.

7. Anyone who notices a trend of "diminishing returns" on their "investment" in their "partnership" is encouraged to choose what's best for them, which may well mean opting out of the "agreement." But "terminating" the "partnership" should be no trouble because the "contract" was already drawn up in advance.

Now, there has never been a "good old days" of marriage. Some of today's most vocal proponents of traditional marriage seem to imagine that it was during the days of their courtship that the standard for proper and holy marriage was set. According to them, it seems that God finally ironed out the wrinkles and perfected the ideal marriage somewhere in America, sometime during the 1950s. "In those days," men worked hard at their jobs and in church, and prayed with, impregnated, and protected their pious wives who stayed home to tend to the domestic duties that the pursuit of happiness entailed. And God had never been more pleased with how perfect things were.

I stand *with* those who stand *against* the narrow, dehumanizing roles that this sort of traditional marriage created for women and for men. The appeal to the values of a utopian "good old days" often means a return to the ways of life of an era riddled with institutionally sanctioned hatred. Many of the things that happened behind the closed doors of many a good Christian home were anything but Christian, and the stamp of supposedly divine approval does not make oppression and patriarchy any less oppressive or patriarchal.

It is presumably the backlash against these sorts of abuses in the traditional family that has caused many a Gen-Xer to write off marriage as a whole. Though most of them still eventually choose to marry, it is less and less likely that they will stay in the relationship for life. "Till death do us part," is an archaism, like manual typewriters and 78 RPM records: some people still seem to enjoy those sorts of things, but probably only if they subscribe to some resurgent vein of neo-Luddite thinking.

But it seems to me that it is the relationship-as-commodity mentality, and not fear of the abuses of traditional marriage, that has fostered today's mood of suspicion towards making a lifelong commitment. Now we are all free to choose which brand of toothpaste to buy, what channel to watch, and to select whatever love seems poised to meet our best interests. The assumption that newer is better means that not only are we free to choose a superior partner if one comes along, but that serial monogamy—which replaces the outmoded idea of marriage—is a more freeing, liberating and superior option to the old ideal of "love, honour, and cherish/'Till death do us part."

Things have not turned out as we might have hoped. One would be hard pressed to argue convincingly that Western culture is characterized any more by love than it was fifty years ago. We are now free to choose whatever we want—from designer coffee to exotic sexual encounter—free to acquire virtually anything except the sort of real love that we want most of all. The presumed right to be free to sleep with a different person every night might very well be construed as genuine freedom, but it will never be mistaken for genuine love.

Love defies measurement, technique, and all guarantees of ease and comfort. Love is fundamentally anti-program, non-rational, and impractical. Love is an untameable impediment to the march of progress; it defies the promises of professionally developed technique, creates inefficiency, and does not guarantee "escalating returns" on "investments." What it does guarantee is challenge, struggle, sorrow, and profound loss. Love is what human beings live for, but like Aslan the Lion, it is not safe, but it is good.

Take, for example, Kevin and Laura, two people who have recently given me the purest example of how love is eminently good but not safe. The two of them met last summer in graduate school. Kevin is from the UK, Laura from Virginia. In the span of four months they started dating, fell in love and got engaged, only to discover that Laura is suffering from Stage 4 bone and lymph node cancer. The doctors laid out for her a spectrum of treatment options, ranging from intensive chemotherapy and radiation to "maintenance" by natural medicine, all with the understanding that none of these things will cure her, only prolong her life with varying degrees of bodily damage. The prognosis was that she would likely not live longer than two or three more years. Now. Any reasonable couple would have carefully considered their options, weighed the costs and benefits of proceeding as planned, and would quite possibly have decided to call the wedding off. But Kevin and Laura chose, instead, to plunge themselves deeper into the insecurity and guaranteed suffering of genuine love: last month they got married, two months earlier than they had originally planned.

The example that these two have set show how the commitment to one person in the vow of marriage "to death do you part" is *absurd*. Whether you end up with only two or three years together—like Kevin and Laura face—or manage to sashay through to your sixty-fifth anniversary, barring some accident that takes you both at once, one of you is going to outlive the other. And the longer the two of you stay together and pour love into one another's lives, the greater the sorrow will be when one of you dies. What then? What reasonable, economic explanation is there for a grieving lover? What words of calculable comfort can one offer the widow or widower? What consolation is there for this sort of return on their investment?

Our culture's version of love-as-commodity represents a fundamental misunderstanding of what love really is. In a culture where everything is supposedly for sale, the implicit understanding of love is that it is a scarce commodity and that you need to gather up as much of it as you can. But love-as-absurd, the kind that Kevin and Laura live by is freely offered to another rather than taken for oneself. The underlying message of true love is: I commit myself to sharing my life with you in a way that furthers *your* well-being. Love is not self-seeking; true love always trusts, always hopes, and always perseveres.

When I pledged my vows to my wife four years ago, I promised to love her "until death separates us." I offered my life for the sake of hers, and she pledged the same to me; now my well being is her well being is my well being. In saying this one "yes" to marriage, I said "no" to a long line of other options, and to my "freedom" to continue to select from an endless number of other choices. I gave up the freedom to "consume," because I chose to love this one person, not simply until the returns began to diminish, but to the very end.

I soon discovered that this was not an entirely comfortable experience. More than the petty arguments about the toilet seat or clothes on the floor, what was most painful was the discomfort of being known. My wife is like an honest mirror that reveals to me who I really am. She encourages me to foster my strengths, but she also helps me to see my weaknesses. She sees me very clearly, and like every normal human being I have plenty that I would prefer to keep all to myself. But ignoring my fundamentally unhealthy ways of living is no more helpful than ignoring a gangrenous limb: it does not go away, and it certainly does not get any better. Love brings to light my diseased ways of living and says: "Look, some of these things are really quite bad, but all is not lost; we still have hope for you. The thing is we will need to do some major surgery, and it's going to hurt. But there is really no other way that you're going to get well."

Each time that this sort of diagnosis occurs, I have, as far as I can see, three options: the first is divorce, which would supposedly be a quick and permanent solution. But because we made a commitment to a lifelong relationship, we're stuck; there is no getting out. This brings me to the second option, which is to do nothing at all, to ignore every challenge and simply let the marriage take whatever course it chooses, which will inevitably lead to a miserable relationship. I have known too many couples who refused to take the steps that love asked them to do, who lived with their personal and relational diseases because it was easier than making a painful change. There is a cold comfort in a familiar malady, even when you know it's killing you. This leaves me, then, with a third option. It is the riskiest of them all, which is why most people opt for either of the first two. The only real option for me is to plunge into absurd love, and into the uncertainty of the changes that love asks me to make.

The commitment to lifelong love provides a crucible that burns off the dross and refines the gold of the human soul. There are no shortcuts, and the only absolute guarantee is that it will hurt. The longer that two people work on their absurd love, the more they will one day hurt. My wife and I talked about the reality of this again just last night, confessing to one another that we didn't know if we had what it would take to survive without the other. I said that the thought of her dying was more than I could bear, and she said she felt the same about me. And now that we have a baby on the way, the thought of losing each other is even more painful and the risks of continuing to love are even greater. What should we do? Cut our losses and get out before it hurts even more? Start making ourselves safer and less vulnerable? Or continue doing all we can to deepen what we have, and continue to love each other in a way that ensures that we *will* suffer?

If deepening our love means we must one day suffer, so be it. Love is still the only thing worth living for. If I dazzle and entertain the masses, or if I become the richest man in the world, even if I live a life of miracles and service, but I do not have love, then I have gained nothing.

This ring on my finger is a symbol of my decision to live against the ways of the consumer world that tells me fidelity is no longer fashionable. Marriage is one part of my stubborn, angry, defiant no to those who offer the hollow promises of so-called freedom. My lifelong commitment to bind myself to my wife is a stand against the consumer culture and its dehumanizing ways. I choose to defy the advertisers' lies that tell me my happiness depends on the freedom to choose from 250 television channels, or to pick whatever relationship is best for me.

No. I am married. For good.

IV

The Word Speaks to Life

10

Guess Who's Coming to Dinner
Sitting at the Table with the Prodigal Son

Joel B. Green

"Will only a few be saved?" According to the Gospel of Luke, a bystander addressed this question to Jesus during his long journey up to Jerusalem (Luke 13:22). Jesus' answer bordered on the elusive. In fact, Jesus routinely responds to questions addressed to him by turning them around and upside down.

For his conversation partners, that must have been an annoying habit, but it allowed Jesus repeatedly to set his own agenda. If Jesus was to reform how those around him understood and related to God, he would have to find ways to reshape what people were talking about, and how. Who is God? What is the nature of God's people? Those were fundamental questions that had to be addressed, and Jesus found various ways to turn a conversation toward them.

"Lord, will only a few be saved?" On the face of it, that was an honest, albeit predictable question. Queries like this belonged to the repertoire of topics one might address to any visiting rabbi. The number of those redeemed comes to 144,000 in the book of Revelation, for example. While folks in the first century and since might puzzle over the calculus of the Apocalypse, another book from that period, the Jewish writing we know as 4 Ezra, insists more simply that "the Most High made this world for the sake of the many, but the world to come for the sake of only a few" (8:1).

"Will only a few be saved?" Jesus' answer was baffling. Rather than tallying the number of those who would be saved, he focused instead on the number of those who would be disqualified: "Strive to enter by means of the narrow door," he replied, "for many, I tell you, will try to enter and will not be able." Ultimately, a curiosity about "how many" turns into a call to struggle now, in the present, in order to show that we are well suited for future salvation.

A bystander raised a question. Abruptly, the tables were turned. Now Jesus was the one asking the questions. How many will be saved? That is not the issue! What sort of people will be saved? That is the question, and with it, Are you among them?

In this way, Jesus brought to the surface the concern that occupied him throughout this section of the Gospel of Luke (13:10—17:10): *Who will participate in the kingdom of God?* The issue is underscored again in Luke 14. Jesus' teaching on eating habits and dining invitations was interrupted by another onlooker: "Blessed is anyone who will eat bread in the kingdom of God!" (14:15). "Yes," we can almost hear Jesus say, "but *who* will eat the kingdom bread?" Who will participate in the kingdom of God? Jesus' answers revolve around the related motifs of table fellowship, celebration with shared meals, and the extending of hospitality.

This is where a big surprise in Jesus' teaching comes. In essence, people were asking, Whom will God invite to the end-time banquet? The question Jesus asked is somewhat different: Whom do you invite to your luncheons, parties, dinners, banquets? Jesus' way of shaping the discussion, even after almost 2,000 years, is striking in its unpredictability, perhaps even off-putting for some of us. How could he turn a question, about whether we will be invited, into an examination of the lists of whose whom we invite?

Whom do we welcome at our tables? To whom do we extend hospitality? What sort of people are included in our circle of friends? In this constellation of issues rests the focus of this mid-section of Luke's Gospel, and, more particularly, is the point at issue in Jesus' parable popularly known as the parable of the prodigal son (Luke 15:11–32). Following repeated attempts to reorient the attention of his audience around the character of God and to redirect their thinking about the nature of God's people, he turned again to the wisdom of a parable.

Here is a message about God and the shape of those who reflect his image. In order to grasp the depth and urgency of this parable, we need to see how the Gospel of Luke prepares us to hear it.

EATING WITH ABRAHAM

Let us return to the initial question, "Lord, will only a few be saved?" Jesus' answer was significant in part for the way he began to develop the notion of salvation in relation to eating at the table of Abraham, Isaac, Jacob, and the prophets in the kingdom of God. In that way, he touched on a variety of issues related to the importance of meals.

Most clearly, Jesus built on the longstanding notion in Israel that the consummation of the kingdom is a great feast. In Luke's narrative we hear reverberations of the banquet scene in Isaiah 25:6–9, with its portrait of an end-time repast of majestic proportions (see also Isaiah 55:1–2; 65:13–14; Zechariah 1:7). In the world of Roman Palestine more generally, meals had a further function. Sharing bread signified acceptance. Hospitality entailed the offer of friendship. People were united in good will and camaraderie at the dinner table.

The combination in this passage of those ways of understanding meals is striking. That is because Jesus clearly anticipated the inclusion of Gentiles at the end-time banquet, as though Jesus expected that Abraham would extend hospitality even to them. "People will come from east and west, from north and south," Jesus asserted, drawing on the imagery of the four winds to represent the four corners of the earth, and thus including not only the scattered remnant of faithful Israel wherever they may be found, but also the faithful of the world. Isaiah had promised as much, observing that, in the end-time, all the nations would exult, "Let us be glad and rejoice in our salvation" (Isaiah 25:9).

Jesus' message at this juncture would be most troubling to those who were self-assured of their prior reservation at the table of the kingdom banquet. Remember: those surrounding Jesus lived in a world where "just desserts" were determined above all by birthright, by kinship ties. It is shocking, then, that the owner of the house in Jesus' short parable could assert, "I do not know you, where you are from" (Luke 13:25).

But this position is fully harmonious with the teaching of John the Baptist and Jesus. Repeatedly they have insisted that "children of Abraham" are recognized not by their birthright but by their behavior

(Luke 3:7–14). The question is not, do we have privileged status on account of our family heritage? Rather, the question is, do we live lives that demonstrate that our faith is like Abraham's?

Within this passage from Luke, the question of "faith like Abraham" is all the more interesting if we recall that Abraham was known in the Old Testament and Jewish tradition as a model of hospitality. A little later in Luke's narrative, Abraham would welcome to his side the poor beggar, Lazarus, in order to receive comfort (16:19–31). This reminds us that yet another significance of meals—but one we are likely to forget in our search for the profound—is their importance for addressing the basic need for food shared by all humans. We eat because we must. What of those with no food? "God has filled the hungry with good things," Mary proclaimed (Luke 1:53).

Meals should serve a further purpose. The dining table ought to be a kind of "safe space," apart from the give-and-take of power plays and status-seeking that might otherwise occupy folks. Meals should provide an opportunity to make friends, and to open one's circle of friends to others.

As Luke 14 opens, Jesus was in the house of a leader of the Pharisees, sharing in a meal. How could this be? Was Jesus among friends? From the point of view of the Pharisees, Jesus' presence at the table must have been motivated by the question, "Isn't this man Jesus one of us?" After all, Pharisees, more than most, would have observed their table norms with care, and would not have jeopardized their ritual purity by extending hospitality to one outside their number.

From Jesus' point of view, if this meal scene is typical, his decision to join these leading Pharisees for a meal must have been motivated by the persistence of his offer of divine restoration. Sitting at the table with these companions constituted an opportunity to establish a redemptive community with them. Jesus had not turned his back even on persons like these Pharisees, who so often opposed his behavior as outside the will of God as expressed in the Law of Moses.

Such a meal would have been governed by time-honored, widely accepted conventions. The dining table doubled as a kind of status symbol, by which one advertised and reinforced one's position in the community. The guest list, then, would have included only those whose presence at the table could preserve or, even better, enhance one's status in the community. Given the teaching of Jesus here, it is not coincidental that one would therefore avoid including the hungry, the marginalized, and the outcast on one's invitation list. On the one hand, such an invitation would have no value in the currency of esteem and social position. On the other, to invite others to one's house was to place them under the obligation to return the favor of an invitation—an obligation that the hungry and outcast could never fulfill.

Even at this meal, issues of status and respect were at center stage, with seating arrangements carefully navigated so as not to offend those of higher honor or to encourage unnecessarily those of lower.

Social practices of this sort are not far removed from some of our own, of course. Anyone who has planned the seating arrangements at a wedding banquet, or listed guests to invite to an intimate gathering of friends, has experienced to some extent the agony of the social symbol of a dinner party. Magnify those feelings to account for a social system grounded in values of honor and shame, and we have a clearer sense of what was at stake here.

When viewed against these horizons, the strangeness of Jesus' teaching comes into sharp relief. First, he counseled,

"When you are invited by someone to a wedding banquet, do not sit down at the place of honor, in case someone more distinguished than you has been invited by your host; and the host who invited both of you may come and say to you, 'Give this person your place,' and then in disgrace you would start to take the lowest place. But when you are invited, go and sit down at the lowest place, so that when your host comes, he may say to you, 'Friend, move up higher'; then you will be honored in the presence of all who sit at the table with you."

Then, he continued, "When you give a luncheon or a dinner, do not invite your friends or your brothers or your relatives or rich neighbors, in case they may invite you in return, and you would be repaid. But when you give a banquet, invite the poor, the crippled, the lame, and the blind. And you will be blessed, because they cannot repay you, for you will be repaid at the resurrection of the righteous."

With those two utterances, Jesus pulled the rug out from under two of the most central, taken-for-granted aspects of the Roman world. The first was the importance of social status and social stratification, the maintenance and broadcasting of one's relative prestige in the community. The second was the gift-and-obligation system that quite literally tied together every person—slave or free, male or female, emperor or child—into an intricate web of reciprocal relations. Clearly, Jesus had a different understanding of meals and dining conventions than those shared by his contemporaries.

Meals, in his view, were opportunities to extend mercy to the hungry and hospitality to outsiders. They were gifts to be given, without strings attached. While still at the table of the ruler among the Pharisees (Luke 14:15–24), Jesus told the story of a wealthy householder, who extended hospitality to the very persons of whom Jesus had spoken in his counsel about dinner invitations. Providing a meal to the blind, the lame, the crippled, or the poor, this wealthy householder modeled Jesus' instruction. What he has did would not enhance his prestige, or provide him with any monetary or social reward. He had participated in an altogether different social order, the one in which the community of God's people is founded in gracious and uncalculating hospitality.

CALLING FOR NEW BEHAVIORS

It is not for nothing that the man in Jesus' story was a wealthy householder, with slaves to carry out his bidding. Undoubtedly, he was the sort of fellow to whom a ruler among Pharisees, like Jesus' host, might relate. Jesus described this wealthy householder as a model to his table guests. "Be like him," he was saying to his companions at the large table, setting before them the implicit challenge to embrace the values and behaviors of a new community.

We see here what Jesus was presenting to his antagonists: new behaviors rooted in new values and commitments. If his table companions, and others like them, would embrace this value-set, these new attitudes and commitments that Jesus placed before them, then their lives would change as well.

The problem is, the call to new behaviors is never enough. Neither is the invitation to adopt a different set of values. Something more is needed —a shift, a tectonic shift, in how we understand the nature of God.

We know that Jesus' teaching fell on deaf ears when we read the opening of Luke 15: "Now all the toll collectors and sinners were coming near to listen to Jesus. And the Pharisees and legal experts were grumbling and saying, 'This fellow welcomes sinners and eats with them'" (Luke 15:1–2).

Here, on the one hand, is evidence of Jesus' unequivocal rejection of the interests and norms of those who had extended hospitality to him, but never lost sight of their own commitments. In Jesus' view, their commitments set them at odds with the ways of God. But Jesus thereby created a problem for himself. His own practices had begun to shape a new community, one whose openness to the least and left out of society would raise an unflattering, even threatening voice against the status quo. Here is evidence, too, of growing hostility against Jesus.

A line has been drawn. How would Jesus respond? Set within this context, the parable of the prodigal son serves as a kind of self-defense. Jesus told this parable in order to defend the nature of his ministry. He wanted to say something pivotal about God. He wanted to paint yet again the nature of God's people, whose form of life would reflect the faithfulness of Abraham.

JESUS IN THE DOCK

Jesus was clearly in the dock for his table habits (Luke 15:1–2). By summarizing the charges against Jesus in this way, Luke borrowed from one of his most pervasive "frames," that of meals. We have seen that, along with providing food, meals serve significant social functions. Presence at the end-time meal means participation in the kingdom of God (Luke 13:22–31). Meals establish "in-group" boundaries and embody values of status and purity (Luke 14:1–24). In these texts, dining together manifests concerns for honor and acceptance.

In a way consistent with his own teaching, Jesus had a habit of flaunting these social and religious protocols, repeatedly eating with the "wrong" people. We see evidence of Jesus' troublesome behavior in the inclusion of toll collectors at the table (Luke 5:20–32; 7:34, 36–50; 19:1–10), and of the socially and religiously marginal (Luke 14:1–6, 13, 21, 23). Meals obviously foster existing bonds of community, but in Luke's portrayal Jesus used table fellowship to establish new and unexpected bonds.

Given the social and religious importance of meals, it is not surprising that Jesus attracted hostility for his table practices. Given the flow of the Gospel of Luke thus far, it is not surprising that the Pharisees and scribes were the sources of that hostility. Though Luke can speak more positively of the Pharisees when they appear with the scribes, they nonetheless function as antagonistic monitors of Jesus' behavior. They repeatedly concluded that he neglected the law of God and they consistently opposed his ministry.

On the one hand, then, Jesus' frequent disregard for the usual conventions helped to construct a people who, like these toll collectors and sinners, heard and heeded his message. "Let anyone who has ears to hear listen!" Jesus proclaimed (14:35), and immediately these social outcasts are presented as persons who "listen to him" (15:1). On the other hand, this new community of Jesus' followers by its very existence raised a threat to the attitudes and practices embraced by Jesus' adversaries.

Jesus had a lot to answer for, and the parables of Luke 15 now defend the character of his ministry. In fact, in the parables of the lost coin and lost son, Jesus highlighted his ministry as the necessary complement to God's own character. To put it differently, Jesus raised the stakes in his encounter with these legal experts and Pharisees. The positive response of toll collectors and sinners as they gathered around him constituted a restoration of the lost that would result in heavenly joy, would call for earthly celebration, including feasting. In welcoming such persons as these outcasts to the table, Jesus expressed the expansive grace of God. By calling his behavior into question, these scribes and Pharisees were actually calling into question the character of God.

WHOSE PARABLE?

Turning to Luke 15:11-32, the most rudimentary question to address is, Whose parable is this? We have long assumed that Luke 15:11-32 concerns a father with two sons—a view that draws immediate support from the opening phrase, "There was a man who had two sons." In fact, activity in this parable particularly revolves around the younger son.

Note, for example, that Jesus' parable has two segments, each allowing the same sequence of events to be recounted—fully by Jesus (15:11-24) and in summary form by a slave (15:26-27). The first concentrates on the younger son's loss and his father's celebratory response at his return. The latter emphasizes the younger son's loss and his brother's indignant reaction. The turning point of both accounts is an emotional response to the return of the younger son: compassion on the part of the father (15:20), anger on the part of the elder son (15:28).

What we are beginning to see is that the focus of the parable falls on *how one responds*. The other two parables in Luke 15 heighten this emphasis. The critical motif of "celebration" is highlighted throughout this chapter: the recovery of what was lost led to joy (vv. 6, 9, 23-24, 27).

Indeed, the father elevates joyous celebration and repast to the level of divine necessity (vv. 32, 7, 10).

Why should Jesus focus in this way on the contrasting responses to the younger son? Here we should recall that Luke 13–17 repeatedly underscores the importance of boundaries among the people of God: with Pharisees, legal experts, the wealthy, and those who act like them, excluding those who live on or beyond the social and religious margins of community life.

Who will sit down at the table of the kingdom banquet? Not those who assumed that the end-time banquet was included among their just desserts, not the "first," but the "last." Whom should one invite to one's home? Not those whose presence would bolster the host's status in the community. Not those capable of reciprocating with invitations of their own. Rather, the marginal, the crippled, the blind, the lame, and others whose diseased state and low status had relegated them to life beyond the walls.

Use what you have to include peripheral folk among your closest friends, Jesus advised, so that you may be welcomed into eternal homes. Care for those like Lazarus—that beggar covered with sores, whose hunger and sorry state placed him at risk from rogue dogs that patrolled the village streets—and so hear and heed Moses and the prophets. Throughout this section of Luke's narrative, the question of how one responds to people like the younger son is front and central.

THE YOUNGER SON

But is it correct to identify this younger son with the marginal, the crippled, the ulcerated, and the like? Jesus' parable actually went to great lengths to make just such an identification. This young man broke with his family and was therefore without kin. His request to his (living) father for the disposition of his estate was tantamount to wishing for his father's death. After the estate was divided, the younger son pushed still further, requesting the right to dispose of his share, heaping further insult on his father. Breaking relationship with his father in that way entailed breaking relationship with his brother also, and with the village as a whole.

Later, he found himself in a distant country, penniless, hired to care for pigs. His shocking breach of familial ties thus lead from one level of infamy to the next: a Jew who lived as though he were a Gentile. His deteriorating situation was exacerbated by the onset of a famine, in a culture outside Jewish influence, where charity for the needy was widely regarded as a waste of time. Plautus remarked, "He does the beggar a bad service who gives him meat and drink, for what he gives is lost, and the life of the poor is prolonged to their own misery" (*Trinummus* §339). This younger son had fallen victim to the ease with which persons in an agrarian society might experience downward mobility.

From his enviable status as the son of a wealthy landowner, he now numbered among society's "unclean and degraded." Such persons had nothing but their bodies and brute energies to sell, so they either accepted occupations that quickly destroyed them or spiraled them downward further to the class of "expendables," for whom mortality was all but knocking at the door. As another barometer of the depths to which he had fallen, this younger son could now imagine himself as a day laborer, a hireling whose day-to-day subsistence was vulnerable to the forces of nature, the whims of the estate manager, and the seasonal needs of a farm. Only someone on society's bottommost rung could see such a life as a step *up* the ladder.

Again, even if this younger son has been cast in the tattered garb of misery, an outcast, can we fairly identify him with those of whom Jesus spoke when he counseled respected persons about their invitees? After all, this fellow has made his own bed; shouldn't he have to lie in it? He humiliated his father, his family, his village. Why should he be met with open arms of reconciliation? He got only what he deserved, did he not?

That is exactly the point. Throughout much of the central section of Luke's Gospel, Jesus was trying to transform how people understood God. A transformed picture of God would lead to new forms of behavior. As he had already stated, God "is kind to the ungrateful and the wicked." Given those adjectives, the younger son clearly qualified for God's kindness! Jesus had also said, "Be merciful, just as your Father is merciful" (Luke 6:35–36).

WHO EATS AT YOUR TABLE?

Here is where the father of Jesus' parable models an appropriate response. He looked with compassion at the bedraggled man walking toward his former household. The father's response was emblematic of the honorable restoration to the family of this one who had snubbed, abandoned, and cut himself off from them. The humiliating act of running through the village, kissing the boy again and again as a sign of reconciliation and forgiveness, instructing the servants to dress his son in a manner befitting a king, and throwing a feast large enough for the whole village—these behaviors gave expression to the depth and breadth that signal renewal and reconciliation.

This father has adopted an alternative view of God, a renewed set of commitments and attitudes that are grounded in God's character. He reflects the image of God that Jesus has been articulating throughout the Gospel. Those who believe, really believe, that God is the gracious Father whose beneficence is turned toward his people are liberated to give freely even to those who have no claim on our love or care (Luke 11–12).

In contrast, the elder son responded with anger and refused to join the gala. Like the Pharisees and scribes who grumbled about Jesus' eating with toll collectors and sinners, he stood outside the house complaining. Though he still lived on his father's estate, he had learned little about his father or from his father. In his behavior toward his brother, who had so dramatically cut himself off from his family, the older son revealed his own need for revitalization. Although his behavior made sense in the world in which he lived, it was out of step with the new world being ushered in through Jesus' ministry.

Indicted for his receptivity to those who came near to hear and heed his words, Jesus responded by asserting the divine necessity of joyous responses to the recovery of the lost. Like the father of this parable, Jesus recognized the gravity of receiving as a table intimate the lost who are recovered—whether the lost come in the guise of a son whose behavior has divorced him from his family or of those identified by social and religious conventions as beyond the reach of divine grace. "We had to celebrate and rejoice, for this brother of yours was dead and has come to life; he was lost and has been found."

"Indeed, those who are last will be first, and those who are first will be last."

Jesus' parable is cast in the form of a defense, but it is more than that. It is a challenge. The parable of the prodigal son is open ended—and so is the invitation.

11

Theological Themes in the Fiction of C. S. Lewis
Good and Evil in the Chronicles of Narnia

Earl F. Palmer

C. S. Lewis was a theologian as well as a storyteller. The moment we dare to say, "I believe," or endeavor to explain to someone what we believe, we are then doing theology. Clive Staples Lewis played that role in just about everything he wrote—even his personal correspondence.

When asked why he wrote children's stories, Lewis answered, "I turned to fairy tales, because that seemed to be the form that certain ideas and images in my mind seemed to demand, as a man might turn to fugues because the musical phrases in his head seemed to him to be good fugal subjects. When I wrote *Lion* I had no notion of writing the others. Writing children's stories modified my habits of composition. It imposed strict limits on my vocabulary; it excluded erotic love; it cut down reflective and analytical passages; it led me to produce chapters of nearly equal length for convenience in reading aloud. All those restrictions did me great good."

Three grand themes are present in every one of Lewis's chronicles, and each is theological in the way it looks at the possibility of the existence of God.

The first theme is the affirmation of life seen in Lewis's respect for the earth itself and for the human beings who become characters in the story. The characters are made in God's image and are given freedom to choose, in small and large ways, just as God has freedom to choose. Great stories respect that goodness in creation. Without that fundamental respect, there would be no possibilities for a story where love happens, or for heartbreak and crises to happen. It is this first ground rule that makes all adventure (or even romantic) stories possible.

The second theme in every great story is the understanding and realistic portrayal of the crises of bad choices and harmful decisions. Whether the story is a fantasy or a real-world story, that depiction of a crisis and its harm to the characters is at the heart of every adventure and of every scene of danger.

The third grand theme is the portrayal of the good that emerges in the story. Even in a pessimistic tale, where tragedy is the end line of the final chapter, there nevertheless must be a counterpoint of good that stands in contrast against the wrongness that seems to win because of the author's artistic decision.

In every great story these three themes need to appear, and this means that a battle of epic consequences between good and evil is under way. When we read the Chronicles of Narnia, the seven stories that C. S. Lewis wrote for us, we find that they contain all three of these grand themes. They begin with the innocence of children exploring an old house and then, because of a game of hide and seek, the youngest of the children stumbles into a wondrous, beautiful new world of snow, a glowing lamp-post, a friendly Faun, and an act of protective kindness toward this little girl Lucy by that Faun named Mr. Tumnus. She meets up with a strange kind of goodness, but soon in the story when her brother Edmund enters that charmed world, the second theme appears. It is not the problems of youth getting lost in a forest, but of something more ominous and threatening. The children meet up with a grave danger—with evil. The expert storyteller that Lewis is gradually draws us along with the four English children into that danger in Narnia. What is it they find? First they find the beauty of Narnia, but soon a second theme unfolds: the reality of evil.

Evil is not portrayed as a formless, mindless force, or as simply human avarice or human wrath. Nor does Lewis see it as a natural disaster, like earthquakes or fire. Lewis accepts the Biblical portrayal of evil as a moral, cosmic, personal will against the will of God. "Cosmic (that is to say, spiritual) and moral (not just natural, as in tornadoes), it is a personal will intentionally against the will of God." C. S. Lewis in the 1960 preface to *The Screwtape Letters* says:

"Now; if by the 'devil' you mean a power opposite to God and like God, self-existed for all eternity, the answer is certainly no. God has no opposite . . . the proper question is whether I believe in devils. I do. That is to say, I believe in angels, and I believe that some of these, by the abuse of their free will, have become enemies of God."

We need to ask what characteristics of evil are portrayed by Lewis. In *The Lion, the Witch and the Wardrobe* and in *The Magician's Nephew*, evil is cold. It is interesting that Lewis used an image of coldness and ice to refer to the devil, whereas it is common to think of the devil with the language of fire. Even in Dante the devil is encased in ice. So perhaps Lewis was influenced by Dante. In *The Magician's Nephew*, the deplorable world is cold, and in *The Lion, the Witch and the Wardrobe*, when the children first come into Narnia, they learn that for many, many years it has been winter without Christmas, and everything is cold. When we think about that coldness we find that it makes things work well for the winter Queen. Her castle is a vast ice sculpture. Sleighs work well on the cold snow.

A second way in which evil is portrayed by Lewis in these novels is its role in the winter Queen as the one who is the tempter. Evil tempts by deception. In *The Silver Chair*, in one incredible scene the Emerald Queen tempts the children, trying to make them think that what they knew in the above ground world as the real sun is not the sun. Rather the sphere she holds and sways before them is the real sun. She tempts them by deception. In *The Last Battle*, we have the most blatant temptation, where a donkey has a lion's skin put over him by his master. This false Aslan is marched before the people who are directed to bow and to worship him.

Evil tempts with desire. The first temptation in *The Lion, the Witch and the Wardrobe* is when the winter Queen tempts Edmund with Turkish Delight. He gets a taste of it with one delicious piece that magically appears, but he never gets any more. His desire is made intense because of the memory of that one taste. In *The Screwtape Letters* Lewis portrays temptation as "an ever increasing appetite for an ever decreasing pleasure." Edmund hears the promise of more Turkish Delight, but he never receives it.

There is also the temptation to virtue. This temptation is perhaps the most subtle of all. We see that in *The Magician's Nephew*. Digory was sent on a mission by Aslan to bring him an apple from a hidden garden in the north of Narnia. At that garden he is tempted by the witch Jadis to take the apple and not to bring it to Aslan. He is told by the witch that, were he to keep the apple, it would help his mother get well. The witch tells him, "If you'll take the apple, it will cure your mother." So Digory is tempted to distrust Aslan in order to help his mother. Each of these temptations becomes a part of Lewis's whole portrayal.

Evil is also portrayed as the destroyer. We see that in *The Lion, the Witch and the Wardrobe*, when Lucy comes back to Mr. Tumnus's house and finds that it has been destroyed, and later Edmund discovers that Mr. Tumnus has been turned into stone.

In every great story the heroes and other characters must fight against evil, fall under its spell, or combinations of both. We see this in *Perelandra*, where the deadly battle between Ransom and Weston becomes a good/bad struggle down into the nethermost parts of the earth, with the final victory of Ransom. In *That Hideous Strength*, we also see the battle between hideous evil and the true reality of good.

Evil is portrayed by Lewis as powerful, but not permanently powerful. This is an important and continuous theme. There is a cumulative power and growth of power in *That Hideous Strength*. Evil gets stronger and stronger over Mark, a young scientist who falls more and more under its control. We watch how, in single steps, evil gathers momentum. But in the end, evil suffers from inner collapse. In *That Hideous Strength*, the marvelous surprise happens at the banquet, when chaos begins to develop: a new tower of Babel, then the horror of confusion, and the inner collapse of cruelty in the end. It's what happens to evil. In the Chronicles of Narnia, evil is powerful but Aslan is more powerful, and evil is finally judged. Rabadash is judged—judged redemptively, but judged. And, finally, in *The Last Battle*, Tash is defeated.

The Apostle Paul said it in Romans 5, "Where sin increased, the grace of God increased more." The best adventure stories in their own way are a commentary on that sentence.

One question always hat to be faced. Should we read stories of the marvelous that dare to portray the reality of the crisis of evil? In thinking of the fantasy elements of stories like the Chronicles of Narnia or the Lord of the Rings by J. R. R. Tolkien, the Harry Potter series by J. K. Rowling, or even a book like *The Shack*, should we encourage youth to read books that feature the battle between good and evil in the territory of human imagination? Yes, I believe that they are a part of a healthy diet of every reader, including children. There are always age-appropriate questions but children who are deprived of healthy fantasy will nevertheless still be fascinated with fantasy. The key is not to ask if fantasy should be in their reading diet, but rather what kind of fantasy, good or bad.

The third theme is also present in the stories of C. S. Lewis. Lewis believed in the existence of ultimate good, and that became the major theme in all of his writings. The sense of ultimate good is present in the "space trilogy"—*Perelandra, Out of the Silent Planet,* and *That Hideous Strength*—in a more hidden sense. In Tolkien's marvelous trilogy, the ultimate good is also hidden yet present. In the Chronicles of Narnia, Lewis decided to dare to show ultimate good as really knowable by mere men and women, boys and girls. The hiddenness and the mysterious element of ultimate good is still present, but he dares to portray good in profoundly knowable, personal terms, yet preserving the mystery and the wonder. Good becomes specific and concrete in the great lion, Aslan.

We see it in the description of Aslan in *The Silver Chair*, when Jill first sees Aslan:

> It lay with its head raised and its two forepaws out in front of it, like the lions in Trafalgar Square. She knew at once that it had seen her. For its eyes looked straight into hers for a moment and then turned away—as if it knew her quite well and didn't think much of her.
>
> "If I run away it will be after me in a moment," thought Jill. "And if I go on, I'll run right into its mouth." Anyway, she couldn't have moved if she had tried, and she couldn't take her eyes off it. How long this lasted, she could not be sure; it seemed like hours. And the thirst became so bad that she almost felt she would not mind being eaten by the lion if only she could be sure of getting a mouthful of water first.
>
> "If you're thirsty, you may drink."

That was the voice of Aslan, the ultimate good in the Chronicles of Narnia. Aslan is the "son of the Emperor beyond the Sea."

Notice how we meet this profound, personal good. At first, we are unaware that a meeting is to take place. Aslan calls people into Narnia and there's always a sense of surprise and wonder and excitement when they actually meet him.

Aslan is encountered first through the words of others about him. That's just like how we first meet Christ, by words said about him. The Scriptures are words about Christ. Perhaps somebody tells you about him. Remember in *The Lion, the Witch and the Wardrobe*, Mr. and Mrs. Beaver tell the children about Aslan. And then it slips out that Aslan is a lion. Who would want to meet a lion? "Is he—quite safe?" Susan asks. And then comes one of the great lines of C. S. Lewis, when Mr. Beaver says, "Safe? . . . Who said anything about safe? 'Course he isn't safe. But he's good."

Aslan is not a tame lion. He's not safe, but he's good. So here they meet him first through what others say about him.

In *The Lion, the Witch and the Wardrobe*, the children next meet him by signs that they miss at first, or don't understand. This is one of the subtle, important themes in the Chronicles, that there are signs about Aslan that people miss. You remember the first sign; everybody misses it until they read *The Magician's Nephew*. That is the lamp-post. Five novels later you realize why the lamp-post is there. It's a sign hidden though present: a sign of evil and a sign of good. The second sign in *The Lion, the Witch and the Wardrobe* is the mysterious thaw. The slush and the mud are signs that Aslan is moving in the East. When he is moving, the winter begins to thaw. The beautiful thing about the thaw is that when it first comes, the sledge has a terrible time moving. Finally, it ends up in pure mud and slush and guck, and that's a sign that Aslan's there. He can be uncomfortable to have around.

Then, of course, in the most definitive way we discover who Aslan is by what he does. Here C. S. Lewis is in agreement with the theologian Karl Barth. Barth argues that we cannot divide the words of Jesus from the work of Jesus, They're inseparable. Lewis portrays the same thing in his stories: the words and the work are inseparable. We know Aslan by what he does: the creation of Narnia itself. In *The Magician's Nephew*, Aslan sings, and while he sings, the world of Narnia comes into being. This may be a portrayal of Genesis 1 when "God said, 'Let there be light.'" Lewis changed the speech to a song. As Aslan walks and sings, Narnia grows into existence.

Second, we learn who Aslan is by what he does in redemption. He doesn't speak the word of forgiveness to Edmund who is the traitor; he takes Edmund's place. And in all of The Chronicles of Narnia the most terrifying scene is that moment when Aslan surrenders himself to the winter witch in place of Edmund. A victory seems to be won against this humiliated lion. In Lewis's story that act of redemption is never repeated. Aslan dies once; he doesn't die over and over again. And from then on, everything builds on that singular redemption. A little later, Eustace becomes a dragon and has a painful need to be de-dragoned. It is Aslan who de-dragons him. Only Aslan can do it.

So we know Aslan by what he does. We learn of the gift of healing grace as Eustace tells Edmund what it was like to be de-dragoned:

"I took all these scales off. Aslan said to me, 'Undress.' And I tried to undress to get into that pool of water, and I kept taking off scales after scales after scales of dragon. And I looked around and there I was. I could repent, but I couldn't get all the dragon off. And finally Aslan said, 'Lie down.' So I lay down. And then he took his great claw . . . and it hurt . . . I felt like he was putting his claw all the way through to my heart. And he ripped off the dragon. And there I was like a peeled onion underneath."

That's the language of Lewis. "And he took me, and I was sure smarting . . . and he took me, a boy again, and he threw me in the water." There isn't a word spoken, Aslan does something. Redemption by Aslan is not a word spoken but an event that occurs. Jesus Christ died for us. What ultimate good is and what ultimate good does are now united in Lewis's theology.

Now, finally, Edmund (and we) discover who Aslan is.

Lewis portrays his healing grace in *The Horse and His Boy*, where the boy Shasta is alone on a mountain pass, "and being very tired and having nothing inside him, he felt so sorry for himself that tears rolled down his cheeks. It is then that he encounters a large lion, and at first is very frightened, feeling very sorry for himself. Then he encounters a large lion and at first he is very frightened. But, in a Large Voice, the lion says, "Tell me your sorrows." Shasta recounts his ordeals, including being chased by lions.

> "I do not call you unfortunate," said the Large Voice.
> "Don't you think it was bad luck to meet so many lions?" said Shasta.
> "There was only one lion," said the Voice.
> "What on earth do you mean? I've just told you there were at least two the first night, and—" [here Aslan interrupts him].
> "There was only one: but he was swift of foot."

> "How do you know?"
> "I was the lion."
> As Shasta gaped with open mouth and said nothing, the lion's Large Voice continued. "I was the lion who forced you to join with Aravis. I was the cat who comforted you among the houses of the dead. I was the lion who drove the jackals from you while you slept. I was the lion who gave the Horses the new strength of fear for the last mile so that you should reach King Lune in time." . . .
> "Who are you?" asked Shasta.
> "Myself," said the Voice, very deep and low so that the earth shook: and again "Myself," loud and clear and gay: and then the third time "Myself," whispered so softly you could hardly hear it, and yet it seemed to come from all round you as if the leaves rustled with it.

That is Aslan, who makes himself known. Lewis has broken new ground: he has dared to portray ultimate good as knowable.

A fourth major theme might be described as the "dynamics of discovery," referring to the faith-and-grace tension: the dynamics of faith. In Lewis's novels our freedom and our doubt are never either ridiculed or ignored. Faith develops by gradual steps in every case. We see this in Shasta.

That same sort of dynamic discovery appears in most of the characters. In *Prince Caspian*, the meeting with Aslan takes time. Lewis seemed to see discipleship as a thousand single steps. He knew this from his own life, and it is portrayed in his novels. Also, in every case Lewis points out that the role that others play in aiding us. In *The Lion, the Witch and the Wardrobe*, of course, it's that inquisitive and funny-looking professor. And when we finally read *The Magician's Nephew*, we discover who that professor is.

I have often thought that if I were going to teach a course on evangelism, one of the most helpful portrayals of what an evangelist should be like is the professor and the way he relates to those children. He knows that Aslan must finally answer our questions and prove himself, but the professor helps the children keep their minds open and keep asking questions.

In all the novels, Aslan himself is the one who must assure us and must "qualify" us. In *The Last Battle*, it is Aslan who finally calls those who enter the small doorway Farther in and Farther up. Only Aslan can de-dragon Eustace and turn him back into a boy.

In the dynamics of belief, the thing that's important to see is that each faith journey takes time. It's a gradual, growing discovery of who Aslan is, and it is Aslan who has the final word.

A fifth major theme in C. S. Lewis's fiction is what may be described as the "way of discipleship." So far we've looked at his teaching about evil, about ultimate good, about faith, and now we'll look at his teaching about the lifelong implications of it all.

How are we to understand the way of discipleship? What does it mean to follow Aslan? In Lewis's understanding of the Christian life, our freedom is not swallowed up or blurred or overwhelmed by Christ's authority. We see this very important theme all through *The Screwtape Letters*. The enemy writes of God: "He will not ravish, he will not cancel out this creature. He wants their free decision, their free choice." Christian faith is a "may," it is not a "must" in Lewis.

We see this in the novels, too. It means that our decisions are vital. Lewis is not in the vague theological world of universalism. For him, it's terribly important that we make decisions, which means that we have a journey to discover who Aslan is. Notice that it's uniquely our discovery. When Shasta wanted to know about Aravis's scratches, Aslan said, "I tell no one any story but his own." We're all inquisitive, and we want to know everybody else's story. But we won't find it out from Aslan.

This is a New Testament theme too. Peter won't find out from Jesus what role John should play. "You follow me," Jesus says. That's just another way of saying that our freedom and uniqueness and dignity are preserved for us.

But our decisions are vital. In *The Magician's Nephew*, Digory is given a mission by Aslan, but Aslan does not command him to do the mission unless he agrees, and he does agree. In *The Silver Chair*, just after Jill has her encounter with Aslan, she also is given a mission. She is offered four things to remember as an assurance, and she accepts the mission.

The Christian life is an experience made up of a mixture of ups and downs. For Lewis, the Christian church moves through history in obedience and in disobedience, in understanding and misunderstanding what's been said to it. That's actually how Karl Barth described the Christian church, but C. S. Lewis could have said it, too.

Here I want to make an important point about Lewis and his characters: There are no superheroes in Lewis's fiction. Every hero is flawed. If you've read only *The Lion, the Witch and the Wardrobe* and *Prince*

Caspian, you might say, "Ah, but what about Lucy?" Lucy is about the closest to a superhero in the Chronicles of Narnia, but by the time we get to *The Voyage of the Dawn Treader*, she too reveals her character flaws when she is too quick to write off friends who disappointed her. But just in time she hears the growl of Aslan. There is ambiguity, complexity, about every single character, and I respect this realism that we see in Lewis. His view of the Christian life, of Christian sanctification is as growth in Christ taking time.

Lewis is in agreement with the apostle Paul's autobiographical statement in Romans 7. Every single character disappoints you in the Chronicles of Narnia. In *The Screwtape Letters*, you see that Lewis feels that way about the people who make up the church. The "patient" comes to church immediately after becoming a Christian. As he walks into the church building and looks around he sees just that collection of neighbors he's been avoiding all week. Marvelous! We're a part of the church as the body of Christ because Christ calls us here, not because we have so much in common with each other. No, we're all in trouble; we all live our life with ups and downs.

Here we see a related theme in Lewis's stories. The Christian life is lived alongside and in fellowship with other Christians. There are no Lone Rangers. Jill and Eustace in *The Silver Chair*, even with their earnest sincerity, don't pay much attention to detail. They can't even keep track of three of the four signs they were to remember. Then they meet a cranky character named Puddleglum. Puddleglum—the apparently negative, pessimistic, and in the end, beloved Puddleglum. These unlikely co-workers need each other. Jill and Eustace are at first optimistic and enthusiastic—when they hear from a beautiful lady that there is to be a marvelous autumn fair and spring feast: "Come to the feast. You are special guests." What they don't know is that they're to be the feast. It was Puddleglum the Marsh-wiggle who didn't want to go to that feast in the first place who objected. And they say, "Oh, you're so negative, a wet blanket on everything. Come on and enjoy yourself." But in the kitchen they discover from a talkative cook that they're on the menu.

Jill and Eustace need Puddleglum because of his realism and, in the great temptation scene with the Emerald Queen, if it weren't for Puddleglum they would have all been in the gravest danger. He put his foot in the fire, and the bad smell of burnt Marsh-wiggle cleared their heads.

They needed him. But Puddleglum needed them too. The young prince Rilian has been lost for many years; and everyone knows he's lost; he's trapped somewhere. Puddleglum's been sitting by his fireplace; and he's never gone after him. He is gloomy and sad about the lost prince. It took Jill and Eustace to come along, impetuous enough to want to look for Prince Rilian. Because of them Puddleglum becomes involved in the search. They don't know the dangers and they're blundering into all kinds of dangers ahead. When they first meet the evil queen, they think she's beautiful. It took Puddleglum with his realism and his crankiness to keep Jill and Eustace balanced.

That's the Christian church. Lewis needed his brother, W. H. Lewis, and in a strange sort of way his dad, too. His father was a disappointment to him, but three of the most beautiful letters in *Letters of C. S. Lewis* are letters he wrote to his brother when their father died, when he realized that even though his father had been in some ways absent for him, his father also made a great mark on his life. Lewis needed people. The Christian needs people: we need the church. That's a great theme in these stories.

The Chronicles of Narnia also teach us that although mission is crucial, it is not ultimate. That's an important theological concept to get hold of. Just as evil's power is strong but not ultimate, so our mission is crucial but not ultimate. Our sins don't do ultimate mischief. They don't destroy the story or the grand mission. Aslan is still able to cope. Digory and Polly are the biggest examples of failure in the Chronicles of Narnia. In the deplorable world, horror of horrors, they ring the bell and start everything off in a bad direction. And then they bring Jadis into the innocent world of Narnia, almost as an Adam and Eve story. But, even that sin, ringing that bell–which they should never have done—even that is not the last word.

Our failures when they occur (and they do occur) are not the last word. The last word belongs to Aslan. Lewis saw that clearly. If you and I could get hold of this, it would set us free in our Christian discipleship. We have terribly important things to do in the world, and we shouldn't fail our task. But when we fail, our failures are not the last word.

Another central theme is that Aslan always keeps his own authority, even when we wish it were different. He keeps his authority even when it upsets us, as when Shasta wants to know why Aravis was scratched. I don't blame him for wanting to know: he's upset. As a matter of fact during the chase scene he stood up and drove the lion back. Shasta is a pretty tough kid when you get right down to it. And so he wanted to know why the lion scratched his girlfriend, whom he's going to marry later. But Aslan won't tell him. He wants to know it, but he doesn't need to know it, so therefore a distinction is drawn. Aslan doesn't always give us what we want, but he gives us what we need. The authority of Aslan is preserved. Even when we can't understand what's happening, his authority stands.

The most moving example is in the last of the novels, *The Last Battle*. It's the story in which everybody seems to lose. All the way through the story we're wondering, "When is Aslan going to come?" But the adventure becomes sadder and sadder because Aslan does not come. The battle gets harder. The terror intensifies. The deception becomes more complete, but he doesn't come. Finally, death itself confronts us at the small doorway. And then we meet him, by surprise. He's there. At that marvelous scene as Aslan surprises everyone, he calls in people we didn't expect to see. He surprises us all by calling in the stars. He's Lord of it all. He keeps his authority to the end and beyond.

12

Care of Souls in Today's America

Robert Bellah

GIVEN THE KIND OF society we live in, it is not hard to understand why people come to church for therapy. They certainly don't come to church to learn economics or sociology or political science. If anything, people come to get away from those subjects.

In *Habits of the Heart* I described how already in the nineteenth century the church was more involved in binding up the wounds that a developing capitalist society was inflicting on its members than in calling that society into question. So what should we do?

Should we tell people that they're making a big mistake to come to church looking for therapy when what they need is a good analysis of our social institutions? That is probably a recipe for going out of business fast.

I want to argue that while the church must not ignore the disruptions and traumas in people's lives, what it most authentically has to offer is not therapy but care of souls. In the face of meaninglessness and despair we can offer a God who is with us as Father, Son, and Holy Spirit, a God in whom we live and move and have our being.

In the face of the brokenness and uncertainty of every human relationship, we can offer a Community that was here before any of us was born, that will be here after all of us die, and that binds us to one another because it binds us to Christ—the vine of which we are the branches.

In the face of self-doubt and personal emptiness, we can offer an understanding of ourselves not as isolated atoms in danger of dropping into a personal abyss, but as souls created by God and destined for community with God, with other human beings, and with everything that is.

There is much talk in the therapeutic church these days about "my personal journey," and the metaphor of pilgrimage still has much to teach us. But it is the essence of ourselves as souls that we are created in and for relationship, that we will find out who we most deeply are only when we find out simultaneously who God and other beings are.

Thus, properly understood, care of souls does not mean confining ourselves to comforting the wounded—though that is often enough the place where we begin, but attending to the whole pattern of relationships that must be transformed if we are to find salvation. The soul will not find salvation except through conversion, but that conversion, that being born again, is to be converted into, to be reborn into, a transformed understanding of our relationship to the whole world.

The idea that salvation comes when I am alone in the garden with Jesus is, as Harold Bloom has written, not Christianity at all, but gnosticism. The word *soul* has become popular of late, partly because nobody quite knows what it means. It has even become a code word for the therapeutic understanding of the self. If we would authentically reclaim it we must understand it in its true Biblical and theological meaning. In short, I think we can undertake a genuine care of souls only when we proclaim an orthodox, full-blooded Christianity, and when we show forth in our lives what we profess by our faith.

But in our society such a faith is not easy to understand. Many people come to church because they want clear answers in the face of the confusion in which they live. But salvation as the Bible understands it is a radical transformation of the person in a radically transformed world. It cannot be reduced to a set of cognitive propositions or simple moral imperatives. Some of our evangelical friends like to say "Jesus is the answer," and indeed he is. But even more deeply, Jesus is the question, the one who calls into question every aspect of our personal and interpersonal lives, and who shows the inadequacy of every answer that claims divine sanction for human claims.

The faith we proclaim does not make sense in human terms: think of 1 Corinthians, chapter 1. The wisdom of the wise, the wisdom of this world, today, is a scientific, objectivistic positivism. To attempt to reduce our faith to quasi-scientific terms is to abandon it, to choose the wisdom of the world over the folly of the cross.

The faith we proclaim comes alive when it is lived in community, above all when it is lived in worship, in the word and sacrament that heal us, and transform us, and that reaffirm our membership in one body. I am not saying we don't need intellectual resources. We have a rich theological heritage, and good work is being done today, but theological truth will come alive more readily in the worshiping, witnessing life of the church than in the solitude of the study.

But people don't come to church just for answers. They come to church for warmth and acceptance. They want a personal atmosphere: some of our Pentecostal friends have abandoned the traditional architecture of the church in favor of the living room, or better the talk-show set. People today want a minister who will be someone they can relate to, who will share some bit of autobiography in every sermon. They want Bible study groups where they can talk about their personal problems more than about what the Bible is saying.

We must, of course, meet people where they are, but to turn the Christian message into therapy is to abandon its content. Somehow or other (and here we must be wise as serpents) we must help people to see that if they are to find what they most deeply want, they must go beyond themselves. In short, they must lose themselves in order to find themselves. And long before that, some of them will move on to another congregation, where they hope to find a warmer, more personal atmosphere.

If we are surprised at the fragile hold we have on many of our members, we shouldn't be. This fragility is only an expression of general problems in our society that affect all forms of relationship. The problems in the area of religion are endemic to the culture as a whole, and are especially clear in the areas of family and marriage, and politics— and acutely, at the moment, in the occupational sphere. In every case the viability of a coherent form of life is endangered by uncertainty and insecurity, which pressure individuals to put a priority on individual self-interest at the expense of long-term loyalties.

Nowhere is this clearer today than in the occupational arena. A recent *New Yorker* had a cartoon in which a person is being interviewed for a job. The personnel manager says to him, "We expect little loyalty. In return we offer little security." One of the people we interviewed for

Habits of the Heart said that right after he got out of college he went to work for AT&T. "It wasn't very exciting," he said, "but at least I knew there would always be an AT&T."

In contrast, last year, after a huge number of layoffs at AT&T under the leadership of its CEO, Robert Allen, the gossip at the company was that AT&T would soon stand for Allen and Two Temps. We hear more and more of companies, after vigorous downsizing, hiring back former employees at much lower salaries, often part-time and without benefits. One wonders how the companies handle the resentments such employees must feel.

With decreasing job security, people have to learn what today is called "personal responsibility," that is, they have to hustle for themselves. A recent PBS *Frontline* program earlier this month focused on average Americans who invest in the stock market. With declining benefits and inadequate salaries, many people are looking to the stock market to meet their future needs: the education of their children and their own retirement. Often they invest what they call "blood money," that is, money that is not really surplus but that they have to save out of near necessities, because they believe that the market will give them a security they would not otherwise have.

Most of them have never known a down market. Few of them know or want to know that there have been periods of bust as long as the boom that we are now in, indeed that the present boom was immediately preceded by a fourteen-year period in which the market did not regain its 1968 level until 1982.

These changes are affecting not only big corporations and their blue- and white-collar employees, but the professions as well. Doctors live in uncertainty as the hospitals where they work and the HMOs for whom they work merge and change the rules every few months. What services they can provide and how much they will be paid for them are constantly shrinking. In law firms, long-time partners are fired if they don't bring in enough business. In my own profession, higher education, tenured professors have not, or not yet, been fired, but tenure itself covers an ever smaller proportion of the profession. More and more teaching is done by part-time and short-term instructors. In a recent article entitled "Anger in the Academic Workplace," Judith Sturnick describes the feelings that arise when those called to university teaching find things changing rapidly beneath their feet:

> The academic workplace as we knew it, and to which we committed our professional lives, is slipping away from us. The process of change has left us in the grip of grief, and anger is a particularly strong phase of that mourning. Restructuring, which was merely a threat four years ago, is now a reality . . . Although our much-vaunted autonomy may have been as much fiction as fact, we no longer believe we have control over our own destiny. Public support for higher education is a tattered garment. Downsizing has left us with fewer people and more work to be done. The quality of our lives has been affected at every level . . . The destruction of the mythos of community has cut a wide swath across our collective psyches . . . (*The Academic Workplace*, 7, 1, Fall/Winter 1996, p. 5).

The university has never been a particularly egalitarian institution, but the inequalities we are experiencing today mirror what is going on in the larger society. Robert Reich's three-class typology now applies to higher education. The most striking feature of this new class system in the university is the appearance of a genuine underclass. We have sensed for quite some time that such a thing existed but the evidence now is overwhelming.

In a recent article in *Academe*, Cary Nelson describes the plight of very large numbers of graduate students today. He begins by asking a riddle: "In three letters, what is the name of a lengthy and expensive cultural enhancement program for term employees in the academy—employees, in other words, who have been hired for a fixed term and no longer? . . . The answer is the Ph.D." (*Academe*, November-December, 1995, p. 18).

The crushing fact is that many, perhaps most, of these PhDs who staff our courses in any large university will never get a tenure-track job (Nelson says graduate students teach over two-thirds of the courses, about 500 courses a year, in his English department at the University of Illinois).

Heavily exploited before receiving the degree, afterwards they may spend some years as itinerant part-timers and eventually, after 8 or 10 or 15 years, they will have to find a different line of employment. At what cost to their self-esteem and the viability of their families we can only imagine. This growing body of temporary or term employees is our academic underclass.

If anxiety and uncertainty have appeared everywhere in the occupational sphere, it is not surprising that they are widespread in the realm of marriage and the family. The young sociologist Karla Hackstaff wrote a recent dissertation at Berkeley on what she calls "the divorce culture." She argues that a generation or two ago we had a marriage culture, and now we have a divorce culture. This is not a matter of the statistical prevalence of divorce but of its cultural meaning and the expectations it creates for everyone: not yet married, married, and divorced alike.

She gave a seminar on her thesis topic to Berkeley seniors and discovered that most of them wanted to use the seminar as group therapy rather than as a sociology course. The majority of the students were from families of divorce and they wished to share the anger and pain that their parents' actions had caused them. But when Karla asked whether divorce is morally all right, the students could only say, of course, people have to be free to do what they want.

As a French jurist has written, "Instead of the individual 'belonging' to the family, it is the family which is coming to be at the service of the individual." The most obvious indicator of the growing fragility of the family is the rising rate of divorce. Since few of us want to return to a situation where individuals are condemned to spend their lives in unhappy or even abusive marriages, we have hesitated to discuss the cost of the rise in divorce to children and to the whole society. Psychologist Judith Wallerstein, however, in her study of the long-term consequences of divorce for children has drawn a picture which should give us pause:

> Divorce has ripple effects that touch not just the family involved, but our entire society. As the writer Pat Conroy observed when his own marriage broke up, "Each divorce is the death of a small civilization." When one family divorces, that divorce affects relatives, friends, neighbors, employers, teachers, clergy, and scores of strangers. Although more people stay married than get divorced, divorce is not a *them* versus *us* problem; everyone, in one way or another, has been touched by it. Today, all relationships between men and women are profoundly influenced by the high incidence of divorce.
>
> Teachers from all over the country tell me that their students come to school wide-eyed with fear, saying that their parents quarreled the night before and asking in terror, "Does that mean that they are going to divorce?" Radical changes in family life affect all families, homes, parents, children, courtships, and marriages, silently altering the social fabric of the entire society.

Just as the family is now seen less as something we belong to than as something at the service of the individual, so politics is increasingly seen less as a means of democratic participation than as a source of interest maximization. Just as we have consumer Christians, so we have consumer voters. The market as the master metaphor of all aspects of life undermines both any sense of objective morality and any need to think of oneself as deeply involved with other people. But the politics of interest is as unhealthy for our political life as the divorce culture is unhealthy for our family life.

In the political sphere, too, a profound sense of uncertainty and lack of trust undermines long-term political loyalties. Candidates run on their own much more than as representatives of a party or an ideology and they spend enormous amounts of money, much of it in attacking their opponents. This leads to profound dissatisfaction with our national political system, which then results in a long-term decline in the percentage of eligible voters who actually vote—and a widespread cynicism.

The rise of so-called political independents parallels the rise of religious independents and of divorce. All are symptoms of social and cultural disengagement and anomie; all are symptoms of a society which, pollsters tell us, most Americans think is "not on the right track."

When we take these reflections back to the question of the meaning of the church in America today we can well ask, when we teach the words of the creed and the catechism, what do they mean? In a society where group boundaries are weak, where families are often incoherent, where individuals do not feel innerly connected to their roles, and where the language of feelings and reasons is much more pervasive than the language of symbol and meaning, then it is hard for people to understand the very idea of the church. Without a sense of what might almost be called the physicality of the church, the church as the body of Christ, people have a very privatized idea of religion, disembodied, psychological, and finally consumerist.

The looseness they feel toward their occupation, family, political party, and even friends, is extended to the church. Individual psychological reward becomes the measure, leading to an incredibly distorted notion of discipleship: Take up your cross and follow me: it'll make you feel good. Without a strong sense of what it is to be the church, it is very hard for people to understand the faith, the liturgy, and, ultimately, what we are called on to be and to do as disciples of the crucified Christ.

If the church is not alone in the faintness of its grasp of its own membership, if occupational, familial, and political relationships are likewise fragile and uncertain, it is clear that we need not only church renewal, a "rebirthing of congregational ministry," but a renewal of fundamental human solidarity at every level of our common lives.

We need a reformed economy that will provide not just material well-being, though that is a high priority especially for our poorest citizens, but occupational security and meaningful work.

We need a revival of marriage culture in the face of the reality of divorce, and a wider understanding of the solidarities essential to family life.

We need a renewed politics of principle and long-term accountability, and politicians who can look beyond the next election to deal with the enormous social, economic, and ecological problems that loom ahead.

To make any sense, church renewal must be undertaken with an awareness of the enormous need for a renewal of solidarity at every level, and not just in our own society but in the world.

But we have to start from where we are, and I want to consider what we can do specifically within the church itself, always mindful that to opt for a purely private spirituality is to abandon our faith altogether.

We have to begin where people are. They come with injured and needy selves; they must be shown that they are souls in need of salvation. What they find or ought to find in church is God. As Marcus Borg puts it in his book, *The God We Never Knew*: "Congregations that are full of God are full of people." (I read this book in manuscript because I was asked to write a blurb for it. I was doubtful at first because of Borg's association with the Jesus Seminar, about which I have more than a few reservations. But I found the book to be both orthodox and contemporary and I will draw from it in some of the things I want to say.)

There is more than one way, even within the parameters of the Bible, to speak of God. In fact there are many ways. The Bible is rich in metaphor and narrative, and God eludes any one kind of language. The variety of forms of reference and address suggests that, while we are wholly encompassed by God, our understanding is never complete and always open to new insight.

But, as Borg points out, there is one way of speaking about God that has dominated much of the church for a long time, since its rise to dominance in the seventeenth century. That way of speaking about God is one with which he, and I, and I suspect many of you, grew up.

It is what he calls the monarchical model of God. In this model the Biblical metaphor of God as king becomes all-pervasive: the central understanding of the divine-human relation becomes one of domination and submission.

In this version of the monarchical model, God is distant, "up there," a ruler, law-giver, and judge. The monarchical model of God carries with it, says Borg, a performance model of the Christian life: that is, the Christian life is one primarily of "meeting requirements" and "measuring up."

Since Borg was raised a Lutheran, he certainly heard about God's grace. But in this version of the monarchical model, God's grace reinforces only the performance model. God's mercy is as arbitrary and remote as his commands. The monarchical model is inevitably authoritarian and it easily reinforces existing authorities in state, church, and family, all seen as powerful, distant, and male.

The monarchical model also tends to subsume the equally Biblical metaphor of God as father, making fatherhood remote, authoritarian, and monarchical. Let me say at once that these understandings of God as king and father are not wrong, though they are one-sided. They become wrong only when they override other understandings of God that modify their one-sidedness.

And they are not even the only versions of God as king and father. God as king can mean, and did mean in ancient Israel and in much of Christian history, that the one true king is God, that all earthly kings are under God's judgment, and that resistance to human authority is sometimes required as true obedience to God.

Our authority is not from man but from God. And God as father need not be remote and monarchical. He can be parental, nurturing, and intimate.

But, Borg argues, there is another model for the understanding of God. It is just as pervasive as the monarchical model and in many ways speaks to us more directly today. This is what he points to when he speaks of "the God we never met," the model of God as spirit. This is the model of God in the fourth Gospel: In the beginning was the Word, and the Word was with God, and the Word was God.

God is spirit, word, wisdom; *nous* in Greek, that which links our innermost self, our soul, with Being itself. Borg has been profoundly influenced by Paul Tillich, but Borg's language is not philosophical. It is the concrete language of the Bible. In the model of God as spirit the central understanding of the divine-human relation is relationship, belonging, membership. We are all members of one body. "For in the one Spirit we were all baptized into one body—Jews or Greeks, slaves or free—and we were all made to drink of one Spirit" (1 Corinthians 12:13).

If God as spirit is gendered, the gender is as often feminine as masculine. But God as spirit may not be anthropomorphic at all. God is wind, breath, life. God is fire and light. God is a rock, firm and sheltering (Rock of ages, cleft for me). God in Christ is food, drink, the bread of Heaven, the water of life. If the metaphor is anthropomorphic it may be God as mother, a hovering or brooding bird, a woman in labor giving birth, a woman caring for or comforting her children.

God may be a companion, perhaps an unrecognized journey companion, as on the road to Emmaus. Or God may be lover, as in Isaiah 43, "You are precious in my eyes and I love you."

If a congregation is full of such a God, a God with us, then the care of souls can take place.

Those who want an exclusively monarchical God can certainly find churches that will take them in, but I don't think that is the problem in your church or mine. Rather the problem for us is that we have become so intimidated by the dangers of an exclusively monarchical imagery that we are almost afraid to talk about God at all. Instead of powerful God language we speak the language of psychology. Instead of referring to St. Paul, we refer to Carl Jung.

But if we recover with vitality and joy the full spectrum of Biblical "God language" we may begin to help our members (and ourselves) see that God goes far beyond "meeting my needs." God transforms our needs, speaks to us as souls, and offers us salvation.

When we are hesitant to speak about God we almost never speak about salvation. Again, Borg shows that not only is the language of salvation central to the Biblical world view, but the overwhelming reference of salvation language in the Bible is not to an afterlife (almost missing in the Old Testament though present in the New), but in both Testaments to this world. In the fourth Gospel, eternal life is not something in the future but something here and now in Jesus Christ. In the Synoptic Gospels, the kingdom of God is at hand, is already among us.

In this perspective God's grace is not some arbitrary remission of a deserved punishment, but God's will that we participate in salvation through Jesus Christ. In the model of God as spirit, the Christian life is centrally about participating in God's salvation.

Borg spells out the meaning of Biblical salvation as God's will for our liberation, reconciliation, forgiveness, enlightenment, and acceptance. God's will is not just for our individual well-being but for the well-being of the whole of creation. We could say that God's salvation is our solidarity with the whole of creation.

The central place for the celebration of the Christian life as participation in God's salvation is the act of worship. Word and sacrament combine to make this understanding come alive, to make this transformation actually happen.

But once we begin to experience salvation, once we see ourselves as souls unbreakably connected to God in Christ, and so unshakably members of the church as the body of Christ, and not as transient visitors in search of having our needs met, then we are bound to ask about all the rest of our lives. About our jobs, families, politics, and the loyalties that should sustain them. Richard Harmon speaks of raising the "pressure" question in individual and group discussion.

What are the pressures in our society that limit our enactment of the Christian life as participation in salvation? What are the pressures on our families that keep them from being cells in the body of Christ, sustaining all their members and not just being an instrumentality for individual members?

What are the pressures in our occupational life that keep us from seeing what we do as a calling from God to fulfill ourselves through contributing to the common good?

What are the pressures that prevent our political life from engaging us in common concerns, trusting that our fellow citizens share those concerns enough to struggle with us?

When we seriously face these questions we are propelled to consider the transformation of every sphere of our common life.

In short, a joyous, God-filled congregation is not just a hospital for the injured, but a place that sends us out to do the work that God has given us to do.

V

Art and Soul

13

The Need to Pay Attention
Darkness, Light, and the Visionary Eye

Luci Shaw

I WAS TRANSFIXED, ONCE, during a dinner party I was hosting for friends, by the sudden sight, in my own dining room, of a green vine spiraling up artistically out of the spout of a blue-and-white teapot as it sat on a shelf next to the wall. It had a look of astonishment as if to inquire, "What am I doing here?" Closer investigation (after the guests had departed) revealed its source as a dried pea hidden inside the teapot. My conjecture was that in some time in the dim past one of my young sons had been prodigal with his pea-shooter in the dining room, and the vagrant pea, nurtured at last by moisture of unknown origin, had been encouraged enough to sprout and wind its way in the dark towards the tiny star of light which shone through the teapot spout.

And the young plant shrouded in the soil "knows," senses, that its task is to reach the light. That it is destined for resurrection after its long burial—that to arrive in the light will mean life and health and growth and fruitfulness.

Light is there for our seeing. Eyes and light working together result in sight.

The Gospel reading in the Anglican lectionary for the 23rd Sunday after Pentecost is from Mark 10. It tells the story of blind Bartimaeus, who had the encounter of his life on the road out of Jericho. Hearing the story read in church, once again sitting there in the pew I was taken aback by the simplicity and urgency of the blind man's entreaty to Jesus—"*I want to see*," a request which I have been making on and off for most of my life. With Virginia Stem Owens, I have pleaded: "Give me phenomena . . . Give me pictures and models . . . The one thing I cannot take is the denying darkness and the blind man's eye." All of us, Christians, with a mission of living the truth that compels, of focusing the light and dispelling the darkness— all of us acknowledge the need to *see* and in order to see truly and deeply we need to learn how to *pay attention* to both seen and unseen worlds.

Another Bible story, very similar, shows up in the ninth chapter of John's Gospel where an unnamed blind man receives sight from Jesus. It triggered this poem for me:

> *The Sighting*
>
> Out of the shame of spittle,
> the scratch of dirt,
> he made an anointing.
>
> Oh, it was an agony—the gravel
> in the eye, the rude slime, the brittle
> clay caked on the soft eyelid.
>
> But with the hurt
> light came leaping; in the shock and shine
> abstracts took flesh, and flew;
>
> winged words like view & space,
> shape & shade & green & sky,
> bird & horizon & sun
>
> turned real in a man's eye.
> Thus was truth given a face
> & dark dispelled, & healing done.[1]

How do we *see*? What is vision? How may we condense into vivid words what we see? How, in the Christian's life, may words and language be redeemed and abstracts "turned real?" How is "truth given a face?" How is the physiological faculty of *seeing* connected with the more profound insight (*in-sight!*) of spiritual and intellectual perception? And what part has the human imagination in this play of glimpse and gleam,

---

1. Shaw, *Polishing the Petoskey Stone*.

of hide and seek, of light and shadow? These were some of the questions on my mind in as I sat, several years ago, looking up from a pew in St. Fridewide's Chapel, in Christ Church Cathedral in Oxford:

A Chiaroscuro God

In this ancient place
one section of the fresco
ceiling has been left
to peel, a puzzle, half
the pieces lost. As from
the bottom of a well I stare
up, waiting for revelation.
A raw plaster frowns
from the past, a closed sky, murky
as thunder, traced with

gold shreds—a snatch
of hair, a broken chin line,
wing fragments in red, in blue.
My eyes are busy—deepening
pigment, filling in the detail
of hands, feathers, touching up
the face of an angel. But nothing
changes. The terrible inscrutability
endures, deeper than
groined arches. Tattered

seraphim flash their diminishing
edges, like the chiaroscuro God who,
if we believe Michelangelo, touched
Adam into being with one finger,
whose footprints crease the blackness
of Genesaret, whose wing feathers
brush our vaulted heaven, purple
with storm, whose moon
is smudged—a round of window glass,
an eye moving between clouds.[2]

Do we worship a chiaroscuro God? The word itself is an oxymoron. It means "clear/obscure," juxtaposing two very opposite elements. The term is used to describe a style of painting in which each of the bright and the dark elements of the work are shown up by the strong contrast each gives the other. It is a term that can also apply to writing, and even

2. Shaw, *Writing the River*.

to musical composition. It has been my own personal experience that God sometimes allows me to be in darkness for a while, hiding his face, so that when his light reappears to me, it is unmistakable. I have learned a great deal through this chiaroscuro, this contrast.

We still, in the human condition, "see through a glass, darkly." Yet in spite of our present failure to know as we are known, to see with the clarity and breadth we long for, Jesus tells us: "If your eye is single, your whole body will be full of light." This promise implies that what is demanded of us is a clear, sharp focus, without the blurring of myopia or double vision. Such seeing requires our deliberate, intentional joining-in-one of the separate images of our two eyes—a convergence. It calls us to be in a state of *attentiveness*.

Annie Dillard, on being asked to write a paragraph for *Life* magazine on, of all things, "the meaning of life," came up with this: "We are here to abet Creation and to witness it, to notice each thing so each thing gets noticed. Together we notice not only each mountain shadow and each stone on the beach, but we notice each other's beautiful face and complex nature, so that Creation need not play to an empty house." I've been reading Marilynne Robinson's *Gilead* in which again and again she seems to affirm this need to love and embrace the things in existence.

For us to participate in this drama presupposes our need to pay attention, (and the word "pay" is significant—time, and awareness, love, concentration and penetration are the price of seeing.) The details of God's creative activity are ubiquitous and all too often unnoticed. In Thomas Merton's words: "When the sun is always shining you forget that it is God's gift, and you don't pay attention any more." But to ignore these evidences of God's magnanimity, or view them as insignificant, is to deny or demean the creative energy of God.

The word "attention" is derived from the Latin *ad-tendere*—to stretch toward. Attending implies *inhabiting*. This is not a spectator sport. Paying attention cannot be done in passivity. It demands intentionality, choice, and awareness. And that, too, is costly. Especially in the Gospel of John the command, "Look!" draws our attention to significance. Behold! Wow! Christian spirituality demands that we stop in our tracks in order to see what's happening, to read its meanings and to attend to them.

Thomas Howard has observed in a commentary on *Out of the Silent Planet*, "The will of God (of Maleldil, or of Aslan) may well present itself to us in the most unobtrusive of circumstances, but the ready servant will be *alive to it*. Most of us miss our cues repeatedly."[3] Or, as Sherlock Holmes commented to Watson: "You *see*, but you do not *observe*." Artist Thomas La Duke notes that: "Some things are so common that they disappear. They're all around us, but they vanish." Missing our cues, we fail to notice the fingerprints of the Creator in the ordinary textures and phenomena of living because we are distracted by daily urgencies, by things we consider more important, which in the end may prove to be both trivial and transient.

Mary Oliver tells us that:

> If you notice anything
> it leads you to notice
> more
> and more.[4]

All these lovers and breathers of life make up my good companions. They tell me I am not alone.

Four years I spent two and a half weeks in the South Island of New Zealand. I recorded in detail my experience during the days we spent in the sub-tropical rain forest of the west coast. Most of the time I was alone, by choice, with camera and journal, porous as a sponge to multiple sensations and impressions. My journal chronicled it for me:

> Giant tree ferns arch over me, and enormous rata trees, scarlet with blossoms. But I find myself enthralled, filled with the joy of *small things*. My camera lens, with its zoom magnification, helps me to see what I might otherwise merely glance at and move on. The microcosm of moss gardens among the boulders along the forest paths, minute, damp velvet fronts like green sea anemones—small, low, unknown, unnamed greens, lie lavish in their rich diversity and texture. Minuscule star flowers punctuate the green of the ferns, jeweled with dew. Pebbles lie under water in the stream, strangely uniform in size and roundness and color, the color of a rain cloud. My need is to stop, to be still, to focus, to be aware, to pay attention, to let the microcosm speak—the world of negligible, unnoticed things. I realize how powerfully, given time, light speaks from such phenomena when seen through the magnifying lens of careful scrutiny.

---

3. Schultz and West, *C. S. Lewis Readers' Encyclopedia*.
4. *Poets & Writers*, March/April 2000, p. 24.

We tend to think of God in terms of the infinitely huge—mountains, oceans, galaxies, universes. But as God is beyond gender and time, so is he beyond size. Like Mary Oliver, once again (a favorite poet of mine, because she brings details to my notice),

> ... The dream of my life
> Is to lie down by a slow river
> And stare at the light in the trees—
> To learn something by being nothing
> A little while but the rich
> Lens of attention.[5]

Later. I am astonished that when I mention the intricacies of moss, or the uniform roundness of pebbles in the stream, or the dark, lacy foliage of New Zealand black birches to my companions, when we rendezvous, they are puzzled. They hadn't noticed. Deeply committed to the Christian church's world mission, they had been discussing global strategic initiatives. Though they are aware, and appreciative in a general way, that this subtropical landscape is "beautiful," they haven't noticed trivialities such as pebbles or varieties of moss. They haven't been watching where they walked.

And here is where the whole incarnational approach to faith kicks in for me. As a poet and a sacramentalist I am learning to recognize pointers to transcendent realities in almost anything I see. Thomas Aquinas put it like this: "We arrive at the knowledge of God from other things." In Thomas à Kempis's *Imitation of Christ* we learn that, "If your heart is straight with God, every creature will be to you a mirror of life and a book of holy doctrine." Or, as St. Anthony put it: "My book . . . is the nature of created things, and whenever I wish I can read in it the works of God." It's not that we are inventing our own ideas about the Almighty, but that we are exploring and examining the body of evidence already made available to us. I find I need to take an annual wilderness retreat as a cleansing of the eyes. John Stott calls the created universe "God's second Bible." The psalmist recognized it in the opening verses of Ps. 19. St. Paul recognized it in Romans 1: "Since the creation of the world God's invisible qualities—his eternal power and divine nature—have been clearly seen, *being understood from what has been made.*" Or,

---

5. Oliver, "Entering the Kingdom"

as Eugene Peterson has paraphrased it, "The basic reality of God is plain enough. Open your eyes, and there it is! By taking a long and thoughtful look at what God has created, people have always been able to see what their eyes as such can't see; eternal power, for instance, and the mystery of divine being."

So our seeing must be on at least two levels if we are to take seriously the prayer of St. Paul for the Christians at Ephesus—"that the eyes of [your] hearts might be enlightened." I believe that this enlightenment is linked to the discussion Jesus had with his followers as recorded in St. Matthew 13—"Blessed are your eyes for they see"—a seeing that takes in both the surface realities and the more profound meanings that lie beyond them. I'm reminded of George Herbert's verse:

> A man may look on glass—
> Or it may stay his eye—
> Or, if he pleaseth, through it pass,
> And then the heaven espy.

And I believe that in the parables Jesus was setting forth the pattern for light and vision. I'm convinced he was saying in the Sower and Seeds story, "Yes—I want you to notice the way seeds grow, or don't grow. I love it when you're exhilarated by the marvel of green life springing from my Father's hand, and it's worthy of notice. Celebrate it, and then move on. It's your soul growth that I'm after. What rocky soil causes your heart to wither? What weeds are choking the life and beauty out of you? What cynical scavenger birds are pecking your truth away, seed by seed? What will help you develop from seed to sprout to plant to a multiplication of seeds—the miracle of the loaves over and over again, out there in the harvest field?"

The aging apostle John, exiled on the island of Patmos, was given an unearthly vision of "one like the Son of Man." Not surprisingly he was stricken with the paralysis of fear—fear of something other, fear of the unknown and the unknowable. But twice he was reassured, "Don't be afraid. *Write what you see* on a scroll."[6] A friend of mine, knowing my addiction to journal-keeping, once gave me a blank journal with the admonition on the front page (an echo of the mandate to St. John) "Write what you see, *and what you can't see.*" A bi-focal vision is called for. It

---

6. Revelation 1:11

tells me to pay attention to the surface of reality, but it could also mean a brilliant epiphany to be glimpsed beyond it.

In this context it is well to remember Emily Dickinson's admonition:

> Tell all the truth but tell it slant—
> Success in Circuit lies
> Too bright for our infirm Delight
> The Truth's superb surprise

> As Lightning to the Children eased
> With explanation kind
> The Truth must dazzle gradually
> Or every man be blind[7]

I am sitting by an east window in my home. It is early—the sun not yet up, and the house quiet enough for me to hear nothing but the ticking of our antique clocks in adjoining rooms, and the refrigerator's gentle hum through the kitchen door.

But I am not here to listen to the language of my house. This is supposed to be quiet time, vision time, when I can see and hear God and my own thinking as I respond to his ideas entering my mind. Sometimes this really happens. I sense the freshness, the pang of a thought from a source other than my own experience or intelligence. Often, as I meditate, or concentrate on the groups of words on the pages of the book in my lap—the Bible—I see pictures in my head, or I hear a new meaning in the familiar phrases. Or I notice a link between them and the events and circumstances and relationships that swim every day into my awareness. Correspondences are waiting there to be recognized—patterns of cause and effect, of comparison and contrast—in which my mind interacts with the thoughts of another human mind—the biblical writer, long dead—and through him (can I believe it?) with the mind of God.

Somehow this all seems incongruous. Me in my flannel nightgown and slippers taking in ideas, seeing colors and shapes and scenes in the ancient words, with the Almighty focusing and clarifying them for me

---

7. Dickinson, *The Complete Poems*.

right now, on this twentieth century morning—how is that I am relaxed and calm, even cozy, in The Presence? Why am I not crouched in terror on the living room rug? Is it possible that I am hearing from God, and yet remain unshrivelled by the blast of divine reality?

But the room is tranquil. The clocks tick on. Upstairs someone is waking and moving. God is with me in this room, and while I am on the edge of my wing-back chair with anticipation, I am not even nervous.

Now the sun is over the horizon, burning through the fringe of cedars to the east of the house, its light flowing through the window not just with a general burgeoning of brightness but in multi-colored flakes of muted radiance that touch the walls, the piano, the leaves of the plants. The skin on the back of my hand has turned turquoise. I glance up at the window sill with its rank of cut glass bottle stoppers of varied shapes and sizes that I have collected. It is through these multiple prisms that the sunlight is being refracted now, split into splinters of coral and garnet and amethyst and topaz and aquamarine that lend the room their gem-like brilliance.

I am aware, quite suddenly, of the arrival of an idea. I am seeing a connection. I am realizing that just as this familiar room of mine is being lit up and decorated with rainbow light at dawn, the Bible—like an old and familiar house—is lit up with the colorful rays of metaphor, symbol, analogy, poetry, story, parable, imagery, projected into all its rooms through the old leaded windows with their beveled edges. Though the light that is pouring through the glass is plain, white, ordinary daylight, because of the prisms the light appears to me in its primary spectral colors. A fascination of changing hues illuminates me with a perception of the true nature of light in its iridescent parts as well as its diffused, white wholeness. I remind myself that the Scripture is not just information, data, exhortation or proposition from God. Nor is it merely a series of abstract principles or concepts linked by pedestrian factual narrative. It is truth often deliberately framed in words that project brilliant images into our thinking, like a series of slides onto a screen.

It is not only difficult but dangerous to look the sun in the eye. (Think of the squares of smoked glass or the strips of exposed film we are obliged to use as we watch the progress of a solar eclipse.) Even now, as I look through my window towards the gold glare moving like a fire between the tree trunks and branches, igniting the surface of the creek, I look away again, squinting in discomfort.

It is that kind of reaction to unfiltered light that reminds me of a verse in Exodus that tells me that "no one has seen God at any time," an idea echoed in St. John 1:18, "No one has ever seen God." We learn that "the appearance of the glory of the Lord was like a devouring fire on the top of the mountain" (Exod 24:17), and that even Moses, God's intimate friend, when invited to scale a mountain and converse with Yahweh, was forbidden a face-to-face encounter for his own preservation. Like me, like blind Bartimaeus, pleading for a true sighting Moses cried out: "Lord, I want to see. I pray you, show me your glory." What he got was a promise that God would *make his goodness pass before him*, would even proclaim his name, the un-pronounceable, un-write-able Tetragrammaton, to him. To hear that holy name articulated, and to learn what that name stood for, (for to God all names have meaning) was to be invited into The Presence. Yahweh was even willing for Moses to see his "back parts," or, as the Cambridge Bible puts it, "the afterglow which trails behind him" (Exod 23:33). But from the full, blazing impact of deity, Moses needed to be shielded in a rock crevice in the shoulder of the mountain, with the hand of God covering him. Even in that shelter the high-voltage proximity of the Almighty must have felt for Moses like being exposed to the blinding power and force of a nuclear explosion.

C. S. Lewis put it like this, in *Mere Christianity,* "God is the only comfort; he is also the supreme terror: the thing we most need and the thing we most want to hide from. He is our only ally and we have made ourselves his enemies. Some people talk as if meeting the gaze of Absolute Goodness would be fun. They need to think again."[8] Lewis again: "The Christian religion . . . does not begin in comfort; it begins in . . . dismay . . . In religion, as in war and everything else, comfort is the one thing you cannot get by looking for it. If you look for truth you may find comfort in the end: If you look for comfort you will not get either comfort or truth—only soft soap and wishful thinking to begin with and, in the end, despair."[9]

A Presbyterian friend of mine remembers talking with a Baptist colleague who had become a high church Anglican; he told this new convert that he found all the liturgical apparatus distracting, that it got in the way of his direct experience of God. "Of course it does, you dummy!" his friend replied. "That's what it's there for. God is too glorious to be

---

8. Lewis, *Mere Christianity*
9. Ibid.

apprehended directly. The liturgy, the robes, the incense, the chanting, are to enable you to stand in the presence of God without being bowled over by the power."

And I, if I were to receive (as a body receives a bullet, or a land mass a meteor) the shock of the reality of divine glory and truth without the protection of imagery, the veil of metaphor, I would be flattened, paralyzed, annihilated. Yet here I am, hale and whole, and every day God shows *me* his goodness. It is visible not only in the Bible pictures he gives me of himself (shepherd, mother hen, protective fortress, banner) but in the very fact that *they are pictures*. Every day I am shown, if my eyes are open and focused, new meanings of the name of God, new dimensions of his person. But a full, frontal view of God, the Almighty One, swift as light, sharp and intense as a laser, with the energy of the universe flashing from his eyes, and with the Earth (and me on it) cradled like a marble in his palm, would be too much for me in my humanity.

It was almost too much for Moses, for Gideon, for Daniel, for John the Apostle on Patmos. Like them we are finite, longing for the touch of divine reality, yet vulnerable and small and trembling. As Isaiah puts it, we are tender as field flowers and as easily cut down as meadow grass. And so God, knowing our fragility, parcels out his truth to us in small gifts of metaphor, shows himself to us in clumps of words, in the sacraments, in the natural theology of Creation. I am growing accustomed to the grace of gradual illumination, so it is a delight, and no real surprise, when I see God's messages to me in the scattered rainbows on my wall at sunrise.

Robert Farrar Capon, in referring to Jesus' way of approaching truth through story, in the parables, comments, "These are mysteries aimed at the Great Mystery..."

Yes, because the Jesus-stories call us to pay attention by speaking to us in images deliberately chosen to be perceived and entered by way of imagination and the senses. As with good poems, the multi-leveled, vigorous metaphors of the parables will be understood by those who pay attention, those with eyes to see and ears to hear. St. Mark, in his Gospel, tells us that "with many parables he spoke to the people... he did not speak to them without a parable" (Mark 4:33). When his friends asked him why, he told them (and here I quote again from Eugene Peterson's translation, *The Message*): "Whenever someone has a ready heart for this, the insights and understandings flow freely. But if there is no readiness, any trace of receptivity disappears. That's why I tell stories: *to create readiness*, to nudge people toward receptive insight. In their present state they can stare till doomsday and not see . . . I don't want Isaiah's forecast repeated all over again: "Your eyes are awake but you don't see a thing . . . the people screw their eyes shut so they won't have to look . . ."[10]

The more we see and accept of divine revelation, the more we will be shown on earth and the better we will be prepared for the brilliance of heaven. Persistent *rejection* of or indifference to the messages carried by God-story and metaphor will, conversely, so atrophy our inner optic nerves and block our souls' auditory canals that true perception becomes impossible. But for the open-eyed the stories of Jesus speak vividly. Because they are expressed in terms real enough to be *felt*, we can take them in without the kind of clinical analysis which renders them lifeless and abstract, living organisms cut apart.

I am reminded of one of my youngest daughter's experiences in her high school biology class. One of her assignments was to dissect a grasshopper. "As if *that's* how you learn anything about grasshoppers . . ." she exclaimed in disgust when she got home. For her the truth and meaning of a grasshopper was better seen in a midsummer field as it arced through shimmering air, than on a lab table, a scatter of small, dry body parts under a scalpel.

A principle, a proposition, a formula, even a systematic theology, tends to gather things together and then smooth them out again, ignoring minor inconsistencies, overlooking exceptions. The general systematic statement about reality, whether in science or theology, has much the same effect on us as a view of the earth from a satellite, or the topography found in a map. It may supply us with certain otherwise unobtainable information, but if we soon lose interest it is because much of the detail has been lost.

The microcosm, by contrast, fascinates us endlessly because it reveals specifics and idiosyncrasies, and is generally less predictable. (One of the characteristics of good poetry is surprise.) If you have ever watched a silkworm spinning a cocoon on the underside of a mulberry leaf, or red blood cells skittering through capillaries under a microscope, you know what I mean. The value of maps or charts or diagrams lies in the grasp they give us of broad spatial or rational relationships. Concrete images allow us to experience a crumb of reality in a different way. Where

---

10. Peterson, *The Message* (from Matthew 13).

proposition twirls the table model of the globe, imagination focuses on the single blade of grass, on the grain of wood in a floorboard, on the helical unfolding of a shell, or the spears of frost across a window.

It was C. S. Lewis who coined the phrase: "the tether and pang of the particular."[11] And in re-reading all of Lewis's fiction this year, I realize that this is how he builds a story. He allows the larger principles which he wants us to recognize as important to grow out of the very particular, unique, concrete details which he describes.

I am fascinated to realize with Marc Chagall, that "any moral crisis is a crisis of color, texture, blood, and the elements of speech, vibration, et cetera—the materials with which we are, like life, constructed." Capon talks of "mysteries aimed at the great mystery." Last year during Advent I heard a choir sing Gabrielli's "O Magnum Mysterium"—"O greatest of mysteries and O most wonderful sacrament, Jesus, lying there in the manger for all creatures to gaze upon. O blessed virgin, whose womb was deemed worthy of bearing Christ, the Lord Jesus. Alleluia!"[12] An intense sweetness filled the space in that auditorium as the singers' voices, deep, strong, high, clear, resonant, reverent, moved up from the stage and enfolded me. As music and words combined in human voices, the harmony, and an all-encompassing sense of the meaning of the words, which went beyond mere intellectual assent, pierced me like a sword.

And it was the Incarnation which *showed us* that "pang of the particular," which *demonstrated* before our eyes simply, clearly, concretely, in memorable detail, in a human body, what would otherwise blind us— Jesus, Logos, metaphor of God, Word that both tells and shows, accessible yet mysterious, essence as well as sacrament, actuality and analogy both, the glory of God channeled through flesh so that we could see and touch him without being shattered by divine power. With Lewis, "If we look for truth we may find comfort in the end."

God and his truth are like a sun that fills the sky. Huge verities flare off from its center like the flaming tongues of a corona, utterly overwhelming us in our insignificance. Yet he may become visible to those who *pay attention*, whose eyes of belief and imagination are open, in a form as unthreatening and taken-for-granted as a baby, or a seed, or a dove, or a lamb, or a loaf of bread, or a flick of rainbow color on a wall.

---

11. Lewis, *The Pilgrim's Regress*.
12. 10 Quoted from the concert program notes.

14

The Rich Legacy of Christian Music

Donald Heinz

Since I am coming to that holy room,
Where, with thy choir of saints for evermore,
I shall be made thy music; as I come
I tune the instrument here at the door,
And what I must do then, think here before.
—John Donne ("Hymn to God my God, in My Sickness")

Some to church repair
Not for the doctrine, but the music there.
—Alexander Pope

HANDEL'S *MESSIAH* WAS BORN for the commercial hall and slowly migrated to the Church. Bach's liturgical music arose in Church and has ended up in the concert hall. But today, neither Bach nor Handel nor an entire Christian culture is deemed usable in modern churches. Has music's role as artistic receptivity to God now become inoperative? Have the fine arts come permanently loose from their historic moorings in Christianity? Has the treasure once stored on Christian premises been abandoned and sold to a museum uptown? Has the far-reaching audacity of the Incarnation come up short in the modern world? Or is it all a false alarm, a failure to understand that contemporary Christianity, too, plays the arts, and God still consents to ever shifting shapes?

MESSIAH'S VERNACULAR LEGACY

Handel's *Messiah*, a religious and even patriotic totem in the English-speaking world, is the most popular piece of classical choral music ever written. Every Easter or Christmas, one can hear *Messiah* performed by choral societies which arose simply to perform it annually, at immense sing-alongs, from professional choruses with symphony orchestras in great concert halls, from early music groups doing it in acoustically perfect churches, and in the settings of homely church choirs having at it with music that is belovedly beyond them. In December 2002, I heard it in Beijing, directed by a young Chinese Christian conductor amid a huge audience of Chinese and Westerners. The tune of the "Hallelujah Chorus," especially its four jaunty opening notes, is an icon for all seasons, including advertising and parodies.

Handel left his German Lutheranism behind to seek his fortune composing operas in London. When London lost enthusiasm for opera, Handel turned to oratorio, a hybrid of religious texts amidst operatic soloists, chorus, and orchestra—but without scenery, costumes, or staging. At age 56 and long since a naturalized British citizen, Handel began work on *Messiah* in 1741—composed in a hurry, for quick cash, and on spec. Its first performance was in Dublin, where it premiered at 12 noon, April 13, 1742, the Tuesday before Easter. Women were requested not to wear hoops and men not to wear their swords, so there would be sufficient room for a 700-person audience gathered for a charity fundraiser.

In the London performances the following year, King George II may have stood up during the Hallelujah Chorus; a very long tradition since has audiences rising to their feet at that moment, except, of course, those for whom jumping to their feet would seem suspiciously religious or musically unsophisticated. There has never been a year since 1742 when *Messiah* was not performed. A performance in a chapel of Foundling Hospital established the long tradition of charity performances and also helped, in the face of religious concerns, to identify *Messiah* as sacred music appropriate for performance in church. In 1784, at the twenty-fifth anniversary of his burial at Westminster Abbey, five hundred performers came together to sing *Messiah*. By 1857, five thousand singers did *Messiah* at the Crystal Palace in London.

The setting in which *Messiah* (and Handel) first flourished is suggestive of how Christian culture emerges in any age. (It's best to remember, as when contemplating the making of sausage, William James's admonition, "Judge by their fruits, not their roots.") As Puritan religion and government began placing restrictions on theatrical performances by prohibiting operas during Lent, oratorios could be distanced from their operatic origins by adopting a concert style of presentation. Music could happen in Lent! Like many a religious festival, "Messiah" was responding to cultural and commercial opportunities. Serving two masters, church and theater, oratorios were made not as church music but for an entertainment venue. Still, God was the hero and humans the objects of divine action. Today's mega-evangelical churches do not have the church vs. theater problem, since they have turned themselves into theaters.

People wanted to make Handel, as well as *Messiah*, a Christian musical icon, but it is not common to attribute Handel's music to his religious faith. One finds his piety where one can. On being complimented on the entertainment of *Messiah*, he is said to have replied: "I should be sorry if I only entertained them, I wish to make them better." While composing the "Hallelujah Chorus," he later wrote: "I felt as if I saw God on his throne, and all his angels around him." He always hoped to die on Good Friday and wake up in heaven on Easter; in fact he died on the Saturday between Good Friday and Easter. He is buried in Westminster Abbey, where a monument shows him writing the aria, "I know that my redeemer liveth."

BACH'S DIFFICULT-TO-TRANSLATE LEGACY

In *Bach and the Heavenly Choir,* Johannes Rüber tells a story about a French abbot who was also a great violinist. When he becomes Pope, he wants to canonize Bach. All the obstacles but one are cleared away. It must be demonstrated that Bach had performed miracles. When the Pope plays Bach on his violin, the music itself is perceived to be the miracle. But the paradox of Bach is that he seems to epitomize a Christian musical tradition no longer able to work its miracles in church—even as he is available to the entire musical world as one of the two or three greatest composers in the Western tradition.

At Christmas or Easter, Bach's *Christmas Oratorio* or *St. Matthew Passion* is most likely to be heard in every German town and in many American concert halls, but rarely in its original venue, Christian worship. There is no doubt that Bach is a direct heir of Luther's legacy that gave music eminent place in the life of Christianity. While other Protestant traditions insisted they could not move beyond what is precisely authorized in the Bible, Luther's principle was that whatever is not forbidden is permitted. Luther understood himself to be giving the mass back to the people and bequeathing them starring roles as hymn-singers. *Luther kept open, and widened, the sluices through which the Incarnation flows into the arts.* Bach is the pay-off on that wager.

But much of the art sedimented into Christian culture is not easily digested today. Merry carolers avoid thinking about the words they sing. Those who come to Bach (or even Handel) for sheer aesthetic joy may not wish to linger on the texts. When Mendelssohn in the nineteenth century was reviving Bach's *St. Matthew Passion*, after a hundred years neglect, one critic complained that the biggest obstacle to enjoying Bach was the "atrocious German chorale texts full of the polemical earnestness of the Reformation and disturbing the mind of the non-believer by smoking him out with the dense fumes of belief which no one really wants nowadays." But for many, Bach can be swallowed whole, not stopping to chew on the theology. Bach himself did not care for the distinctions between sacred and secular; he gave it all to God. The second *Brandenburg Concerto*, with no whiff of sacred text, is a miracle, too.

Into Bach (like Dante) flowed all high art, and out flowed a distinctive Christian culture. Perhaps he understood that a millennium of Christian music was coming to an end in his work, that perfect blend of passion and intellect. His calling, whether in court or church, was to a metaphysics of art. He wrote for God's ears, and his own—never mind what his superiors and his contemporaries called for. He has been named the "fifth evangelist."

MUSIC AS CHRISTIAN CULTURE

Everyone knows that angels sang *Gloria in excelsis* over Bethlehem. The New Testament set Christ's birth to music. Christ *was* music: the early church called him God's song. Borrowing from Israel's musical traditions, early Christianity carried forth into the praise songs of Easter.

New Testament songs have laid down a rich deposit in the worship life of Western Christianity. Mary's praise song is a form of musical outburst rooted in the Old Testament where response to divine surprise calls forth "musical shout." Since the fifth century the *Magnificat* has been the chief song at Vespers, sung by every generation of monks and by many other Christians who gather for evening worship. It has inspired innumerable musical settings, culminating in works like that of Monteverdi, whose operatic treatment was meant to impress the listener with the power and majesty of Christ and the Catholic Church, and Bach, who made it a jewel of liturgical worship. At the naming ceremony for John the Baptist, his father Zachariah's tongue is untied to sing of John's mission as the forerunner of Jesus in God's plans and purposes. His *Benedictus* ("Blessed be God") has for centuries been sung at morning prayer in monastic communities and by many other Christians. At the presentation of Jesus in the temple and the purification of Mary, the old prophet Simeon, representing expectant Israel, acclaims Jesus to be God's agent of salvation and registers the passing of the old order into the new. This third song in Luke's nativity narrative is called the *Nunc dimittis* ("Let me now depart"), and since the fourth century it has been sung at Compline or evensong, and at many funerals.

Around AD 105, Pliny the Younger, spying on the Christians, reported to Emperor Trajan that they were accustomed to meet early in the morning and sing hymns. The New Testament alludes to Christian hymn-singing (Mark 14:26; 1 Corinthians 14:26; Acts 16:25; Ephesians 5:19; Colossians 3:16), and elegant Christian poetry set to music flourished in the early centuries of Christianity. Hymns as a verse form within the liturgy sung to specific tunes began to proliferate in fourth century public worship, so that Christmas and Easter acquired rich musical accompaniment.

Pope Gregory the Great, who reigned from 590 to 604, gave to the church of Rome and to missionary efforts far beyond an orderly liturgy in a Christian Year. By the time of the Carolingian renaissance of the 8th and 9th centuries, musical creativity infused Christian worship, especially in Gregorian chant. Its eight "modes" became the form through which monks chanted their way through all 150 psalms each week, in the seven daily services of the Divine Office. The Gregorian impulse was restless and fertile. The final "a" in a chanted alleluia became a vocalization of human striving for heaven and an artistic impulse to ever greater musical complexity, elongating into ingenious melodies, which then acquired fresh texts as well. Musical improvisation became the germ of drama and street theater and the stimulation for Christian poetry. The mystic Mechtild of Magdeburg would regularly have heard such music and more than the music when she herself sang:

> As the Godhead strikes the note
> Humanity sings.
> The Holy Spirit is the harpist
> And all the strings must sound
> Which are touched in love.

Western Christian music gave us the "heightened speech" of a Latin vernacular perfectly molded to Gregorian melodies and then moved on to an ever widening outpouring of song and instrument emerging from the Church's dynamic worship life. *The endless musical expansion of earlier, simpler forms paralleled the endless human ornamentation of the Incarnation that made God bloom in every art of lived Christianity.*

BUT CAN WE BEAR IT?

Whether classical Christian music arises from the secular world (Handel) or from Christian worship life (Bach), it scarcely survives in American churches, even as it flourishes outside them. Few aspire to "bring every thought (art) captive to the obedience of Christ." To mention Handel or Bach today is to realize that no student in a high school or college choir, nor any modern concertgoer, escapes the fact that the overwhelming preponderance of the great choral music of the West is Christian. A remarkable fact of university life is that the most likely second job for the university organist or the music department's choral director is as a minister of music in a local Christian Church. Is this a remaining, frail contact between church and academy?

The Christian culture of the arts is a many-coursed banquet available in many venues, but it is, or would be, a significantly different experience within lived Christianity. In the churches, no one hears it; in concert halls, no one "gets it." Rich legacies take considerable work to appreciate; Goethe said every generation must make itself worthy to "own" the past. College music programs work very hard to offer the public a taste of an authentic Christian musical culture. Shakespearean dramaturges try to duplicate the experience of the original Globe Theater for modern play-goers. The early music movement that arose in the last century attempted to recover the "performance practices" of earlier times—how much vibrato was allowed in a soprano's voice, how many singers were employed in Handel's first performance of *Messiah*, how the "original instruments" sounded.

If it is difficult to recover what was heard, it is far more so to imagine the hearers themselves. Historic "audience practices" are a world away from the present, so it is difficult genuinely to hear Christian culture today. Bach's self-consciousness and the environment in which he worked can scarcely be imagined any longer. His implied listeners were written into the score, but a great paradigm shift has occurred since then, and the modern listener, certainly in a concert hall, is far removed from most of those who heard Bach's music in Leipzig. As far removed as those who stare admiringly at Christian art in a museum are from those who reverently kiss icons, museum docents know that an understanding of past religious art requires *a retrieval of knowledge lost and an un-learning of knowledge assumed.* Of course, neither concert halls nor museums were the seminal sites for Christian culture. The Church was the original theater for the performance of Christmas or Easter. While Bach's legacy in the musical world keeps growing (during the ten days leading up to Christmas 2005, BBC Radio 3 broadcast the entire Bach corpus with only newsbreaks), the aural landscape of Christian music has grown ever more constricted. Is artistic retrieval impossible, the legacy of Christian culture too heavy to bear?

It is clear enough that secular music-lovers come to Bach (or even Handel) not for their religious messages but for sheer aesthetic joy. But what of Christians for whom these texts would be congenial? Contemporary Christianity is not comfortable with its heritage. Its high art makes many Christians uneasy. An English critic has remarked that the glories of English church music evident at King's Chapel Cambridge is wonderful for musicians, but its performance is more of a concert than a worship service. Meanwhile, pious churches down the road are singing music that seems bad to musicians but is apparently good for worshippers. In this view, good music is bad if connoisseurs get it but the congregation does not. And bad music is good if it inspires worship of God and fosters spiritual uplift in the community, even if musicians belittle it.

Many Protestants and Catholics precisely reject the Church's musical past because it now seems elitist and no longer easily usable. They are unwilling or unable to open artistic gifts from the past. Their notion is that contemporary worship music must be "popular," instantly intelligible to anyone just through the door. Music's assignment is to carry texts whose everyday obvious meanings remove all barriers between the church and its visitors. This music avoids liturgical settings and associations because they are perceived as distancing and possibly rote. The hallowed *Dominus vobiscum* ("The Lord be with you") is improved with, "Good morning, how are you feeling today?" Music is a feel-good tool fit to carry instant messaging. "Real musicians" and liturgical guardians, meanwhile, sniff that such music aspires to the genre of commercial advertising jingles set to billboard messages. They insist that some worship music should be difficult, so that people do not escape the idea that salvation is a long process learned with fear and trembling, or that God and the Incarnation may be more complex than can be grasped at first hearing. They note that colleges insist on instilling in recalcitrant first-year students the glory of arts and humanities past—because it is good for them. Can the Church do less? But this leaves aside the glaring fact that very few Catholic church choirs are capable of performing a Palestrina mass, and almost no Protestant church choir could ever mount Bach's *Christmas Oratorio*, with its huge demand on choir, soloists, and a panoply of instrumentalists. Some performances by church choirs of Handel's "Hallelujah Chorus" are so far off the mark as to be comical. The elaborate resources of mega-churches are put to other, more relevant, uses. The Church seems unable to carry its own legacy in the modern world. Nor is music the only instance of this.

ART AND INCARNATION

Why bother? If the arts have abandoned or scorned religious faith, are Christians merely returning the compliment? As we have to the intellectuals as well? Left alone, or jettisoned, the arts lack the overtones of spiritual searching and become—not purer, but more beholden to other influences. Christianity, meanwhile, loses the capacity to deepen its experiences and understanding and also to speak convincingly to an unevangelized world. It has not always been this way.

Though not without cautions and hesitations along the way, the history of Christianity sacramentalized nearly every human artifact, not holding back divinity from earthly imaging, not keeping Christ from every art. The Christianity that went public after the conversion of Emperor Constantine soon fostered connections to the cultural opportunities outside the churches. Nevertheless, the old suspicion that when people lose their faith in God they turn to the arts to construct graven images of the divine, or to substitute for lost religious meaning, lingers in Christianity as well. Augustine, however, remembered that the precious metal used to construct the golden calf was later melted down to adorn the ark of the covenant.

Could the Incarnation still dance its way into new forms and rhythms? Modern musicians believe that music grants immediate communion with what lies beyond us, perhaps God. The arts free the spirit to meanings beyond empirical ways of knowing. *Music forms the human capacity to listen for God.* Is good music a way to recover the organic connection between the arts and religious seeking?

But doesn't the reigning "art for art's sake" exclude the arts as handmaiden to religion? In fact, the modern period did not really set the arts free to live in unencumbered splendor. The visual arts and much film-making are produced in an environment of art (economic) appreciation, of buying and selling and impressing, and recently of shocking entertainment. Set free from spiritual seeking, the arts became available for the commodification of culture that is consumer capitalism's all-day sale. Unencumbered (pure) creativity scarcely exists in any of the arts, nor does unencumbered appreciation.

It is still possible that the arts open a window on, among other things, larger meanings. A replete aural landscape could, in fact, invite people to *hear religiously* again, to detect more than what is on sale. Artistic beauty has always been an avenue for the mind's ascent, for its quest for more. Music is not reducible to religion and not to commerce, but it can serve either. In a post-religious age, music is as close as many get to God, their clearest experience of being grasped by something precious and good and other than themselves.

Where to go from here then. Roman Catholic authorities once attempted to make normative one historical period, Gregorian chant and Palestrina's High Renaissance masses. Lutheran musicians get edgy when modern praise songs begin to edge out classical Lutheran chorales from their hymnals. Did either of these historic traditions drop like rocks from heaven, or were they both vernacular evolutions of Incarnation on native soils, dreamt by committed artists—as when Luther taught God to speak German. Can there be a definitive music for all times when the Incarnation itself is so relentlessly indigenous? Aren't we to expect that Christ keeps spinning God into every imaginable art?

This is not to say that we do not need to become worthy of our past. There lies infinite generativity, an indispensable gene pool from which infinite joint ventures between God and humanity are waiting to be born. The required creativity will, however, require the presence of artists, if we can find them. Once, in the fourteenth century, a Pope condemned the musical innovations of *Ars Nova* and unintentionally contributed to the development of secular music by driving the best musicians away from the service of the Church and into the employment of wealthy and cultured princes. It still happens.

If that is the artistic dilemma, the theological question is touchier. Are we perhaps unsure about the arts because we are unsure about the Incarnation? Early Christianity was audacious and risk-taking when it imagined Christ as the *logos spermaticos* who infuses the creativity of God in every art and matter. Much more risk averse, we are inclined to protect God from excessive immersions. God, who requires no protection, was willing to make the immense journey to earth, while we are afraid to cross the street for fear of secular contamination.

15

The Art of Worship
Breaking Our Tools to Receive God's Gifts

David and Susan Fetcho

There used to be an old argument between two competing metaphors for art. Is art a hammer, or is art a mirror? Does it shape culture, reflect it, or a little of both? It was the sort of question that seemed designed to pester freshman Art Appreciation students into their first serious considerations of the role of art in culture. It was also a question being asked by Christians coming for the first time to believe that art might have some relevance to their faith. Can one use the arts as a kind of high-pressure nozzle for the pneumatic force of the Spirit to drive home the Christian message? Or is that too close to propaganda, the alternative being to use the arts to reflect back to us our best values and deepest spiritual commitments?

It always was an unanswerable question, though it's one that still rattles in the background of numerous Christian discussions on the role of the arts in worship, missions, evangelism and education. Which is regrettable, since neither of those two metaphors comes remotely close to picturing the nuanced and complex relationship of art and Christian faith. What's more, they really are not all that different from one another. They are more like the yin and yang subsets of a dominant metaphor for the arts that has severely limited Christian thinking about the subject.

Our first clue to this metaphor is that sneaky little word "use" that shows up in the first paragraph. A tiny word, and so easy to ignore. But it's like an invisible, radioactive molecule. If you're not careful, it can mutate everything.

The very idea that we can *use* art either as a hammer *or* a mirror suggests that one of our core assumptions about the arts is that "art is a tool." And whether it's a mirror, hammer, prod, or downy comforter, analgesic or amphetamine, the tool metaphor for the arts generates a myriad of misunderstandings—some quite damaging—that have kept the Western church from fully embracing the arts on their own terms.

In a sense, our story of working in the area of "the arts and worship" over the past twenty years is always first about dismantling this metaphor as a way of clearing the ground before we can even set up camp.

That's because art is made from a way of engagement with the world that depends for its life on discovery and risk, surprise, gift, and grace. It's never about exercising mind *over* matter. It's always about discovering the mind *of* the matter. When it succeeds, it extends that way of participating to the viewer/audience—enlivening, reorienting (or disorienting), and reforming our sense of being in the world. Which means that whatever else it sets out to accomplish, the primary role of art in worship is to help set up the conditions for the congregation's own original insight and discovery. Not simply to reinforce or decorate (to retool) all our foregone conclusions.

The other big problem with this metaphor is that as long as art is a tool, it will never be seen as intrinsic to the act of worship. The arts may be imported like an undocumented nanny to sing us some sweet songs, but that's about as close to citizenship as they can get.

That seems more than a little removed from the Bible's portrayal of our worshipping heritage. Biblical descriptions of worship range from the Hebrew Testament's processions and feasts—full of both noisy and subtle instruments, poetry readings and dancing, and clouds of incense blended from sacred formulas—to the democratized and unpackaged, Spirit-orchestrated potluck worship of the early church, perhaps with invitations sent out for everyone to bring a song or a prophesy or a prayer. If such events were able to weld the community's imagination again and again to the Presence of God with them, it is because they immersed their participants in metaphor, and so functioned both as worship *and* as art.

Walter Brueggemann refers to biblical worship as "constitutive metaphor," in that it both forms and feeds the heart of the community. Behind all the diverse liturgical and denominational traditions of worship we encounter today, this remains our deepest spiritual legacy, the abiding tradition of responding—with all our hearts, multi-intelligences and senses—to God's own self-expression in the multi-media forms of the world. The arts belong in worship because they allow us to join the conversation of creation and revelation in God's own vernacular.

This is to suggest that the arts and worship share much of the same vocabulary and syntax—are speaking the same language, in fact, with only a slight difference in dialect. And not even the anthropologists, as they trace the near simultaneous appearance of primitive forms of art and worship, can decide which is a dialect of which.

It's a distinction the Bible never bothers to make. Just as Jesus spoke in parables not because it was a nifty technique, but because Jesus thought in metaphors, the arts belong in worship the way your heart belongs in your chest. Without them, it's all tubes and gurneys and pumping machines.

If it's true that worship and the arts are as closely related as two dialects of a single language, we need to ask just what sort of language it is. Accustomed as we are to think of language as exclusively made up of words that are containers for data or information, a quick dip into the Bible's own pool of metaphor might help refresh our understanding.

"The heavens are telling the glory of God; and the firmament proclaims God's handiwork . . ." So begins Psalm 19 with this great proof-text for the beauty of creation (or is it the other way around?). But in the next couple of verses our semantic assumptions begin to lose their grip, and our thoughts ping-pong like a cartoon bullet off the strange surfaces of the text. "Day to day pours forth speech, and night to night declares knowledge. There is no speech, nor are there words; their voice is not heard; yet their voice goes out through all the earth, and their words to the end of the world."

Of course, everybody loves a scenic overlook, and "the beauty of nature" can work like a mega-dose of aesthetic vitamins to recharge our souls. But this text suggests that it's actually *telling* us something. Not only that. This communication of "knowledge" is taking place in creation via a mode of "speech" far removed from our modern notion of language as an envelope for data or ideas. The psalm asserts that creation itself is a text of God, whose power and clarity are self-evident. It is the word of the Lord.

And when the Word becomes flesh in Jesus, we should not be surprised at his choice of two direct metaphors to sum up the incomprehensible mystery of Incarnation. "This is my body. This is my blood." These words—meaningless apart from the taste and texture and act of chewing and swallowing the bread; the slight sting as the wine goes down, full of its fruit and strength—anchor us once and for all in the metaphor of the world, released at last to be filled with the presence of God.

Too bad that some churches have, in effect, turned Jesus' words into "this is my cracker pellet, this is my grape juice." For them, the engaging metaphor has been boiled down to a mere symbol. Sensual participation in the reality of the meal as a felt sign of Christ's substituting his life for ours is reduced to an intellectual assent to the abstract ideas of incarnation and atonement that are referenced by this tasteless, watered down excuse for food.

Placed at the core of our worship, the metaphor of the Eucharist does what all metaphor does. It allows for participation in the real. The arts are intrinsic to worship simply because they draw us into the same level of participation in the mystery of metaphor as do the bread and the wine. Or as does the shouting firmament.

What does it take to allow the arts their rightful place at the table of our worship? To afford them more space than just the "special music" slot in our liturgical planning? In our experience as liturgical artists, the most "successful" pairings of the arts and worship we've seen have been in special worship celebrations (liturgical "high holy days," conferences, ordinations, retreats), where the liturgical requirements of a normal service have been relaxed. These services have given us a vision of what's possible when the arts, and artists, are let out of the corral of "this is how we've always done it." Likewise, they've shown us what's needed in liturgical planning for the artists to be fully empowered to bring their gifts.

First of all, the artistic elements are woven into the thematic architecture—the artists are there at the groundbreaking. Right from the start, the structure of the service is built as a latticework of multiple inferences toward its core images. Each element in the service is allowed to speak in its own voice, to mean what it means in its own way of meaning; to settle, saturate, or disturb. (Occasionally this will mean suspending the assumption that the "meat" of the service will necessarily be borne by the sermon.) Early on, careful consideration is given to the design of the physical space, its untapped possibilities and its rigid constraints, such as light and sightlines. When possible, the seating is rearranged to allow freer movement through the space for both dancers and worshippers, to break down the barrier between "performers" and "observers," and to encourage a fuller bodily participation in worship. Attention is paid to the relationship among the media, to the dramatic considerations of flow and segue, rhythm and dynamics as the worship leaders attempt to lay out the markers for the congregation's journey toward meaning.

Finally, time must be allowed for each artistic offering to resonate in the worshippers' hearts and minds. A common misunderstanding is that in advocating for the arts in worship we're arguing for more stuff to be jammed into the service. But the way artists work is more like sculpting time and space and silence. The way a stone creates a pool in a swiftly flowing stream. It takes a certain quality of interior quiet to fully encounter a work of art. And it takes a period of external stillness to afford the time to really absorb what one has encountered.

When this all finally cooks, there comes into existence a kind of mutual permeability, wherein the interface/juxtaposition of all the elements in a service creates a synergy of meaning that surpasses the evocative power of any element by itself. Imagine a multi-part choral work. But instead of sopranos, altos, tenors and basses, you have sound, sight, smell, the kinesthetic empathy of bodies in motion as well as all the cognate powers of the mind working together within a multi-sensual metaphor of God's loving presence. It doesn't often get a chance to happen, but when it does, you never forget it.

A comment we've heard many times following one of these services sums it up: "This is the church I want to go to! Where is it?" The truth is, it could be any church that gives its artists broad enough permission to do their best work, to offer their best gifts, not in isolation but in collaboration.

In our work over the years advocating for and designing liturgy that seriously incorporates the arts, we've come to realize that, really, we're not talking about the arts at all. What we hope to find through the arts is nothing more than an approach to meaning that is more resonant with the "way" of God's own self-disclosure.

This is the big secret of God that Jesus reveals. It's all metaphor; it's all a poem. It's all the meaning of God completely embodied. It's a language that takes all our senses to understand. In their small and limited way, the arts are a light into this hidden subtext of God's own speech—the mysterious coinherence of meaning and metaphor that renews our imaginations and redeems our intuitions, energizing them toward the possibility of a new creation.

VI

Spiritual Formation

16

Sabbath Living

Susan S. Phillips

> *If you refrain from trampling the Sabbath,*
> *from pursuing your own interests on my holy day;*
> *if you call the Sabbath a delight*
> *and the holy day of the LORD honorable;*
> *if you honor it, not going your own ways,*
> *serving your own interests, or pursuing your own affairs;*
> *then you shall take delight in the LORD,*
> *and I will make you ride upon the heights of the earth*
> *and feast on the inheritance of your father Jacob.*
> —Isaiah 58:13–14 (NRSV)

UNLIKE THE OTHER TEN Commandments, Sabbath-keeping often is treated as optional. Adults who grew up in Christian or Jewish families with strict Sabbath practices tend to recoil from Sabbath. It connotes prohibition, weekend days unhappily spent in submission to beliefs and practices imposed by parents, frenzied cooking one day to allow no cooking the next, historic television shows missed (like the Beatles on *The Ed Sullivan Show*) because of a "no entertainment" rule on the Sabbath.

Some argue passionately against strict Sabbath observance, quoting Jesus' warnings against hollow legalism. Others, not similarly marked by childhood exposure, may simply say, "It's not really one of my personal spiritual disciplines." A few express mild curiosity, wondering if perhaps there's an opportunity for prayer that they've missed. On the whole, complaint, dismissal, or tepid interest are not the responses elicited by "Thou shalt not kill" and the rest of the Ten Commandments.

Not growing up in a strict Sabbatarian home I had little interest in the subject until recently. My family had always practiced "Sabbath lite": going to church, not going to work or school, and spending the day according to personal choice. As an adult, I spent many Sunday afternoons working at home, with no sense that I was "trampling the Sabbath."

The last few years have been different. With children off at college, work has mushroomed, increasingly encroaching on even my minimal Sabbath expectations. I love my work—most of which has to do with supporting and accompanying people as they listen for and follow God—and I appreciate the monastic rhythm of dividing the day into "*Ora et labora*" (prayer and work). Yet I began to notice signs of excessive *labora*.

My back ached from sitting for many hours every day. I less frequently saw my garden in daylight. And then one day I forgot an appointment with a person coming to see me for spiritual direction. I took that grave lapse of responsibility as a divine stop sign, and decided to keep the Sabbath day holy. Isaiah 58 has been a guide in doing that.

STOP—REFRAIN FROM TRAMPLING THE SABBATH

The Hebrew word *Shabbat* means, simply, "Quit . . . Stop . . . Take a break"[1] The word *Shabbat* itself has no religious or spiritual content. Stop. Empty your hands. Sit down. Breathe. Look around. Notice. This is the invitation.

In Genesis 2:1–4 we read, "By the seventh day God had finished the work he had been doing; so on the seventh day he rested from all his work. And God blessed the seventh day and made it holy" (the first use of the word *holy* in Scripture). God made many things, and they were good. The seventh day arrived, and God made it holy.

---

1. Peterson, *Christ Plays in Ten Thousand Places*, 109.

When we observe the Sabbath, we, like God, stop from our doing, and experience our being. We join God in what God has made holy. This can be done everyday in Sabbath moments, as well as every seventh day and every seventh year (sabbatical), but most significantly we are encouraged by the Creator's example to stop on the seventh day of the week.

At the beginning of the Sabbath as the sun sets Friday evening, Jews kindle the light. As dinner begins, the woman of the house lights two candles and prays: "Blessed are you, Lord our God, King of the universe, who has set us apart by his commandments and commanded us to kindle the Sabbath lights."[2] Two candles are lighted in remembrance of the two mentions of Sabbath in the Law (Deuteronomy 5:12–15 and Exodus 20:8–11).

There is great wisdom in the Jewish observance of Sabbath from sundown to sundown. Most of our spiritual disciplines are under our control. We establish their frame and rhythm (for instance, writing in a prayer journal each morning, or an evening prayerful review of the day). We can negotiate with these practices: "Well, I'm tired tonight, so I'll review today in the morning." I was once on vacation with a person who was "catching up" on months of neglected journaling, writing each day's entry retrospectively as though on the day long gone. How many of us hurriedly play catch-up when we fall behind with our scheduled daily Bible reading?

A sundown Sabbath cannot be postponed. It arrives. There is anticipation, readying and, perhaps even the tingle of desire. In some Jewish synagogues it is as though the bride is coming. All of us who welcome Sabbath on Friday or Saturday sundown, stop and wait, much as we turn expectantly at the opening notes of a wedding march such as Wagner's "Bridal Chorus" from the 1841 opera *Lohengrin*.

Stopping isn't easy. We notice what things inside and outside ourselves keep us busy and preoccupied. My mind goes to Jesus, who stopped in the midst of all kinds of urgent, important affairs, crowds of people, and the urging of friends to keep moving. When Bartimaeus cried out, "Jesus stood still and said, 'Call him here'" (Mark 10:49). Jesus stops for us. When we stop for him, we often discover what's going on in our minds and hearts. The distraught couple on the road to Emmaus, questioned by the stranger "[s]tood still, looking sad" (Luke 24:17). On

---

2. Baab, *Sabbath Keeping*, 127.

the Sabbath, we can choose to stand still, notice what we're feeling, and anticipate encountering God.

TURNING TOWARD—CALL THE SABBATH A DELIGHT AND THE LORD'S HOLY DAY HONORABLE

Stopping prepares us to turn toward God. We "call the Sabbath a delight and the Lord's holy day honorable." This is an avowal, an affirmation, an acceptance of God's sanctification of the day. Isaiah doesn't write, "call the Sabbath a chore and the Lord's holy day onerous." In fact, the word *delight* appears twice in this short description of Sabbath living. Savoring that delight is part of the commandment. How we do that is personal and relational, and we discover more and more about it with practice. God takes the first step by creating the holy day and inviting us into it.

The Sabbath sanctifies time. So often we think of space as sanctified. We create a temple or church in which to contemplate God. The Sabbath is a "temple in time." The great rabbi and theologian Abraham Joshua Heschel claimed that "The Sabbaths are our [Jews'] great cathedrals ... which neither the Romans or Germans were able to burn."[3] The Ten Commandments do not command the building of a temple or altar; they do command sanctification of the seventh day. In times of persecution and times of thriving, in the Holy Land and in captivity, Jews were to observe the Sabbath. God made the Sabbath holy, and no person can demolish that sanctuary.

One of the most distinguished words in the Bible is *qadosh*, "holy," a word first applied to Sabbath, and one that "more than any other is representative of the mystery and majesty of the divine."[4] On the seventh day, God rested, blessed, and hallowed the day. We experience it as holy, but it is objective, not subjective holiness that we encounter. It is not merely a sensory experience; it is a relationship. We stop and turn from our occupations and preoccupations in order to orient toward God.

Whatever our circumstances, this Sabbath temple constructed of time is available to us. This temple of the Holy Spirit is there for us in our solitude as well as in community; even in solitude we enter that temple of time with the universal communion of saints. Sabbath-keeping turns

---

3. Heschel, *The Sabbath*, xv.
4. Ibid., xvi.

my mind to God's saints throughout time and around the world, and sometimes inspires me to contact some I've been blessed to know as friends.

Stopping and turning toward God is the foundation of contemplative practice of all kinds. The practice of the presence of God is "an application of our soul to God, or a remembrance of God present, which can be made either by the imagination or by the intellect."[5] This is Sabbath delight.

In all contemplative disciplines, receptivity is essential. We open our minds, hearts, and senses, to God, not knowing how God will be experienced. Perhaps as a wind, an earthquake, a fire . . . or a gentle whisper. Resting in that openness to God may be the day's grace. By stopping, we honor God's holy day and discover the way it shapes our time. Unlike other time that we manage, make, take, give, spend, and organize, consecrated Sabbath time arrives for us to enter—or not.

TURN FROM—PURSUING YOUR OWN INTERESTS, GOING YOUR OWN WAY, PURSUING YOUR OWN AFFAIRS

It's important to notice what we turn from when we stop and turn toward God's holy day. When Jesus talked with people, he drew out their concerns: "What do you want me to do for you [Bartimaeus]?" "What are you talking about as you walk along [on the road to Emmaus]?" In Eastern Orthodox hesychastic prayer (centering or heart prayer) there is a movement called nepsis (vigilance), which involves guarding the heart against fears and doubts that turn one away from God.[6] The people on the road to Emmaus were kept from seeing Jesus. Their questions, fearful fleeing, and roiling emotions prevented them from recognizing what their hearts were noticing. Jesus helped them get in touch with their hearts. Sabbath-keeping can help us do the same.

As we stop, we notice what vies for our attention. We live in a noisy, cluttered culture. Walking down the city street at the noon hour, there's a cacophony of people talking. A close look reveals that each person is, seemingly, talking to him or herself. For a moment the scene seems surreal, even lunatic. Closer scrutiny identifies small metal objects attached

---

5. Brother Lawrence of the Resurrection, *The Practice of the Presence of God*, 88.

6. See, for example, Georgios, Archmandrite. "The Neptic and Hesychastic Character of Orthodox Athonite Monasticism."

to ears, lapels, and pockets. Each person is talking on a phone. What would Jesus have to do to attract the hermetically sealed attention of a person on this road?

What seals us into our own solipsistic bubbles of buzz and hum? Sometimes it's habit. We gradually increase the pace and density of our lives, and barely notice the change. Sometimes fears imprison us: "I'll fall behind if I don't keep up." Pride, too, is encapsulating: "I'm busy; therefore I'm important."

Biblical wisdom about Sabbath alerts us to some particular elements of our lives that we must turn from as we stop and "call the Sabbath a delight and the holy day of the Lord honorable."

HIERARCHICAL RELATIONS

All of Scripture calls us to love one another, love our neighbor as ourselves, and care for the alien in our land. Justice is integral to loving God. The fourth commandment specifically instructs us, on the seventh day, to stop all work, and to rest. This command is not only for each of us, but is also for those who live with and work for us, including animals, and the aliens in our land (and, we might include today, those in other lands who labor for us). This is a practice of justice as well as devotion; we are not to expect others to work for us while we enjoy Sabbath rest.

We are to see this day of rest as a privilege for all who are created by our Sabbath-keeping God. This is radical thinking. Part of the interests and pursuits we put down on the Sabbath are those of class, employment, and ownership relations. In a small way it is like the year of Jubilee imagined in Scripture as occurring every 50 years (after seven times seven years of Sabbaths), during which wealth would be redistributed generously (Leviticus 25:8-17).

The Law offers two grounds for Sabbath rest from the usual social stratification of our relationships. The Exodus 20:8–11 expression of the Sabbath commandment invites us to see God as our exemplar, God who ceased working on the seventh day and invited all of creation into that holy rest. The Deuteronomy 5:12-15 form of the commandment is based on a justice argument: Do not oppress others, because you remember how it was to be a slave before your Lord stretched out his arm and freed you. Keeping the Sabbath holy enjoins love of God and neighbor.

The beautiful invitation to Sabbath in Isaiah 58 is preceded by a clarion call to justice and compassion (vv. 1–12). God exhorts us "to loose the chains of injustice and untie the cords of the yoke, to set the oppressed free and break every yoke . . . to share your food with the hungry and to provide the poor wanderer with shelter—when you see the naked, to clothe him . . . " (vv. 6–7). Jesus echoed those words, affirming the primacy of justice love over insular piety (Matthew 25). The right observance of Sabbath is infused with compassionate care that crosses all boundaries of class, privilege, ethnicity, gender, age, and wealth. We turn from these distinctions on the seventh day, so that all may rest in the holy day we call "honorable."

We need to ask ourselves what forms of relating we need to abandon on the Sabbath. Perhaps there are kinds of serving we do or receive that require suspension. Do we delegate work to others on the Sabbath? Perhaps we think in terms of "getting ahead (of others)," and can be released from those thoughts on the Sabbath. Sunday is often the day homes that are for sale are open for visits. We might ask ourselves if we visit such homes in order to assess our own status or wealth relative to others. If so, that might not be compatible with observing the Sabbath.

WORK

The call to rest from work on the seventh day of each week is, in part, an affirmation of the six other days of work. Work and Sabbath are part of the integrated whole of our lives, in keeping with the life of God as we encounter it from the very beginning.

Genesis opens with God at the work of creation. Notice the verbs describing God in the first two chapters of Genesis: created, hovered, spoke, named, made, separated, gathered, called, made, and formed. God worked. Creation was active: The land produced, trees bore fruit (according to their various kinds), the lights in the sky marked seasons and illuminated the land, the greater and lesser lights had their own domains of governance, fish teemed, birds flew, and all were fruitful and multiplied.

Humankind was made in God's image as ruler of the earth and its creatures. When God put the man in the Garden of Eden it was "to work and take care of it" (Genesis 2:15). The first work we see the man invited to do was to name each living creature. Among the first work we see God and people collaborating on is sewing—God improved upon the flimsy vegetable material the man and woman sewed by introducing leatherwork (3:7, 21). Each workday in creation is called "good." Jesus worked and told us that he and his Father are working (see John 5:17).

Work is essential, *and* God clearly calls us, one day a week, to put it down. This is not an injunction to turn keeping Sabbath into a replacement kind of work, legalistically enforced. Jesus healed the paralytic at the pool of Bethesda on the Sabbath, and was criticized for it. Jesus' actions were in keeping with the justice/love teachings of Judaism. Ancient rabbis did not deify the Sabbath, but rather wrote, "The Sabbath is given unto you, not you unto the Sabbath," and counseled that "Even when there is the slightest possibility that a life may be at stake one may disregard every prohibition of the law."[7] Scripture is a way to life, not an obstacle to it. Sabbath, too, is vitalizing.

One day a week we are to put aside work in order to keep the Sabbath. For many of us it is a challenge to discover what is in keeping with the Sabbath, and what pulls us toward work. I cannot turn on my computer on the Sabbath, even to communicate with friends or read on-line devotionals. Turning on the computer pulls me toward work. I can't talk with certain people at church on Sunday because I get drawn toward thoughts of work. Being with friends and family, reading, gardening, walking alone and with my dog, and many other activities are, for me, compatible with Sabbath delight. As we practice Sabbath-keeping, we discover what we must turn from, in order to turn toward God's holy day.

INSTRUMENTALITY

Romans reacted with contempt to the Jews' adherence to the law of abstaining from labor on the Sabbath (see Juvenal, Seneca, and others). They saw it as self-indulgent, lazy, and counter-productive. (We might notice our own "Roman reaction" to Sabbath-keeping.) Some Jews (such as Philo) legitimated the practice by referring to relaxation as a means to an end. This, too, was Aristotle's view: "[W]e need relaxation because we cannot work continuously. Relaxation, then, is not an end; for it is taken for the sake of activity."[8]

---

7. Heschel, *The Sabbath*, 6, quoting rabbis from *Genesis rabba* 19:3.
8. Aristotle, *Nicomachean Ethics*, Book X, chapter 6, l. 34–35.

Today some have adopted this instrumental approach to Sabbath and rest. Scripture, however, simply commends Sabbath as a practice engaged in by God from the beginning, and commands it in the Mosaic law. Sabbath is to be cherished in and of itself, not as a means to an end.

In the United States (and in much of the industrialized world) we alternate between frenzied striving and mind-numbing disengagement, which we hope will refuel us for our return to striving. We have the longest work-week and work-year in the world, and are proud to call ourselves "busy." Writing about American anxiety at the end of the twentieth century, Pulitzer Prize–winning novelist Marilynne Robinson wrote, "It is as if we took morphine to help us sleep on a bed of nails."[9] The bed of nails is, among other things, our endless working to get ahead. Sabbath is neither a narcotic that enables endurance, nor a pious practice for the sake of heavenly credit.

Jesuit writer Peter van Breemen's words about prayer are apt for honoring the day that God has called "holy": "Prayer cannot be a means to an end. Prayer is the *last* word—there is no word beyond prayer . . . Prayer is not efficient, it doesn't bring about anything—it's the stillpoint, the axis around which everything rotates."[10] To greet the Sabbath, we free our hands of work, roles and responsibilities of authority and rank, and our thoughts of gain.

EXALTATION—TAKE DELIGHT IN AND RIDE ON THE HEIGHTS OF THE LORD

Exaltation is a theological word akin to what some psychologists now are calling "elevation." Exalt, literally, means to lift high. One can be lifted high in rank, pride, power, character, or joy. Isaiah 58 tells us that on the Sabbath we are to delight as God lifts us up.

We read in Scripture that God is a God who exalts the faithful. At the end of his life, Moses sang about how God will bless his people by lifting them to high places (Deuteronomy 32:13). David is called "the man whom God exalted" (2 Samuel 23:1). The expression of God lifting up is most poignantly expressed in Isaiah's song of the suffering servant: "See, my servant shall prosper; he shall be exalted and lifted up, and shall

---

9. Robinson, "Facing Reality," 80.
10. Farrell, foreword of *As Bread That Is Broken*, 7–8.

be very high . . . [though he be] despised and rejected" (Isaiah 52:13, 53:3). Paul echoed this in Philippians 2: "Therefore God also highly exalted [Christ] . . . " (v. 9). There is no contradiction between exaltation and suffering. Being lifted on high is the mark of God's blessing for faithfulness. This experience is sheer gift. We can stop, turn toward God, and turn from distraction, but the experience of exaltation is a gift not subject to our control.

"Exaltation" in the Bible is a relational word. We exalt God, and God exalts the faithful. But we can also exalt ourselves, exalt other gods, and respond to the exaltation of others. Jesus taught that "All who exalt themselves will be humbled, and all who humble themselves will be exalted" (Matthew 23:12). Exaltation is not the aim, but, rather, a possible blessing, of keeping God's Sabbath holy.

Social scientists study the horizontal dimension of intimacy and attachment, and the vertical dimension of relative social status and power. Some theorists are now pointing to a third dimension, which spans the continuum from purity to pollution, and for which we often use vertical concepts of morality (e.g., "low life," "moral stature," etc.), including that of elevation. "Elevation is elicited by acts of virtue or moral beauty; it causes warm, open feelings ('dilation?') in the chest; and it motivates people to behave more virtuously themselves").[11] We might experience elevation when we see Rembrandt's painting *Return of the Prodigal* or see a person give up his seat on the bus for a pregnant woman. Elevation changes our vantage on the landscape of life. On the Sabbath, we behold the hallowed day of the Lord and are moved.

In studies of elevation, people have told of pleasant or "tingling" feelings (often in their chests) which inspire them to want to affiliate with and help others, and to become better people themselves.[12] Is the chest expansion a stretching of the heart, like that about which the prophet Joel said, "Rend your hearts not your clothing" (2:13)? Unlike elevation, spiritual exaltation is relational. Our hearts are made to be stretched by compassion, truth, and beauty, and when they swell in the spaciousness of Sabbath time, they do so in God's embrace.

---

11. Haidt, "Elevation and the Positive Psychology of Morality," 276.
12. Ibid., 282.

COMMUNION—FEAST

The verses about Sabbath in Isaiah 58 end with a promise of feasting, which is based on inheritance. Similarly, in Matthew 22, people are invited to the wedding banquet prepared by the king for his son. The word *sanctify* in Exodus 20:8—where we're enjoined to "remember the Sabbath day to sanctify it"—is the Hebrew word *le-kadesh*. This is the word the Talmud uses to speak of consecrating or betrothing a woman to a man.[13] We put down our work, open our hand to receive the wedding invitation, take off our work clothes, and dress in our best. Then we simply show up, anticipating the beloved.

It is a timeless space, like that of Eden and Kingdom. As a verb *Shabbat* means "to be complete."[14] The holy *shalom* of Sabbath links creation and eternity, as "Eternity utters a day."[15] Eugene Peterson claims that Sabbath links creation and salvation, as "we are interested in God and Christ being formed in us."[16] The Talmud says that the Sabbath is "somewhat like the world to come,"[17] and we savor it. "To men alone time is elusive; to men with God time is eternity in disguise."[18] It is on the Sabbath that we taste this time. That is the feast—a taste of wonder and adoration for God. Like food at a feast, it is ingested and metabolized, nourishing our souls.

In keeping Sabbath, I sometimes think about the Sabbath day long ago when Jesus was in the tomb. Jesus lay still. The forces of creation and salvation joined on that holy day, and there was resurrection. Later, appearing to his disciples in Emmaus, in a room in Jerusalem, on the shore of the Sea of Galilee, Jesus invited those he loved to the feast. They had been bereft and devastated, confused and exhausted. He exalted them, and invited them to eat with him. They ate together. In remembrance of God, and in remembrance of God's Son, we are invited to stop, "take delight in the Lord," and eat. How can we refuse?

---

13. Heschel, *The Sabbath*, 44.
14. Edward Mahler, quoted in note 13, in ibid., 99.
15. Ibid., 43.
16. Peterson, *Christ Plays in Ten Thousand Places*, 116.
17. Quoted in Heschel, *The Sabbath*, 68.
18. Ibid., 93.

17

East Meets West
The Distinctives of Christian Meditation

Steve Scott

Why are so many people still "looking East" today? Thinking people sometimes study religious history and tradition to see if the "great traditions" have any elements that are common property, or to see if their own tradition (in this case, Christianity) might be enriched with insights from the East. "What can we in the West learn from you in the East?"

People on the street, on the other hand, may not have such noble aspirations. They may feel that theologians have taken traditional religion away from them, wrapping it in such phrases as "God in process" or the "theology of ultimate concern." To ordinary people, using a simple nonreligious meditation technique practiced all over the world may look like a way to enrich a faltering faith with some kind of inner experience. Let the theologians talk. After all, a person with an experience is never at the mercy of a person with an argument, as someone once said.

Today an academic theology that capitulated to a metaphysic of radical negation is already grappling with issues peculiar to an Eastern world view, although those issues may appear in Western guise. It seems ironic that non-theological types seeking shelter from that arid speculation should turn to spiritual techniques arising from the very metaphysic they are fleeing. Nonetheless, many Christians are looking eastward with the hope of enriching their faith.

Some writers talk of reconstructing a bankrupt and depleted religious tradition with material drawn from Eastern sources. Jacob Needleman, in his book *Lost Christianity*, suggests that elements taken from the East would restore Christianity to its former vitality, its early purity. Peter Berger, in *The Heretical Imperative*, argues for an encounter between the Judeo-Christian tradition and the great religions of Asia as a "contemporary possibility of religious affirmation." Such a dialogue is by no means limited to our present day.

I am not against dialogue between Christianity and Eastern religions. I think such an exchange is informative and valuable. I am personally convinced, however, that unless Christianity recovers some of its distinctive, Biblical elements, then what will actually occur will be less than dialogue.

I am not against the idea of meditation or of spiritual experiences, but I am convinced that every practice has its philosophical basis and context. A fully Christian and Biblical grounding must be the testing area for the truth-claims of any spiritual technique.

A particular emphasis that has run through the dialogue in all its historical occurrences is the "incarnational presence of Christ throughout created reality," placed in opposition to the "Jesus of history." The problem has been not so much the idea of Jesus as a historical person, but the wider implications of the events of his life and death. Leaving those troublesome implications aside clears the way for emphasis on the "incarnational presence," which is far more amenable to the underlying presuppositions of Eastern philosophy.

It is not my purpose to say that Christianity and linear thinking are insolubly welded together. I hope that the kind of distinctions I am trying to make, the kind I think Christianity makes for itself, will become evident through some brief comparisons. Let me begin with Thomas Merton.

Thomas Merton, a Trappist monk, was known for his books of poetry, his writings on the monastic life and contemplative prayer, and, toward the end of his life, the issue of interfaith dialogue. His books of excerpts from Asian wisdom, such as *Zen and the Birds of Appetite* and the writings of the Taoist sage Lao-tse, reveal a critical engagement in bringing East and West together. As Merton remarked to a fellow participant at the Bangkok conference shortly before his death, "Christianity and Zen are the future."

Merton's early interests in Zen are alluded to in an essay on his book, *The Wisdom of the Desert*. That book, a selection from the sayings and anecdotes of the early Desert fathers contains, in Merton's opinion, ideas comparable to some of the concepts in Zen Buddhism. Merton engaged in correspondence with D. T. Suzuki, a noted Oriental scholar who has done work comparing medieval mystical thought with Buddhist ideas.

Merton's purpose was to pursue the conceptual analogies in order to enrich the Western monastic tradition. He points out that Zen was beginning in China at approximately the same time that the period of the Desert fathers in Egypt was drawing to a close. Also, "There are countless Zen stories that almost exactly reproduce the Verba Seniorum incidents which are obviously likely to occur wherever men seek and discover the same kind of poverty, solitude and emptiness." In dialogue with Suzuki, Merton draws parallels between the "recovery of paradise"—the Desert fathers' desire through asceticism and contemplative prayer to regain the "innocence" lost in the Fall—and the Zen monk's search for "emptiness" as an index of purity of heart.

Suzuki, in his essay "Knowledge and Innocence," pursues the same idea somewhat further. Equating the Judeo-Christian idea of innocence with the Buddhist notion of emptiness, he proceeds to the Fall, i.e., to the knowledge of good and evil. Suzuki points out that such "knowledge" is viewed in Buddhist terms as "ignorance," and "ignorance" obscures the original light "which is emptiness." Discriminatory consciousness is looked upon as ignorance. That which is truly good proceeds from a condition of *suchness*, the void.

Suzuki goes on to align the concept of *suchness* with poverty of spirit as interpreted by the medieval mystic Meister Eckhart. Suzuki extends the poverty to include lack of individual identity. The empirical self, the ego, and its investment in discriminatory consciousness are an illusion, the stumbling block that prevents a return to the state of *suchness*.

Merton strives to find the equivalent for the "emptiness of Zen" in the mysticism of some of the Desert fathers and in the contemplative traditions of the church. With Merton's interpretive approach to the Bible (grounded in those traditions), it is possible to extract such "message" even from the pages of the New Testament. Merton pauses, however, before the radical nature of the void. He sees a tension between that and the "true self" that comes from participation in Christ.

It is here, I suggest, that the first observable breakdown in the Eastern and Christian dialogue comes. Examining the Biblical notion of the Fall and the Biblical concept of anthropology we notice several points. First, God, who is beyond our ideas and concepts, chooses to address himself to us in terms drawn from our realm of experience. That is one aspect of grace. Second, what renders God radically unapproachable is our non-recognition of our moral and existential displacement, i.e., our sin. Third, we are not complete until we recognize our condition, until our relationship with God is restored, and God comes to dwell within us. Prior to that recognition there remains a God-shaped void in our center.

What Merton is striving to articulate is the life of that selfless human who is now no longer clinging to his or her self, but is radically Christocentric. What Suzuki and other schools of thought that hinge on the idea of radical negation are saying is that the interior "God-shaped" void is the primary condition of *suchness.*

That notion of the interior void carries with it an echo of the Greek philosopher Heraclitus' statement about the inexhaustible depths of the soul. It also echoes a passage in the Upanishads that speaks of "The empty space of the heart . . . the bare room of the inner man." The place where the source of all reality wants to come and live is mistaken for the reality itself. And the emptiness that is discovered there becomes the index of wisdom. It is perhaps assumed to be the underlying universal condition.

At that point the analogies start to collapse. It is possible that the monastic simplicity of the Desert fathers is comparable to that of the Zen monks. Why not? Both traditions were possibly informed by a single source. It is possible that their understandings and concepts draw from the same kinds of terminology. But where the incomprehensible fullness of Christ starts to part company with the God of unconditioned negation, the dialogue falters.

Let us pursue the implications of this by looking at the writings of another contemporary contemplative, Dom Aelred Graham. Graham is the author of a number of books, notably *Zen Catholicism* and *Contemplative Christianity*. I want to look at a couple of passages from the latter and add some observations of my own.

In pursuit of a contemplative Christianity, Graham alludes to a "widening of the options," which for him means a new approach to the problem of religion. He says, "Considered within the conceptual framework, every religion may be regarded as the basic symbol system of its respective adherents." Among those symbolic modes he lists Judaism, Buddhism, Marxism, Hinduism, and others as systems not so much of authoritative revelation but of existential verification.

Needless to say, his approach to the book of the Christians, the Bible, is much the same. As a mode of reference it is discredited, except where it can be drawn on to argue for a postconceptual unqualifiable absolute Godhead in which we have a participatory role. As Graham puts it, "God is negated epistemologically but affirmed ontologically." He disapproves of God as "thought about in Old Testament imagery" and is prepared to use portions of Scripture only to verify his philosophical presuppositions.

Just how far Graham is prepared to go in arguing for his particular perspective in the guise of "contemplative Christianity" is demonstrated in this breathtaking reinterpretation of Jesus' death on the cross:

> Jesus was the completely God-centered man; yet we seem to detect in his mind a deepening of his concept of God, until he transcends all concepts. Habitually he speaks of God as his Father . . . on the cross it is no longer Father, simply 'God'. It is 'My God' (Mark 15:34) who appears to have deserted him. Dare we interpret this as meaning that Jesus, in his anguish, had been brought to the extreme point of abandoning any anthropomorphic notion of God? . . . If this were so, Jesus would have mentally broken through, without repudiating, all the concepts of God inherited from his Jewish tradition, to reach God as he is in himself (as theologians were later to express it).
>
> He had passed in his own way through an ordeal far more terrible and self-denuding than St. John of the Cross's 'dark night', to realize the goal of the individual self, self-absence. The Suffering Servant had been transformed into the Spirit, the Jesus of history became the mystical Christ. Do we catch here also an echo of the *neti neti* 'not this, not this'—a reference to the self-manifesting Godhead, 'before whom words recoil?' of the Upanishads, the sunyata (the void) of Buddhism?

The Zen term *satori* is literally "a kick in the eye." A sudden flash of enlightenment—a shift from the discriminatory consciousness of ignorance to the pure consciousness of Sunyata, the void. Quite simply, Aelred Graham is saying that Jesus underwent *satori*, Zen enlightenment, while on the cross. During that moment, according to Graham, the shift occurred from "the Jesus of history" to the "mystical Christ."

It seems obvious that the search for conceptual analogies creates many problems. Although there are many things to be learned from a dialogue between Christianity and Eastern religions, it robs the word *dialogue* of its full meaning when we undermine the distinctive characteristics of our confession by radically reinterpreting them or modifying them in the light of tradition. Nonetheless, those problems primarily occur in the conceptual realm, and of course everything is seen in a new light if we overturn the primacy of the conceptual and argue from an experiential base. Finally, I want to address this "postcritical" approach to the problem.

M. Basil Pennington, author of *Daily We Touch Him*, cites a shift from the conceptual "Gutenberg era" to an era of experience as the reason for the need for "centering prayer." His approach—drawn, as he points out, from medieval mysticism—makes meditative repetition of a simple word or phrase the core of his technique. The aim, again, is to establish the participant in an existential awareness of the "ground of being." Pennington's comment on the similarity between his techniques and goals and those of Transcendental Meditation is this: "What seems evident to me is that we can expect similar methods and techniques to arise in the various traditions, given that they are all concerned with the same human creature and his [or her] basic call to transcendence."

Pennington, of course, assumes that we can all correctly respond to that "basic call" with the aid of techniques borrowed from our "wise friends in the East." After all, he reasons, God has given us "all things" in Christ. It is Pennington's hope that those techniques will push us beyond ideas "about" Christ to the experiencing of Christ in our depths of being. He ignores the problem that those techniques come with a world view all of their own, one that will displace any initial Biblical or Christian presuppositions that a meditator may begin with.

Another writer, Father George Maloney, answering charges that "material techniques" expose the would-be meditator to psychic danger, points out that "No Christian ought to condemn out of hand any technique, be it Yoga, the use of music in prayer, chants, Silva mind control, Arica, T. M., or whatever, unless we ask the question: How is it being used? What are the fruits that come from such use? Does it help us or others to pray with greater consciousness, beyond the habitual, superficial level of controlled, discursive prayer?"

The idea that each of those techniques might have a specific metaphysical context seems foreign to Maloney. He and others like him seem to be grounded in the presupposition that the variety of world views those techniques represent is nothing more than their symbolic mode of existential verification. The question is no longer, "What ideas do these world views have in common?" but "How does it make you feel?"

Ironically, Maloney proceeds to map out some of the psychic chaos that awaits the meditator. Flashes and lights, psychic powers of telepathy, communing with the dead can come forth. What is reality, what is hallucination, before the beckoning forms that whirl over the screen of our consciousness? Voices that we recognize and strange voices give their messages with impelling realism—again what is real, what is false?

Of course, to try to answer questions like that would mean "backsliding" from the experiential to the conceptual mode. It would also require the employment of the discriminatory consciousness so troublesome to the Eastern world view. Elsewhere, Maloney tells us that "The demonic is within all of us." That cheerful message is drawn heavily from the speculative fringes of depth psychology. Maloney strips personified evil and deception of its objective reference. It is all "within," that same "within" that centering prayer conveys us toward in order for us to participate existentially in the "incarnational nature of Christ."

But what do we do if the "ground of our being" turns out to be quicksand? If the ideas drawn from Eastern religion end up radically restructuring the way we read Scripture, the way we understand God, and how we interpret the work of Christ, then the dialogue has been one-sided. If the techniques drawn from those sources have exposed us to a metaphysical order of being that is at radical variance to our Christian confession, then how can we claim that Christianity has been "enriched"?

It is not enough to relegate the problem areas of that metaphysical order to the forgotten corners of the collective unconscious. What if they are objectively real? And what is there in those meditation techniques that will protect us from the more fearsome aspects of that reality? The Biblical writers showed some knowledge of that metaphysical order and were able to describe its true nature. They also counseled against attempts to blend the worship of the true God with "seeking after experiences" in that realm.

The Desert fathers initially employed the technique of the repeated prayer, not in order to descend into blissful awareness of Christ-consciousness, but to guard the mind from the real attacks of the Evil One. They also had the concept of "prelest," the idea of psychospiritual deception that every aspiring monk had to guard himself against.

Prelest was not a formulated mode of discriminatory consciousness or a fully worked-out empirical epistemology. It was acute discernment of the subtle degrees of deception, the visions, the religious feelings, and the auditory hallucinations that befell the young monk, specifically to incite him to pride at his spiritual experiences. One orthodox writer points out that many of the vaunted spiritual experiences of today, sought through a variety of techniques, would have been recognized in the early days of the desert monks for what they were: elementary forms of spiritual deception. Little such discernment seems to exist today.

The differences that should surface in a dialogue between Christianity and the Eastern religions are minimized through strategic reinterpretation of the distinctives of the Christian faith. Further, a foundation is laid for introduction of a variety of psychospiritual technologies that will minimize the differences even more, by empirically confirming an Eastern world view in the minds of meditators.

Whether one meditates on the void or unwittingly pays homage to the deceased Guru Dev, the nature of the deception is the same; the plurality of its manifestations ensures both its cultural distinctives and underlying conceptual similarities. There is no integration point between that and a Christianity that consists of a personal God, a reliable Bible, and a historical Jesus who is also the Christ.

Christian meditation will have to look elsewhere. That is a task before us. The search for a viable approach to Christian meditation will have to be grounded in the distinctive elements of the Christian confession.

It may require a close reading of the contemplative tradition of the church in the light of that confession, separating the wheat from the chaff as the writers labor to articulate their experience in the terms of their faith. More important, it may send us back into the pages of the Bible, where the Biblical context will aid our interpretation of the mystical dimension we encounter there. As we explore the writings of the early church, the spiritual experiences and insights of Peter and Paul, we should be drawn back to Jesus himself, the incomprehensible mystery of God among us as a human person, the Creator among us as servant. He speaks of our mystical relationship to him by comparing us to branches on a vine. He shifts our attention from the void of our own emptiness to the inexhaustible depths of his grace. He draws us deeply, not into an empty, world-negating solitude, but into the very stuff of life.

18

Journal-Keeping
The Poor Person's Art

Virginia Hearn

FAMOUS PEOPLE SOMETIMES KEEP journals and, because of their fame, other people are interested in reading what they write. Just before retiring from the army in 1993, Gen. Colin Powell, the first black man to head the U.S. Joint Chiefs of Staff, signed a six-million-dollar book contract to write his memoirs. I don't know if that well-known and popular general kept any kind of personal journal during his years in the military, as he rose in the ranks, but I have no doubt that his autobiography would make better reading if he did.

George Washington and John Adams also kept journals. In high school or college many of us read part of the nature journals of Henry David Thoreau. The diaries of famous Christians from the past continue to be republished and to intrigue us, like those of Jonathan Edwards, Samuel Johnson, David Brainerd, John Wesley, Søren Kierkegaard. In some of his journals, Wesley even used a secret code, which has now been deciphered.

Because for centuries women were given little space in history books, encyclopedias, and other biographical sources, not much could be known about their everyday lives—were it not for the discovery and in some cases the publication of their long-overlooked diaries and journals.

In recent decades the diaries of Anais Nin (extending over 40 years), Dag Hammarskjold, Anne Frank, Thomas Merton, May Sarton, and Henri Nouwen have been bestsellers.

Some people have become famous only *because* they once kept a journal; it is their journal, or diary, that has set them apart and is the source of their fame. Thirteen year-old Anne Frank, hiding from the Nazis as they overran Holland and tracked down Jews, comes immediately to mind. With the rise of Hitler, Anne's family had emigrated from Germany to Holland in the early '30s, so Anne's diary was first written in Dutch. But within 10 years of its 1947 publication in Amsterdam, it had already been translated and republished in 20 countries.

Not until 1981 did the diaries of Etty Hillesum come to light. She was a young woman in her mid-'20s, also Jewish, also living in Amsterdam during that terrifying era. Both Etty and Anne died in Nazi concentration camps: Etty at Auschwitz, Anne at Bergen-Belson. It is their journals that survived.

BUT *I'M* NOT FAMOUS

Most of us are not famous for any reason, nor are we ever likely to be. Right now you may be thinking, "Who, me? Keep a journal? No way."

On the other hand, after a little reflection you might be willing to admit, "All right, maybe I should have been keeping a journal when . . ."

The person you once were—as a younger adult, teenager, or child—is now largely lost. There may have been periods in your life that you realize were important to your becoming the person you are today. Some of us can date the year, even the hour, when we first understood the gospel, and we point to that as a turning point in our life. We know that it made a significant difference.

Now, as we grow older and mature in faith, we may ponder our past: the choices we made, the friends we were close to. There was the thrill of getting our first real job, and perhaps a second or third; a trip to Europe; our decision to move to another part of the country; years of singleness and the questions raised by being "alone"; perhaps courtship, marriage, the eventual birth or adoption of children. So many details of those life-transforming experiences have faded and are gone forever—unless we were keeping a journal at the time.

On the other hand, there are plenty of things we might not want to remember. Obviously not all the important events of anyone's life are positive. Yet the negative or sad ones may be affecting us still today. It is better to be aware, rather than ignorant, of those influences.

Increasingly many women, and some men, are trying hard as adults to deal with painful memories, often long repressed, of physical or sexual abuse. Most of us have probably had one or more experiences of a special person choosing to walk out of our life—or simply disappearing with no explanation at all. How does one live with the anguish of abandonments?

Even experiences like those, however, can be better dealt with when written down at the time in our own words. That is why so many counselors and therapists ask their clients to keep a journal and bring it to their counseling sessions. Karen Burton Mains writes: "I never enter into a counseling relationship unless the person who wants my help will agree to keep a journal. This diarying stimulates spiritual growth like no other tool I know. It becomes a format by which I can direct my counselees to the One who can best help them, and that is God, the wisest Counselor."

IF NOT NOW, WHEN?

Yes, the thought of keeping a journal "someday" does recur from time to time to a lot of people. But "If not now, when?" the Jewish sage Hillel is quoted as asking. In bookstores and stationery stores, we walk by display racks of expensive, fabric-covered "blank books." On an impulse you may buy one, attracted by the picture or beautiful design on its cover, even if the empty pages inside are a bit intimidating. Or a friend or relative may give you one. And there it is. Your journal.

"Journal-keeping is the poor man's art." Contemporary writer Thomas Mallon came to that conclusion as he described his own experience of journal-keeping, while also studying the writings of other journal-keepers over the centuries.

Some journal-keepers, Mallon said, are *chroniclers*. For whatever reason, they record the day's events, usually briefly. Other persons decide to keep some sort of diary while on a trip; they are *travelers*. Then there are men and women who record a personal quest or spiritual search: *pilgrims*. Artistic types, or *creators*, may use a personal journal as a source of ideas and inspiration. Others, anticipating publication, use their journal to advocate a cause; Mallon sees them as *apologists*. Then come *confessors*, like St. Augustine, and *prisoners*: men (usually) who spend weeks, months, or years reflecting on their lives during their incarceration. Finally are persons suffering long-term illness or disability, who then pass the hours courageously writing about their experience. They are, often, heroic *overcomers*.

You may fit in one of the above categories—or perhaps you see yourself in a combination of several. Although people have always kept diaries, recent decades have brought a surge in journal-keeping by ordinary people like you and me.

This phenomenon can be traced to the tumultuous decade of the 1960s, when a lot of ideas and human relationships were in flux. It was then that a psychologist named Ira Progoff discovered that his clients were helped by writing out possible dialogues between themselves and persons important in their lives. That kind of back-and-forth writing went beyond the "role-playing" now common in counseling practice. The act of writing out such conversations seemed to be more effective than merely trying to verbalize them aloud. Often that imaginary discussion led to unexpected shifts of perception. In time, Ira Progoff devised a series of innovative (though rather complex) approaches to "journaling" and has popularized his methods in workshops held not only in the U.S. and Canada, but around the world.

A BOOK THAT ONLY YOU CAN WRITE

Why write? Why keep a journal?

> Though for no other cause, yet for this,
> That posterity may know we have
> Not loosely through silence
> Permitted things to pass away
> As in a dream. —Richard Hooker

Anyone, of whatever age, can keep a journal—and the majority of those who make that effort describe it as surprisingly helpful. It is a book that only *that* person can write. Through doing so they find new meaning for their lives. Certainly it is a better way to record ideas than jotting them down on the back of an envelope or on whatever scrap of paper is handy. Contemporary journal-keeping, as it has been developed by Ira Progoff and many others, is not the same as writing in a diary as an adolescent.

A personal journal can be a remarkable aid to spiritual growth. In the Bible, God's people were frequently told to *remember* what the Lord had done for them. "Remember that you were a slave in Egypt, and the Lord your God redeemed you from there" (Deuteronomy 24:18). Writing is an aid to memory. As we write, God can speak to us through our memories—as well as give us new insight and direction for the future.

As people of faith we want to discern God's will. We want guidance in making big and small decisions. Sometimes we hope that writing things down will help us sort through what is going on in our lives. At such times it makes sense to take pen and paper in hand, since our thoughts often go further in writing than they would have gone if we just sat and analyzed (or worried about) our circumstances.

As Elizabeth O'Connor has noted, when we keep a journal we are taking something that is inside us and putting it outside us, where we can look at it, ponder it, and pray about it. Later on, when we reread what we have written, we may be astonished to find "diamonds in the dust." No one's life is so prosaic or uninteresting that it is not worth documenting. No one's life is unimportant to God.

HOW TO BEGIN

In 1983 I started leading journal-keeping workshops at a small school in Berkeley, then called New College for Advanced Christian Studies (now New College Berkeley), where I am still a faculty member. I always take my own collection of journal-keeping books in two apple boxes to my workshops, so participants can see the many aids that are available. Although the writers of those books take a variety of approaches to journaling and offer all kinds of helpful advice, I can here list only a few basic points that I have found useful in my workshops.

1. Just walk on by those ubiquitous, tempting blank books. It is more practical to buy an ordinary three-ring loose-leaf notebook for journal-keeping. Such notebooks are inexpensive, and, if you watch

for back-to-school sales, even in the inflationary '90s you can find three-ring notebook paper for a penny a sheet, sometimes less. Then, as your writing continues, and the pages in your journal reach into the dozens (and hundreds), by using ordinary notebook dividers you can easily devise a number of categories or divisions to classify the different aspects of your now-voluminous output. Within those categories, you can still arrange your writing chronologically. Don't be surprised that in time you accumulate a number of journaling notebooks. Finally, should it be become important to do so, you can remove or relocate certain pages without destroying your journal's visual integrity.

2. Always date every page you write. And don't forget the year. Later on, that won't be so obvious as it is today.

3. Most of us seldom have time to chronicle a day's events extensively. Rather, ask yourself, "What was important about today?" Note that down, and then add your *response* to whatever it was. Your journal needs to be more than a long laundry list of day-to-day happenings.

4. From time to time reread parts of what you have previously written, and then also record your response to what you have just read. When you do that, you can revise or soften or qualify what you formerly wrote, now adding the perspective of time and subsequent developments. It is a mistake to erase or white-out what once were your honest feelings.

5. Sooner or later the question of privacy will arise. If you live with other people, keep your journal off the beaten path—not on the living room coffee table. Try to find some place where it is accessible to you, but not to others.

6. Finally, don't let journal-keeping become a new legalism in your life. None of us needs that. Rather, look at your journal as a tool to use when you need it. Of course it's desirable to write something every day, but at times that will be impossible. So don't flagellate yourself mentally when you find you have missed days, weeks, even months. Rather, find a quiet or not so quiet place, calm down and relax, pick up your pen again, and resume. Of course you may regret that expanse of silence, but it won't help to feel guilty about it. Your journal is a friend who is always there—awaiting your return.

Do you think of yourself as "not all that creative," not artistically inclined? Whether you are poor (in wealth, or in spirit) or not so poor, journal-writing is a creative art form that is available to almost everyone. "Diaries [or journals] are the flesh made word," Thomas Mallon wrote. And,

> I've learned that the private fingering of ordinary experience can fill up notebooks as interestingly as musings on great events; . . . My own diaries [about thirty of them now] have outgrown the green strongbox I used to keep them in, and I've outgrown believing I'm such a shocking character that they need to be locked up. . . .
>
> Who needs it? I'll ask myself; but I'll write anyway. . . . It's often on days when I thought nothing happened that I'll start writing and go on for pages, a single sound or sight recalled from the afternoon suddenly loosing a chain of thoughts. I've learned, in fact, that *nothing never happens.*

VII

Media

19

It's a Wonderful Life
Charles Dickens's A Christmas Carol and Frank Capra's Film

Margaret Horwitz

WATCHING *A CHRISTMAS CAROL* every year on television was part of what made Christmas special when I was growing up. That "old movie," made in 1938 by MGM (with Reginald Owen as Scrooge), helped foster a feeling of tradition.

Since then, I have seen many film and television adaptations of this novel, including George C. Scott's in 1984 (with David Warner as Bob Cratchit); Michael Caine in *The Muppet Christmas Carol* in 1992 (narrated by Muppet character the Great Gonzo as Charles Dickens); and a Hallmark production in 1999 (with Scrooge portrayed by Patrick Stewart, who was coming off 10 years in his one-man stage show). Clearly a story that keeps getting retold, a number of writers consider the 1951 British film *Scrooge*, with Alistair Sim in the title role, the "authorized version" of Dickens's novella.

Now, however, for many viewers, Frank Capra's *It's a Wonderful Life* (1946), starring Jimmy Stewart, Donna Reed, and Lionel Barrymore, appears to have replaced *A Christmas Carol* as the quintessential Christmas film. Although not a strict adaptation of *A Christmas Carol*,

It's a Wonderful Life also follows a character who views his past actions and their consequences.

When it was first released, reviewer James Agee compared the film to *A Christmas Carol* and called Barrymore's villain "a hundred percent Charles Dickens."[1] More recently, Stephen Handzo in *Film Comment* described it as *A Christmas Carol* "from Bob Cratchit's point of view."[2] Paul Davis in *The Lives and Times of Ebenezer Scrooge* (1990) charts the editions of Dickens's novel(and the various stage, film, radio, and television adaptations), confidently listing *It's a Wonderful Life* as one of them.

In both of these Christmas classics, the main characters are confronted with their pasts in a way that induces change. In one, an evil man, Ebenezer Scrooge, comes to repentance and reformed behavior. In the other, a good man, George Bailey, finds hope after despairing. In my view, both are Christian stories as well as Christmas stories. I look at *A Christmas Carol* as a story of salvation and *It's a Wonderful Life* as a story of answered prayer. Both of them demonstrate the consequences of selfish, as opposed to compassionate, behavior in relation to community.

Charles Dickens (1812–1870) became famous at age 25 with the publication of his first novel, *The Pickwick Papers*, and then for such works as *Oliver Twist* and *Nicholas Nickleby*. He composed *A Christmas Carol* in a mere six weeks for Christmas 1843. He wrote in a heat of passion, motivated by the comparatively poor sales of the first monthly segments of *Martin Chuzzlewit*, along with being angered by reports on the conditions of child laborers. A facsimile of the first edition reveals a beautiful little volume, whose design and illustrations Dickens oversaw. It was his first novel to be published initially as a single complete volume.

A Christmas Carol was an immediate success, going through 10 editions and as many stage dramatizations in 1844 alone. The book was also popular in the U.S. in pirated form. (The lack of international copyright had been one of Dickens's chief criticisms of America, along with his abhorrence of slavery after his first visit to America in 1842.) Given that the novel has been translated into many other languages and never out of print, Patrick Michael Hearn, editor of *An Annotated Christmas Carol* (2004), refers to it as "the most popular work by England's most popular novelist."[3] In Dickens's "second career" as a reader (performer, really) of

1. Glatzer and Raeburn, *Frank Capra*, 157.
2. Basinger, *The "It's a Wonderful Life" Book*, 72.
3. Hearn, *An Annotated Christmas Carol*, xiii.

his own works, he was heard by admiring audiences in the British Isles, the U.S., and France.

This extraordinarily famous man, who met two American presidents, British prime ministers, and the Queen, was born into a lower middle-class family. At age 12, Dickens worked for a few months in a shoe-blacking warehouse, when his father, mother, and younger siblings were in debtors' prison. That experience horrified him.

Enrolling, for self-education, as a reader in the British Museum, he became a parliamentary reporter before writing sketches for a newspaper. Never losing his investigative zeal, especially on the issues of mistreated children, he also worked with one of the great philanthropists of his day, Angela Burdett Coutts, to provide a home for the restoration of former prostitutes.

G. K. Chesterton wrote that Dickens "really did sympathise with every sort of victim of every sort of tyrant." He prayed for all who were desolate and oppressed[4] and wrote a harmony of the Gospels, *The Life of Our Lord*, for his eight children. In this gospel, not published until 1934, he said of Jesus, "No one ever lived, who was so good, so kind, so gentle, and so sorry for all people who did wrong, or were in any way ill or miserable, as he was."[5]

A Christmas Carol expresses a Christian perspective in many ways, some of which are evident in the film and television versions. In almost all of them, Scrooge's nephew Fred enters his office on Christmas Eve, cheerfully greeting him with "A Merry Christmas, Uncle, God save you!"

Most versions end with Fred's defense of Christmas. But none of them fully quotes his entire speech (shown here in italics): "But I am sure I have always thought of Christmastime, when it has come round—*apart from the veneration due to its sacred name and origin, if anything belonging to it can be apart from that*—as a good time; a kind, forgiving, charitable, pleasant time; *the only time I know of, in the long calendar of the year, when men and women seem by one consent to open their shut-up hearts freely, and to think of people below them as if they really were fellow passengers to the grave, and not another race of creature bound on other journeys.*"[6] Those omitted words identify Christmas as a celebration of

---

4. Chesterton, *The Victorian Age in Literature*, 37.
5. Dickens, *The Life of Our Lord*, 1.
6. Dickens, *A Christmas Carol*, 6–7. All quotations from the novel are cited from the 1962 paperback edition (in the Apple Classics series) published by Scholastic Press.

Jesus Christ, and refer to the Biblical view that all men and women are equal before God.

Scenes near the beginning of the 1951 British film show that Scrooge believes that happiness is based on wealth. Yet his clerk, Bob Cratchit, in spite of being poor and ill-treated, is joyful after Scrooge leaves the office. This sequence and others portray a unique quality in Alistair Sim's Scrooge as being horrible and funny at the same time, in the Dickensian fashion of combining "humor with pathos." Sim doesn't raise his voice, speaking words of utter insensitivity in a matter-of-fact tone. He rebukes Cratchit for saying "Merry Christmas," when he is only a poor clerk with a large family. Sim's performance shows an entire range of emotions during the course of his gradual softening in this "conversion narrative."

In all the adaptations I've seen, two men who've come to Scrooge's office tell him that many poor persons would rather die than go to the workhouses. To that, Scrooge replies, "If they would rather die, they had better do it and decrease the surplus population."[7] Scrooge's hard heart is certainly an undesirable trait. Later, his pride is criticized by the Ghost of Christmas Present: "Will you decide what men shall live, what men shall die?" In a way, his actions do decide this very thing.

Although Luke 16:19–31 is not mentioned in *A Christmas Carol*, "what if" the rich man who died and went to hell, never taking notice of the sore-covered Lazarus, had then been permitted to go back and warn one of his "brothers"? That happens when the ghost of Scrooge's old business partner, Marley, dead for seven years, arrives that night in Scrooge's chambers. Marley now wears a chain made up of ledger books having to do with his former work, but none of the later adaptations manages to convey the fact that the chain is "long and wound about him like a tail," suggesting the temptation of the serpent. Further, Marley's hair is stirred by an "infernal atmosphere," as from "the hot vapor from an oven."[8] The reader of Dickens knows that he has come back from hell, and Marley refers to Scrooge as "captive, bound."[9]

Ghosts are not a part of orthodox Christianity, but like the ghost of Hamlet's father, mentioned right at the beginning of *A Christmas Carol* in relation to Marley, these ghosts appear in order to right a wrong.

---

7. Ibid., 10.
8. Ibid., 18.
9. Ibid., 23.

Unlike a conventional ghost story the Spirits or Ghosts of Christmas Past, Present, and Yet to Come benevolently serve to enlighten Scrooge, rather than to haunt him. C. S. Lewis does something similar in *The Lion. the Witch and the Wardrobe*, using images from his own cultural heritage within an essentially Christian tale.

In the Alistair Sim adaptation, the Christmas Past section is greatly expanded to show the genesis of Scrooge's wickedness. When his sister Fan (older here) comes to rescue young Ebenezer from school, we learn that his mother's death, after he was born, caused Scrooge's father to be bitter against him; Scrooge himself becomes more hardened when his sister also dies following his nephew Fred's birth. While an apprentice for Mr. Fezziwig, Scrooge had given Alice a shilling ring that he hoped one day would be a gold one. Instead, a "golden idol" replaced his regard for her, and money became his master instead of God. When Scrooge leaves Alice (Belle in the novel), he departs from any positive bond to community.

The Sim version also shows Alice in Christmas Present taking care of people in a shelter, where a minister recites the 1 Corinthians 13 verses about love being more important than any other gift. A poor Irish woman praises Alice for her exemplary kindness, but one senses that Alice had never married, dedicating herself to the poor in reaction to her failed relationship with Scrooge. In the novel, however, Scrooge's fiancée is shown later in life as wife and the mother of a large family. (That change may be an example of *It's a Wonderful Life*, made five years earlier, influencing this version of *A Christmas Carol*. George Bailey's wife, Mary, also never married in the vision he is shown by the angel Clarence of his town in a future without him.)

Evidence of another possible influence of *It's a Wonderful Life* comes with a character called Jorkins, who, like Mr. Potter with George Bailey, diabolically tempts an idealistic man to work for him. In this case Mr. Jorkins asks the young Scrooge to leave Fezziwig and work for him with young Marley. After the death of his sister from childbirth, the embittered Scrooge does just that, forcing Fezziwig out of business and finally taking over a company from which Jorkins has embezzled money. This seems so convincing a depiction of the period, and so Dickensian (including the name Jorkins) that I was surprised to re-read the novel—and find none of it there! Paul Davis contends that there are two texts of

A Christmas Carol, the novel written in 1843, and a "culture-text" which is "the one we collectively remember."[10]

Also added to the Christmas Past of Sim's version is the sequence of a charwoman coming to get Scrooge to visit Marley on his deathbed, which he characteristically delays doing until his office is closed. When Scrooge enters Marley's home, a film-noir-ish shot dominated by stair rails and their shadows reveals an undertaker seated at the top of the staircase rather like a judge in a vision of hell. Marley points a bony finger at Scrooge, gasping out words like "wrong" and "save yourself," part of the salvation theme carried over into the film. Scrooge rejects his warning.

One reference to Jesus always quoted in the Christmas Present section of film versions is Bob Cratchit saying that Tiny Tim hoped that people saw him when they were in church, because "it might be pleasant to them to remember upon Christmas Day, who made lame beggars walk and blind men see."[11] Tiny Tim has the wisdom and spirituality that Scrooge lacks, suggesting a childlike faith. In Sim's version the Ghost of Christmas Yet to Come shows Scrooge a nightmarish scene, with dialogue taken almost verbatim from the novel, of the charwoman, the undertaker, and a laundress selling plunder taken from Scrooge's room and even from his body. This picture of utter abandonment and contempt contrasts with Tiny Tim's family, who mourn and honor him. At the story's core are two lives, Scrooge's and Tiny Tim's. Part of Dickens's brilliance is that their destinies are intertwined in community. Scrooge's transformation literally saves his own life as well as that of the child.

The most satisfying conversion scene of any adaptation, to my mind, is Alistair Sim as Scrooge waking up to find out that he is alive, his bed curtains have not been taken down by the charwoman to sell, and that it is Christmas morning. His exuberance in saying he is as "merry as a schoolboy," part of his rebirth as a Christian, is enhanced by the presence of the charwoman, Mrs. Dilber. He even tries to stand on his head, sending her shrieking from the room. He calms her on the stairs and gives her a coin, not to silence her but as a present. He also raises her salary by five times, in a move that reverses his earlier decision of letting Fezziwig's office boy stay on, but only for reduced pay. Such actions highlight Scrooge's repentance.

10. Davis, *The Lives and Times of Ebenezer Scrooge*, 4.
11. Dickens, *A Christmas Carol*, 67.

Sending Bob Cratchit a large turkey anonymously, also a sign of compassion and humility, Scrooge rejoins community by going to his nephew's house and dancing with Fred's wife whom he had also shunned. Back in his office the day after Christmas, Alistair Sim as Scrooge continues to forge community, laughing contagiously after raising Bob's salary, and pledging, as in the novella, to help him raise his family. Alive and eventually healthy, Tiny Tim runs to Scrooge and they stand under a cathedral-like arch, while we hear most of the last two paragraphs of the book narrated, and a choir singing "Silent Night." The novel is divided into five staves (stanzas) and alludes to a young caroler singing, "God Rest You Merry, Gentlemen," but the film provides an actual Christmas carol. "Sleep in heavenly peace" also conveys the notion of Scrooge's salvation.

Frank Capra (1897–1991) was the producer and director of *It's a Wonderful Life*, and is also listed as its co-writer. This film is the culmination of all Capra had done; and, like *A Christmas Carol* for Dickens, it is the film he would be remembered for.

Like Dickens, Capra came from humble circumstances, born into a very poor family in Sicily. At age six he came with his parents and most of his family to join his brother in Los Angeles, after a harrowing trip described in his autobiography, *The Name above the Title*. He wanted to get out of poverty and, like Dickens, had to work while going to school. He earned a BS from the college that became Cal Tech, and served at home in the armed forces at the end of World War I. Capra nevertheless had difficult years before becoming established in Hollywood. By the thirties, however, he had become a top director, winning an Academy Award for *It Happened One Night* (1934). He also worked with Jimmy Stewart in *Mr. Smith Goes to Washington* (1939) and with Gary Cooper in *Meet John Doe* (1941). During World War II he made the highly respected *Why We Fight* series of documentaries.

Along with success, Capra also experienced tragedy. "Shortly after winning a freshman scholarship at college, Capra was stunned by the news that his father had been killed in a machinery accident at his recently purchased lemon orchard. The family lost the farm, and Capra had to get loans for school expenses and to help support his family."[12] Years later, in 1938, one of Capra's four children died suddenly. So, like Dickens, Capra understood loss in ways that he expressed in his works.

---

12. Maland, *Frank Capra*, 22–23.

Returning to Hollywood after the war, Capra wrote that he picked Jimmy Stewart for the lead role in *It's a Wonderful Life* because he was an actor who could play a good guy who didn't know he was a good guy.[13] Lionel Barrymore, a loveable curmudgeon in an earlier Capra film *You Can't Take It With You* (1938), also became the voice of Ebenezer Scrooge on the radio, beginning in that year.

Capra's own description of *It's a Wonderful Life* is full of Biblical references. He saw it as a "film that expressed its love for the homeless and the loveless; for her whose cross is heavy and him whose touch is ashes; for the Magdalenes stoned by hypocrites and the afflicted Lazaruses with only dogs to lick their sores."[14] The last line in his autobiography is "Friend . . . . hang in there! If doors opened for me, they can open for anyone."[15] I can't think of any other director as concerned for ordinary people, as we see in Capra's films.

It's a Wonderful Life has a present, past, and future like *A Christmas Carol*, although not all the action is on Christmas Eve, Christmas day, or the day after. The timing of the "present" initiates the theme of prayer. The film opens on the sign "You Are Now in Bedford Falls," the main street with Christmas decorations, and we hear people in this community praying for George including his mother, his wife, and two of his children. A succession of buildings and the voices of people praying are accompanied by an organ quietly playing in the background, "O Come Let Us Adore Him." Buildings are important in this film about a Building and Loan Company, in which George builds homes and provides jobs for others, while Mr. Potter builds an empire for himself.

The action travels to "heaven," demonstrating that the prayers are heard, and initiating the "past" of the film, a flashback narrated by Saint Joseph to the angel Clarence. Clarence has his own prayer, as a second-class angel wanting to earn his wings. This notion had meaning as well as humor in post-war society (filming began in April 1946, less than a year after World War II's end).

In a scene from his early life, George courageously rescues his brother Harry from drowning while other boys form a chain supporting him, a picture of community. The next day, the boys walk through Bedford Falls with linked arms, another sign of solidarity. As a boy in

13. Capra, *The Name above the Title*, 377.
14. Ibid., 383.
15. Ibid., 495.

1919, George subscribes to *National Geographic* and wants to be an explorer. But he gives up going to Europe on a boat trip and to college with his friends after his father's fatal stroke in 1928. Instead he goes to work to support the family.

When George marries, he and his wife give away their honeymoon travel money to keep the Building and Loan from closing during the 1932 bank run. All of these are their investments in community. In the informative *The "It's a Wonderful Life" Book*, Jeanine Basinger points out that the film "doesn't suggest that George was lucky to have stayed all his life in Bedford Falls; it suggests [that] his having had to stay counts for something."[16]

A year or so later, a poor family is able to move from "Potter's Field" to a kind of Elysian Fields, by way of a "Welcome to Bailey Park" sign. Under George's management, Bailey Park thrives as something of a utopia, contrasted with Mr. Potter's hell of "Potter's Field." Diabolically tempted by Potter to work for him, with a high salary but at the price of losing the Building and Loan, George resists and is comforted by his wife Mary's saying she is expecting a child.

The voice-over narration of Saint Joseph, "Then came a war," starts a montage sequence showing every character's contribution to the war effort, the Red Cross, the USO, the war bond campaigns. Documentary battle footage portrays the different fronts of the war, where relatives and friends travel not as tourists but as soldiers. George is excluded because of the ear he injured when rescuing his brother as a child. Footage of the home front with rubber and paper drives concludes with people filing into churches to pray. We hear the narrator's voice saying that on VE Day and VJ Day, like everyone else, George "wept and prayed." One sign appearing outside a church reads, "Sunday morning, August 19th, Special Prayers as Requested by President Truman."

Returning to the "present" of the film, Christmas Eve 1945, the whole town participates in a homecoming for Harry, who has received the Congressional Medal of Honor. The sign "You Are in Bedford Falls" appears again just before Uncle Billy foolishly gloats and brags about Harry to Mr. Potter at the bank, setting in motion events leading to the film's crisis in which prayer plays a critical part.

Billy inadvertently misplaces a Building and Loan deposit in the very issue of the newspaper, with its headlines about Harry, that he forces

---

16. Basinger, *The "It's a Wonderful Life" Book*, 75.

on Mr. Potter, who "took over the bank" in 1932. Now Potter becomes an actual thief, keeping that money and peering out of his office window as George and Uncle Billy search desperately. When George finally begs Mr. Potter for a loan, taking the blame for the money he says "he" misplaced (a Christlike role), Potter calls him a "miserable little clerk" (a reminder of Bob Cratchit). George offers his life insurance as collateral, and Potter responds laughing, "You're worth more dead than alive." This time George believes Potter; his hope is stolen along with the money.

In a small bar, the theme of prayer is renewed, as George pleads, "God . . . God . . . Dear Father in Heaven, I'm not a praying man, but if you're up there, show me the way. I'm at the end of my rope. Show me the way, God." His feeling of worthlessness intensifies. He travels to a bridge at the edge of town, symbolically a bridge between life and death. He intends to jump into the river below to commit suicide. But instead, the angel Clarence (now taking part in the narrative) jumps into the water, screaming "Help!" in order to activate George's instinct to rescue others. George does rescue Clarence but then says he wishes he'd never been born.

Science-fiction music accompanies a sequence where the "future" comes in, a film-noir-ish vision of what his home town and community would be like if he hadn't been born, focusing on buildings as well as on people he knows. Then we see a garish neon sign, the town "Pottersville," with prohibitive warnings like "No Loitering," and "Keep Moving," indicating Mr. Potter's oppressive use of power as well as his megalomania in naming the city after himself. This sequence ends with a return to the bridge and with prayer. Returning to the bar, George finds it changed, now with an underworld nightclub atmosphere. He sees Mr. Gower, a man whose reputation he'd saved, as an ex-convict and an alcoholic. The incredulous George then hears Clarence say, "You've been given a great gift, George, a chance to see what the world would be like without you."

Running through Pottersville, invisible in a different way from Scrooge in his "time travels," George doesn't see the Building and Loan and is told "Oh, that went out of business years ago." The town flirt in Bedford Falls, Violet, is forcibly arrested, probably for solicitation at the "Dime a Dance" nightclub, one of several with advertisements like "20 Gorgeous Girls" and "Striptease." His own house, which was a lively place with Mary and four children, is deserted and like a haunted house with cobwebs and broken glass.

Lacking George's support and compassion, everyone closely connected with him has suffered. His alcoholic uncle is in an insane asylum, and his embittered mother runs a boarding house as "Ma Bailey," not recognizing him as her son. He sees the grave of his brother, who would have died as a child without George's intervention in his accident, and a depressed-looking Mary, who has just finished working at the library late at night. George runs back to the bridge, this time embracing life, described at the beginning of the film as "God's greatest gift." He calls for Clarence, and as soon as he prays, "Please God, let me live again," the snow starts falling, metaphorically a baptism or rebirth.

After yelling "Merry Christmas!" George runs back toward the town, this time seeing the sign, "You Are Now in Bedford Falls." He greets not only the people who call to him in friendly recognition, but also the buildings representing faith and community: a movie theater featuring *The Bells of St. Mary's*, the Emporium, and Bailey's Building and Loan. He even runs up to the "Bedford Falls Trust and Savings Bank" (not Pottersville's). The contrast between the two men is never so great as when George calls out, "Merry Christmas, Mr. Potter," to this tyrant who replies, "Happy New Year to you—in jail!" Able even to embrace his enemy in the joy of living in this rediscovered world, George also greets the reporters, the bank examiner, and the sheriff there to arrest him.

But Mary had gotten the word out about his predicament, and now George and his family are surrounded by people whom he has helped, giving back to him with their contributions. When his brother arrives, after flying home in response to Mary's telegram, George says emotionally, "Harry, Harry," to the soldier in uniform whose childhood tombstone he had "seen" in the Potter's Field graveyard. Harry Bailey speaks a central philosophy of the film with his toast, "To my brother, George Bailey, the richest man in town." George is *not* worth more dead than alive; his value is not measured in money, but in compassion. The solution is not to take his life, but to put his trust in God, seeking the kingdom of God first, with all the rest now being added to him (Matthew 6:33).

In conclusion, both stories show the value of self-reflection. In *A Christmas Carol*, Scrooge is confronted with what he would learn on Judgment Day about his life, and then was allowed to reform. The gift of Dickens's novel is that we see the results of selfishness and greed, in contrast to the result of repentance, followed by good works from a newly cheerful giver. By contrast, George Bailey realizes all that he does have, even if facing arrest and imprisonment.

His prayer that God would show him the way is answered. At the end of his own resources, and humbled, God "exalts" him.

George had also been bound by his hatred of Mr. Potter. Now he is liberated by his reliance on God in prayer and worship, expressed in the Christmas carol his daughter plays, "Hark! the Herald Angels Sing."

Both stories illuminate the interconnectedness of people and our responsibility to others. Both show that we reap what we sow, even though these stories aren't strict allegories. And in both stories there are life and death consequences, not only for hard-heartedness, pride, and greed, but also for integrity, self-sacrifice, and generosity.

20

The Gospel Songs of Bob Dylan and Mavis Staples

Dan Ouellette

GOTTA SERVE SOMEBODY
The Gospel Songs of Bob Dylan (Columbia/Legacy Records)

MANY DIEHARD BOB DYLAN fans are still appalled by his "born again" testifying in the late '70s and early '80s. They conveniently disregard this period as an aberration in an otherwise brilliant career. Instead they focus on celebrating his early social-conscience tunes in the '60s such as "Blowin' in the Wind" and "The Times They Are A-Changing" as anthems that helped Americans wake from their '50s slumber. They salute him for his artistic courage in breaking from the folk tradition into the rock world when he traded an acoustic guitar in for an electric. They award him with accolades for such classic recordings as *Blood on the Tracks* (1975), *Desire* (1976) and *Empire Burlesque* (1985). And they applaud him for continuing to record stellar albums, such as his most recent CDs, *Time Out of Mind* (1997) and *Love and Theft* (2001). But when it comes to *Slow Train Coming* and *Saved*, recorded in 1979 and 1980 respectively, many Dylanphiles chalk the discs up among the low points of his pop music career.

But the fact is that at the time the tune "Gotta Serve Somebody" from *Slow Train Running* was Dylan's first hit song in a long spell (it cracked the Top 30) and remarkably earned him his first Grammy Award. And, though his overt evangelism-in-song period only lasted a few years, Dylan continues to perform compositions from his "Christian era" albums. Over two decades after they were first recorded, 11 of these tunes get the full gospel treatment on *Gotta Serve Somebody: The Gospel Songs of Bob Dylan*. Overseen by gospel producer Joel Moss, the collection features an all-star cast of gospel musicians, pop stars and Dylan himself in a duet with Mavis Staples giving new life to his poignant and inspirational Christocentric songs.

Gospel queen Shirley Caesar opens the disc with her funky, Memphis-soul take on the title track, preaching Dylan's fact-of-life sermon (whatever way you slice it, you're serving somebody or something) with house-rocking glee. (A Grammy– and Dove award–winning singer, Caesar sang the song at Dylan's request at the Kennedy Center in 1997 when President Bill Clinton awarded him a Lifetime Achievement Award.) Lee Williams & the Spiritual QC's go the cool, soulful route with an organ-grooved rendition of "When You Gonna Wake Up," inspiriting such Dylanesque wisdom as "Counterfeit philosophies have polluted all of our thoughts" and "Do you ever wonder just what God requires/ Do you think He's just an errand boy to satisfy your desires."

The Fairfield Four gives a harmony-rich a cappella reading of "Are You Ready," Sounds of Blackness (the studio reunion of Dylan's gospel touring band including drummer Jim Keltner and Hammond B3 ace Billy Preston) serves an invigorating interpretation of "Solid Rock" teeming with call-and-response vocals, Aaron Neville sings a slow, heartfelt take on "Saving Grace" (with his sweet falsetto intoning the words "I know I'm going to make it by the saving grace") and Rance Allen emotively renders "When He Returns" with a churchy organ accompaniment.

Highlights include Dottie Peoples singing Dylan's prayer "I Believe in You" with gospel piano/organ embellishments and ringing electric guitar licks and Mighty Clouds of Joy (the preeminent gospel singing group since 1955) launching into a rollicking take on "Saved."

One of the biggest career-spanning complaints about the artistry of Bob Dylan is his thin, reedy and often off-key voice. On *Gotta Serve Somebody*, the full-bodied gospel vocals of the participants beef up the tunes and make them come alive in an entirely new and, perhaps for church folks, more reverent way. Yet the collection blooms in the final track when the rasp-voiced Dylan invites gospel great Mavis Staples to take a hard-rocking spin through "Gonna Change My Way of Thinking." The grit in his throat and the holy fire in her vocals make for a great finale.

Especially hip is the on-record humorous conversation the pair have before they take orbit. "Someone's coming up the road, boys," Dylan tells his band, then invites Mavis into his house where she marvels about his seaside California view. Yep, he replies, "You can sit on this porch and look right straight into Hawaii." Dylan then says, "Mavis, I've had the blues . . . I've been up all night laying in my bed...reading Snoozeweek." She says that's not going to work and then suggests, "Let's sing about it." The festive, blues-steeped session that follows is both a celebratory good-times offering and a glistening spiritual reminder of how hope through prayer shines through the storms.

Gotta Serve Somebody, three years in the making, is a special collection which demonstrates, as drummer Jim Keltner says, that "Bob Dylan is one of our great gospel writers." Pop critic Tom Piazza writes in the liner notes of the CD, "When Bob Dylan let it be known in 1979 that he had been born again, it seemed to some that he had renounced the complexity and questioning of his earlier work in favor of what they saw as the pre-packaged answers of religion. As time has gone by, though, it is clear that Dylan encountered the Gospel the same way he has encountered everything else he has looked into—with the full complexity of a whole human heart and mind."

In one interview about his spiritual conversion, Dylan said, "I guess He's always been calling me. Of course, how would I have known that? That it was Jesus calling me. But God's got His own purpose and time for everything. He knew when I would respond to his call." Respond he has, with tunes that, in my opinion, should be given even greater exposure in churches. Song is central to worship; biblically we're encouraged to "sing a new song to the Lord." In addition to singing the hymn "Be Thou My Vision" and listening to the pipe organ postlude of Johann Sebastian Bach's "Fugue in G Minor" (my experience recently at a music-wise top-notch Sunday service at Riverside Church with the Rev. Dr. James A. Forbes, Jr. presiding), how about an inspired choir working up a rendition of some gospel according to Bob?

MAVIS STAPLES
Have a Little Faith (Alligator Records)

This summer at the Umbria Jazz Festival in Perugia, Italy, the streets of the picturesque hilltop city flowed with music, especially in the expansive stone-paved Piazza IV Novembre in the top-of-the-hill old city center. While I was at the fest covering jazz shows, I became distracted by a gospel show featuring Bobby Jones and his Nashville Super Choir. Jones held sway over the piazza masses with a riveting, slayed-in-the-spirit performance. Curiosity drew me to the stage and exuberance kept me glued. In fact, Jones and co. forced me to miss Burt Bacharach's concurrent appearance in the arena venue down the hill. My consolation prize was the choir dissing war and singing Burt's "What the World Needs Now Is Love." Heavenly.

Upon returning home, I was greeted with more gospel, albeit of a different variety: an advance CD by Mavis Staples, the daughter of the late music legend Pops Staples and a member of her dad's Staples Singers group that was inducted into the Rock 'n' Roll Hall of Fame in 1999. The Staples were known for their gospel-rooted tunes inspired by rhythm & blues seasoning and spurred into action by social and political injustice.

The new Mavis Staples album, *Have a Little Faith*, is her first solo album of new material since 1993 and is a solid roots-music disc of Christocentric material leavened by funk and soul power. On the surface level, the album rocks with a cooking beat, and unlike most "Christian" pop and even the Nashville Super Choir, teaches rather than thumps the Bible. By all measures, her album has been a commercial and critical success, garnering Staples showcase performance opportunities as well as offering her the fortuity of being the opening act at recent Al Green shows.

While music aficionados are re-embracing Staples' grace and vibrancy as a performer, I find that *Have a Little Faith* goes much deeper upon a second round of listening, especially in light of the results of the presidential election. Beneath the pop, there's welcomed wisdom, heartfelt blues and devotional love that trumps the artifice, superficiality and hypocrisy of these dark times. Staples is the real deal—not the new moral-mandate deal that professes belief but glosses over the call to equality, justice and peacemaking.

With her smoky contralto and ease of conviction, Mavis leans back and sings it like it is. And that too is heavenly—a respite from the bracing for the next four years as well as an inspiration for hope. As she sings in the soul-dripping "Ain't No Better Than You," racism is still alive and rampant ("Watching a brother struggle and suffer because of his color . . . You wanna step out but they won't let you in"). Her advice? Stand your ground and persevere: "In this life you stand up and fight/Change will come but not overnight."

Staples recognizes that God is there for those who "hang on" (revealed in her ballad "God Is Not Sleeping") and for those who are blind but still quest (in the funky, slide-guitar spiced "Step Into the Light"). On *Have a Little Faith*, Staples prays for forgiveness ("I Wanna Thank You") and faith ("I Still Believe in You") as well as offers advice for making it through the troubled times on the lightly rocking title track: "Got to fight the good fight/Win that war with love."

The most memorable and catchy number of the batch is "Pops Recipe," a funky tune with Hammond B3 organ flourishes. Staples pays homage to her dad, by detailing his life story (growing up as the seventh of 14 children, picking cotton on a plantation for 10 cents a day, moving from Mississippi to Chicago, fulfilling his dream of playing music) as well as passing on his words of wisdom:

> He said . . . accept responsibility
> Don't forget humility
> At every opportunity
> Serve your artistry
> Don't subscribe to bigotry, hypocrisy, duplicity
> Respect humanity

Pops was indeed a wise man and a powerhouse, but a humble performer. Mavis follows in his path, singing a newfangled gospel from a place of deep commitment and gracefully pointing out that there's much to be thankful for. There's spiritual strength in *Have a Little Faith*, the kind that has the stamina our culture, as it totters on the brink, surely needs.

21

Why Harry Potter Is Not the Chronicles of Narnia

Krista Faries

IN THE FIRST CHAPTER of J. K. Rowling's *Harry Potter and the Sorcerer's Stone*, the name "Harry Potter" is heard spoken in excited whispers on the streets all over England. It is an apt image for the real-life buzz today over the bestselling Harry Potter books.

This British children's series, three of which have been published so far, have topped bestseller lists and have broken records for children's books sales. As of this writing, the three are #1, 2, and 3 on the *New York Times* bestseller list. The fourth book, not yet published, is already #6 on Amazon-dot-com's bestseller list, based on pre-order sales. And these books aren't being bought just for kids. They are also topping the bestseller lists on college campuses across the U.S. In England, a separate edition, with a more subdued cover, was published to cater to the adult audience. Recently, the third book narrowly missed being picked for one of England's highest literary prizes.

For a while it seemed that everywhere I turned, someone was talking about these books. But it wasn't until one person qualified her expressions of delight by calling them "the new Chronicles of Narnia" that I really became curious.

Early in *The Sorcerer's Stone*, we gather from the excited whispering that Harry Potter is "The Boy Who Lived" (as the first chapter is intriguingly titled). Harry's parents, James and Lily Potter, are killed by the evil wizard Voldemort, but when Voldemort turns on their one-year-old son Harry, for reasons that remain a mystery, Voldemort's powers are dramatically weakened and he is unable to kill the boy. This moment of Voldemort's downfall causes the lifting of the former spirit of oppression he had caused throughout the wizard community. Harry becomes a legend, and the mystery of how Harry survived is one of the questions that lingers throughout the series.

Harry himself is both literally and figuratively scarred by the encounter. Voldemort leaves his mark in the form of a lightning-bolt-shaped scar on Harry's forehead, a distinction that makes it difficult for Harry to fade into anonymity. He also bears the psychological scars of the encounter, and his struggles to face his pain and loss are an important theme—perhaps the most important theme—of the books.

Years pass, however, before Harry knows anything about what happened. After his parents are killed, Harry goes to live with his Aunt Petunia and Uncle Vernon Dursley, who are "Muggles" (Rowling's name for non-magic people). His aunt and uncle embody unimaginative dullness and excessive self-indulgence, typifying the worst characteristics of Muggleness. Ever since Harry arrived on their doorstep, they've not only made his life miserable, but have done everything possible to hide his magical history from him, telling him his parents were killed in a car accident. But Harry has inherited magical traits, which insist on bursting out at the most inopportune moments, to their dismay and to Harry's bewilderment.

Just before Harry's 11th birthday, the truth finally comes out. Harry receives notice that he is to enroll in the Hogwarts School of Witchcraft and Wizardry, England's premier institution for the training of young wizards and witches. He will spend the next seven years there, each book in the seven-book series chronicling one year of school.

Hogwarts School becomes for Harry his first real home—a place where he finally receives the love and acceptance he has always craved and where he can begin to learn about himself and his past.

JUNIOR HIGH IN AN ALTERNATIVE REALITY

Hogwarts is, of course, a magical place. An immense castle with wandering passageways, tall towers, and (it seems) a centuries-old history,

Hogwarts is a wide open door for the imagination and full of secrets waiting to be discovered.

What is most striking about Hogwarts, though, is how very human and ordinary it is. Despite the fact that Harry and his friends take classes like Transfiguration, Potions, and Care of Magical Creatures, the teachers, students, and classroom dynamics are uncannily familiar. This is junior high (to put it in American terms), and all the players are there: the class clowns, the bullies, the teacher's pet, the whiny kid, the friends who stick up for you, the teacher who picks on you. Familiar daily routines—science lab, gym class, the lunchroom—are there too, albeit in slightly different form.

The magical world of Hogwarts turns out to be the perfect setting for a parody of adolescence, with all its insecurity and fumbling, as well as of human nature in general.

Rowling's satire can be witty and alert. She captures perfectly the voice of the frustrated teacher in love with his subject and convinced before he begins that his students will fail to appreciate the magic, figuratively speaking, of it. There are some truly vivid reminders of adolescent humor. This is a world where jelly beans are made in every flavor (ear wax, vomit) and where a spell gone wrong causes Harry's friend Ron to burp up slugs for days.

A PSYCHOLOGICAL DRAMA

Somewhere buried amid the humor (sometimes buried too deeply) is a serious story of adolescence: a classic coming-of-age drama. For Harry, being at Hogwarts is about gaining the tools he needs to come face-to-face with his fears and the pain of his childhood trauma. Magic in the Potter series becomes a metaphor for the power of the human imagination to overcome obstacles and to heal the psyche.

The "moral of the story" moments often read like excerpts from popular psychology. In *The Sorcerer's Stone,* Harry encounters an enchanted mirror called the Mirror of Erised, in which he is able to see his mother and father waving to him. But Professor Dumbledore, the wise headmaster of Hogwarts, warns Harry of the dangers of the mirror:

"It shows us nothing more or less than the deepest, most desperate desire of our hearts . . . However, this mirror will give us neither knowledge or truth. Men have wasted away before it, entranced by what they have seen, or been driven mad, not knowing if what it shows is real or even possible . . . It does not do to dwell on dreams and forget to live, remember that."[1]

In their third-year Defense Against the Dark Arts class, Harry and his friends learn how to overcome boggarts, shape-shifters that transform into whatever someone most fears. The lesson is ultimately about learning to face our fears with both courage and a sense of humor.

Harry's boggarts, however, seem to be overwhelming him. His childhood wounds are reopened by the appearance of dementors on the Hogwarts grounds, and these dementors become what he fears most. The dementors, prison guards from the wizard prison, have been brought to Hogwarts to protect it against an escaped wizard criminal. But far from being beneficent protectors, these guards are enactors of despair. In the words of Professor Lupin, Harry's Dark Arts teacher:

"Dementors are among the foulest creatures that walk this earth. . . . they drain peace, hope, and happiness out of the air around them. Even Muggles feel their presence, though they can't see them. Get too near a dementor and every good feeling, every happy memory will be sucked out of you. . . . You'll be left with nothing but the worst experiences of your life."[2] Under the tutelage of Professor Lupin, Harry goes into training to learn how to ward off the overwhelming power the dementors have over him. These sections read like hypnotherapy sessions, including flashbacks to the terrifying moments just before his mother's death.

At the end of each school year, Harry's personal struggles culminate in a scene where Harry once again comes face to face with the enemy who killed his parents. These confrontations are like a final exam, tapping on Harry's magic skills and the lessons he has learned about strength of mind and character. In each encounter, he comes closer to unraveling the mystery surrounding what happened to his parents.

SATIRE AND SECRETS

While reading the first and second Harry Potter books, I smugly thought myself resistant to their reputed charms. By the end of the third book, I was sneaking out to read during my lunch hour and checking the Web

1. Rowling, *Harry Potter and the Sorcerer's Stone*.
2. Rowling, *Harry Potter and the Prisoner of Azkaban*.

to see when the fourth book is coming out. So what is it that makes these books so appealing to kids and adults alike?

First, there's the appeal of the fantasy. Rowling creates a world with wonderfully imaginative things bursting out on each page. For sheer creativity with language and plot devices, Rowling is amazing. This is a world where anything can happen, and you learn to expect the unexpected, as in the best from the genre of kids' mysteries.

To top it off, Rowling has a remarkable knack for hinting, frequently, at secrets she's not going to tell us for a long, long time. By the third book, she has raised the cliffhanger to an art form, and we're dying to know what happens next. Finally, we keep reading because we've grown to love the characters and just want to keep hanging out with them.

I personally began to fall in love with the books, just a little, when they introduced Hermione, a character that Rowling says is a caricature of herself.[3] Hermione is a rule-abiding overachiever desperate to succeed at everything she does and terrified of failure. For Type A personality types like me, her character is both a needed laugh at ourselves and a kind of redemption. Despite her excesses, she proves to be a likable character and at times provides a needed balance to Harry and his friends' more casual approach to life, using her skills to get them out of scrapes and working out puzzles that baffle them.

BUT THEY'RE NOT THE CHRONICLES OF NARNIA

Their entertaining and endearing qualities notwithstanding, the Harry Potter books are not the Chronicles of Narnia. In a sense, of course, that is an obvious statement and an unfair comparison. Rowling is writing her own story, not C. S. Lewis's. But having heard the books compared to the Narnia chronicles more than once, in the media and among acquaintances, I began reading the books with great anticipation. I was disappointed.

In trying to name what sets the Chronicles of Narnia apart from the Harry Potter books, I see two things. The first is that the Chronicles of Narnia are transformational. The characters grow and change, and so do we. The second is, in a word, Aslan.

Descriptions of Harry's dull and priggish Muggle cousin, Dudley Dursley, are reminiscent of the opening of *The Voyage of the Dawn*

---

3. Weir, "Of Magic and Single Motherhood."

Treader, where Lewis describes the Pevensies' cousin Eustace. He and his parents are snobs, "very up-to-date and advanced people," and Eustace delights in bullying his cousins, Lucy and Edmund, who have the misfortune to be visiting for the summer.[4]

For Harry, the story of the troublesome cousin ends when Harry leaves for school and resumes for briefly irritating passages when Harry returns for summer vacation. Eustace, on the other hand, gets sucked into Narnia by accident (or perhaps not by accident) and Lucy and Edmund are stuck with him for the duration. But Eustace, Lucy, and Edmund go through incredible adventures while on board the Dawn Treader, and by the end they and their relationships have changed. Eustace's personal story is, in fact, a powerful allegory for conversion that readers of *Dawn Treader* do not soon forget.

Far from reaching those levels of growth and change, Harry's sour relationship with his relatives drones on and on. The purpose of these scenes is never clear, unless it's to serve as a backdrop to make Hogwarts School seem all the more special. In these encounters, Harry frequently comes off looking bad as he stoops to their level in retaliation. I was disappointed that Rowling chose to end her first book with Harry implying that he's going to spend the summer torturing his cousin.

Even the story of Harry's psychological healing is less about growth and change than it is about self-realization and the discovery that he is special and loved. It often seems that he can do no wrong—and that affirmation of his self-worth is of the highest importance.

That message, about the need for love and affirmation, tells a certain truth, but it doesn't tell the whole truth about what ultimately heals us. The deeper truth, that we are special and loved and that we need forgiveness and change, is a more difficult truth, and it's a truth that few writers can convey with the power and subtlety of C. S. Lewis.

In *Dawn Treader*, Lucy uses a magic spell that is supposed to "let you know what your friends [think] about you," and she is hurt by what she hears her friend say. Soon after, she encounters Aslan, who, with compassion, nudges her to think about making wrong choices. As Lucy learns, those choices—even those that seem too small to make a difference—can have painful consequences.[5]

---

4. Lewis, *The Voyage of the Dawn Treader*.
5. Lewis, *The Voyage of the Dawn Treader*.

Occasionally, it looks as if the Potter books are about to take a turn toward such a "moment of truth." After a series of disagreements with their friend Hermione, Harry and Ron are having tea with the school's gamekeeper, who gently chides them about their strained relationship with Hermione. But maddeningly (and this is a recurring pattern in the books), the subject is suddenly dropped, on a light humorous note, and is never picked up again. Eventually the three friends are talking again, but without ever addressing the problem. Ron and Harry never seem to feel remorse, or sadness, or anything else beyond that one brief moment of discomfort.

Catharsis—transformative power—is a hallmark of great literature, and the Chronicles of Narnia have a cathartic power that the Harry Potter books do not. At the heart of this catharsis is of course Aslan, a personification of God's love and goodness. Aslan's transformation goes deep, not only clarifying our understanding of goodness and truth, but awakening our sense of wonder.

In the Chronicles of Narnia, the battle against evil is inseparable from a belief that goodness has an inherent power and evil an inherent weakness. While the struggle with evil and temptation may be painful and confusing, Aslan always, in the end, brings truth and clarity.

In Harry Potter's struggle against evil, it often feels as if he is groping through the darkness with very little understanding of his enemy. Somehow, at the last minute, he always manages to stumble on the key to defeating his enemy, but it seems random. He could just as easily have not succeeded. There are some vague hints that good triumphs over evil for a reason, but this is part of the great mystery of Harry's past and Harry's destiny, not yet fully revealed. Also, because Harry's enemies are vividly conceived by Rowling and are shrouded in mystery, they become a powerful specter—and have a stronger hold on our imagination than the "forces for good": a group of gangly (and sometimes petty and insecure) 13-year-olds.

There is no question that there is a darkness in the Harry Potter stories. The Narnia chronicles lead us ultimately into hope, and awe and wonder. They lead us to desire what is good and what is greater than we are. When one reads the Potter books, on the other hand, it is easy to feel frightened and confused and lost. With danger and terror and despair lurking so easily in the halls of Hogwarts, we have no clear basis for hope that good will have the final word, and no clear sense of what the substance of that good is.

Harry's story isn't over yet. There are yet more secrets to be unlocked, more mysteries to be unfolded. Since this is a serial drama, and the books aren't all written, we aren't quite sure what it is leading up to. Will the conclusion prove the books worthy of all the buzz and excitement? That remains to be seen.

Contributors

Margaret G. Alter is professor of psychology and Christianity at New College Berkeley. She is the author of *Resurrection Psychology: An Understanding of Human Personality Based on the Life and Teachings of Jesus.*

Kurt Armstrong writes for magazines, newspapers, and radio. He lives in Winnipeg with his wife and their two children.

Robert Bellah has coauthored books, including *Habits of the Heart, The Good Society,* and *The New Religious Consciousness.*

Bob Buford is the author of *Halftime: Changing Your Game Plan from Success to Significance, Finishing Well: What People Who "Really Live" Do Differently,* and other books. He is the founder of Leadership Network (leadnet.org) and Halftime (halftime.org).

Krista Faries is a freelance writer and editor who lives in Albany, California. She often writes and presents on transportation issues.

David Fetcho and Susan English Fetcho are visiting professors of arts and worship and artists in residence at New College Berkeley. As founders and creative directors of foundlight.tv, they bring their experience as performance directors to the creation of compelling video content.

Sharon Gallagher is editor of *Radix* magazine and associate director of New College Berkeley. She is also author of *Finding Faith: Life-Changing Encounters with Christ.*

David W. Gill is an ethics writer and teacher based in Oakland and Berkeley, California. He is the author of books that include *The Word* of God in the Ethics of Jacques Ellul* and *Becoming Good: Building Moral Character*.

Joel B. Green is professor of New Testament Interpretation and associate dean for the Center for Advanced Theological Studies at Fuller Theological Seminary. He is the author of *Seized by Truth: Reading the Bible as Scripture* and many other books.

Os Guinness is an author and social critic. His books include *The Call: Finding and Fulfilling the Central Purpose of Your Life* and his newest, *The Case for Civility*.

Walter R. Hearn is professor of Christianity and science at New College Berkeley. He is coauthor of *Teaching Science in a Climate of Controversy* and author of *Being a Christian in Science*.

Virginia Hearn is professor of communications at New College Berkeley and copy editor for *Radix* magazine. Her books include *Just As I Am: Journal-Keeping for Spiritual Growth*, *Our Struggle to Serve*, and *What They Did Right*.

Donald Heinz is professor of religious studies at Chico State University. He is the author of *The Last Passage* and many journal articles.

Margaret McBride Horwitz is visiting professor of Christianity and literature at New College Berkeley. She often lectures on the novels of Jane Austen and their film versions.

Mark Labberton is director of the Lloyd John Ogilvie Institute for Preaching at Fuller Theological Seminary. He is also the author of *The Dangerous Act of Worship*.

Henri Nouwen was the author of many books and articles including *The Return of The Prodigal Son* and *Here and Now: Living in the Spirit*.

Earl F. Palmer is preaching pastor in residence at the National Presbyterian Church in Washington DC and heads Earl Palmer Ministries. He is the author of many books, including *Prayer between Friends* and *Salvation by Surprise*.

Dan Ouellette is the *Radix* music editor and the Jazz Notes columnist for *Billboard*. He is the author of *Ron Carter: Finding the Right Notes*.

Susan S. Phillips is executive director of New College Berkeley and teaches Christian spirituality at the Graduate Theological Union and other seminaries. She is the author of *Candlelight: Illuminating the Art of Spiritual Direction*.

Steve Scott is the director of CANA (canagroup.org). His most recent book is a revised/expanded version of *Crying for a Vision*, available from alivingdog.com.

Luci Shaw is the *Radix* poetry editor and has published many volumes of poetry, including *The Green Earth* and many volumes of prose, including *The Crime of Living Cautiously*.

Permissions

All the articles listed below were originally published in *Radix* magazine and are reprinted with permission:

The Good Life: Wholeness and Meaning:

"Reflections on a Meaning-Filled Life," by Bob Buford (34:1, 2008); "Wounds of Childhood and the Grace of God," by Margaret G. Alter (24:4, 1997).

Discipleship: Call and Response:

"The Constellation of God's Call," by Mark Labberton (22:4, 1994); "Knowing Means Doing," by Os Guinness (18:1, 1987); "The Earth is the Lord's: Stewardship in an Age of Crisis," by Sharon Gallagher (33:2, 2007).

Contemporary Challenges:

"Modern Technology: Servant and Master," by David W. Gill (30:2, 2003); "Finding Your Way in Science and Faith," by Walter R. Hearn (31:2, 2004); "Why Love Will Always Be a Poor Investment," by Kurt Armstrong (32:1, 2005).

The Word Speaks to Life:

"Guess Who's Coming to Dinner: Sitting at the Table with the Prodigal Son," by Joel B. Green (28:4, 2001); "Theological Themes in the Fiction of C. S. Lewis: Good and Evil in the Chronicles of Narnia," by Earl F. Palmer (34:4, 2009); "Care of Souls in Today's America," by Robert Bellah (28:1, 2000).

Art and Soul:

"The Need to Pay Attention: Darkness, Light, and the Visionary Eye," by Luci Shaw (32:3, 2006); The Rich Legacy of Christian Music," by Donald Heinz (32:4, 2006); "The Art of Worship: Breaking Our Tools to Receive God's Gifts," by David and Susan Fetcho (27:3, 2000).

Spiritual Formation:

"Sabbath Living," by Susan Phillips (32:3. 2006); "East Meets West: The Distinctives of Christian Meditation," by Steve Scott (27:3, 2000); "Journal-Keeping: The Poor Person's Art," by Virginia Hearn (23:2, 1995).

Media:

"It's A Wonderful Life: Charles Dickens's A Christmas Carol and Frank Capra's Film," by Margaret Horwitz, (32:4, 2006); "The Gospel Music of Bob Dylan and Mavis Staples," by Dan Ouellette (31:2, 2004; 30:2, 2003), "Why Harry Potter Is Not the Chronicles of Narnia," by Krista Faries (27:3, 2000).

The article "Intimacy, Fecundity, and Ecstasy" (15:6, 1984) © The Henri Nouwen Legacy Trust. Used by permission. The themes in this article were later expanded by Henri Nouwen and published as *Lifesigns: Intimacy, Fecundity, and Ecstasy in Christian Perspective*. Published by Doubleday Religion, a division of Random House.

Bibliography

MARGARET G. ALTER

Bowen, Murray. "On the Differentiation of Self." In *Family Therapy in Clinical Practice*, edited by Murray Bowen, 467–528. New York: Arnson, 1985.
Coontz, Stephanie. *The Way We Never Were: American Families and the Nostalgia Trap*. New York: Basic Books, 1992.
Coontz, Stephanie. "Where Are the Good Old Days?" *Modern Maturity*, May-June 1996, 13–19.
Fraiberg, Selma. *The Magic Years: Understanding and Handling the Problems of Early Childhood*. New York: Scribner, 1959.
Hoffman, Martin. "Is Altruism Part of Human Nature?" *Journal of Personality and Social Psychology* 40 (1981) 121–37.
Lewis, C. S. "Pilgrim's Problem." In *Poems*, 119–20. New York: Harcourt, Brace, Jovanovich, 1964.
Pippert, Rebecca Manley. *Hope Has Its Reasons: From the Search for Self to the Surprise of Faith*. San Francisco: Harper & Row, 1989.

ROBERT BELLAH

Borg, Marcus. *The God We Never Knew: Beyond Dogmatic Religion to a More Authentic Contemporary Faith*. San Francisco: HarperSanFrancisco, 1997.

BOB BUFORD

Collins, James. *Good to Great and the Social Sectors: Why Business Thinking Is Not the Answer*. Boulder, CO: J. Collins, 2005.
Crabb, Lawrence J. *Inside Out*. Colorado Springs: NavPress, 1988.
Nouwen, Henri J. M., with Michael J. Christensen and Rebecca J. Laird. *Spiritual Direction: Wisdom for the Long Walk of Faith*. San Francisco: HarperSanFrancisco, 2006.

KRISTA FARIES

Lewis, C. S. *The Voyage of the Dawn Treader*; with illustrations by Pauline Baynes. The Chronicles of Narnia. New York: Macmillan, 1952.
Rowling, J. K. *Harry Potter and the Prisoner of Azkaban*. New York: Scholastic, 1999.

———. *Harry Potter and the Sorcerer's Stone*. New York: Scholastic, 1997.
Weir, Margaret. "Of Magic and Single Motherhood." Mothers Who Think. *Salon*, March 31, 1999. Online: http://www.salon.com/mwt/feature/1999/03/cov_31featureb.html/.

DAVID W. GILL

Ellul, Jacques. *The Presence of the Kingdom*. A Seabury Paperback. New York: Seabury, 1967.
———. *The Technological Society*. New York: Vintage, 1964.
Grant, George P. *Technology and Justice*. Notre Dame: University of Notre Dame Press, 1986.
Mitcham, Carl. *Thinking through Technology: The Path between Engineering and Philosophy*. Chicago: University of Chicago Press, 1994.
Monsma, Stephen V., editor. *Responsible Technology: A Christian Perspective*. Grand Rapids: Eerdmans, 1986.
Postman, Neil. *Technopoly: The Surrender of Culture to Technology*. New York: Vintage, 1992.
Tenner, Edward. *Why Things Bite Back: Technology and the Revenge of Unintended Consequences*. New York: Knopf, 1996.

VIRGINIA HEARN

Hearn, Virginia. *Just As I Am: Journal-Keeping for Spiritual Growth*. Grand Rapids: Revell (now Baker), 1994.
(Parts of the above article have been adapted from this book, which is now available at, or can be ordered from, any bookstore.)

Kelsey, Morton T. *Adventure Inward: Christian Growth through Personal Journal Writing*. Minneapolis: Augsburg, 1980.
Klug, Ronald. *How to Keep a Spiritual Journal*. Minneapolis: Augsburg, 1993.
Mallon, Thomas. *A Book of One's Own: People and Their Diaries*. New York: Ticknor & Fields, 1984.
O'Connor, Elizabeth. *Letters to Scattered Pilgrims*. New York: Harper & Row, 1979.
(You'll find two good chapters on journaling in this book.)

Progoff, Ira. *At a Journal Workshop: The Basic Text and Guide for Using the Intensive Journal*. New York: Dialogue House Library, 1975.
(This is the journal-keeping classic, but it's not an easy read until you've been in a Progoff workshop.)

Shaw, Luci. *Life Path: Personal and Spiritual Growth through Journal Writing*. Portland, OR: Multnomah Press, 1991.
Smith, Margaret D. *Journal Keeper*. Grand Rapids: Eerdmans, 1992.

WALTER R. HEARN

Alexander, Denis. *Beyond Science*. Philadelphia: Holman, 1972.
———. *Rebuilding the Matrix: Science and Faith in the 21st Century*. Grand Rapids: Zondervan, 2003.
Barbour, Ian G. *Issues in Science and Religion*. Englewood Cliffs, NJ: Prentice-Hall, 1966.

———. *Religion in an Age of Science*. San Francisco: Harper & Row, 1990.
———. *When Science Meets Religion*. San Francisco: HarperSanFrancisco, 2000.
Behe, Michael J. *Darwin's Black Box: The Biochemical Challenge to Evolution*. 10th anniversary ed. New York: Free Press, 2006.
Dembski, William A. *The Design Inference: Eliminating Chance through Small Probabilities*. Cambridge Studies in Probability, Induction, and Decision Theory. Cambridge University Press, 1998.
———. *The Design Revolution: Answering the Toughest Questions about Intelligent Design*. Downers Grove, IL: InterVarsity, 2004.
———. *No Free Lunch: Why Specified Complexity Cannot Be Purchased without Intelligence*. Lanham, MD: Rowman & Littlefield, 2002.
Giberson, Karl W. *Worlds Apart: The Unholy War between Religion and Science*. Kansas City, MO: Beacon Hill, 1993.
Giberson, Karl W., and Donald A. Yerxa. *Species of Origins: America's Search for a Creation Story*. American Intellectual Culture. Lanham, MD: Rowman & Littlefield, 2002.
Hearn, Walter R. *Being a Christian in Science*. Downers Grove, IL: InterVarsity, 1997.
Johnson, Phillip E. *Darwin on Trial*. 2nd ed. Downers Grove, IL: InterVarsity, 1993.
———. *The Right Questions: Truth, Meaning & Public Debate*. Downers Grove, IL: InterVarsity, 2002.
———. *The Wedge of Truth: Splitting the Foundations of Naturalism*. Downers Grove, IL: InterVarsity, 2000.
Polkinghorne, John C. *Belief in God in an Age of Science*. The Terry Lectures. New Haven: Yale University Press, 1998.
———. *The Faith of a Physicist: Reflections of a Bottom-Up Thinker*. Gifford Lectures 1993/94. Princeton: Princeton University Press, 1994.
———. *The Faith of a Physicist: Reflections of a Bottom-Up Thinker*. Theology and Science. Minneapolis: Fortress, 1996.
Ramm, Bernard. *The Christian View of Science and Scripture*. Grand Rapids: Eerdmans, 1954.
Russell, Robert John. *Fifty Years in Science and Religion: Ian G. Barbour and His Legacy*. Ashgate Science and Religion Series. Aldershot, UK: Ashgate, 2004.
Templeton Foundation. *Who's Who in Theology and Science: An International Biographical and Bibliographical Guide to Individuals and Organizations Interested in the Interaction of Theology and Science*. New York: Continuum, 1996.
Templeton, John Marks, editor. *Evidence of Purpose: Scientists Discover the Creator*. New York: Continuum, 1994.
Wells, Jonathan. *Icons of Evolution: Science or Myth? Why Much of What We Teach about Evolution Is Wrong*, illustrated by Jodi F. Sjogren. Washington DC: Regnery, 2000.
Witham, Larry. *By Design: Science and the Search for God*. San Francisco: Encounter, 2003.
Woodward, Thomas. *Doubts about Darwin: A History of Intelligent Design*. Grand Rapids: Baker, 2003.

DONALD HEINZ

Rüber, Johannes. *Bach and the Heavenly Choir*. Translated by Maurice Michael. Cleveland: World, 1956.

MARGARET MCBRIDE HORWITZ

Basinger, Jeanine, in collaboration with Trustees of the Frank Capra Archives. *The "It's a Wonderful Life" Book*. New York: Knopf, 1986.
Capra, Frank, director and producer. *Frank Capra's "It's a Wonderful Life."* Presented by Liberty Films. Screenplay by Frances Goodrich, et al. Los Angeles: Republic Pictures Home Video; distributed by Artisan Home Entertainment, 1998. DVD.
———. *The Name above the Title: An Autobiography*. New York: Macmillan, 1971.
Chesterton, G. K. *The Victorian Age in Literature*. Thirsk, UK: House of Stratus, 2001.
Davis, Paul. *The Lives and Times of Ebenezer Scrooge*. New Haven: Yale University Press, 1990.
Desmond-Hurst, Brian, producer and director. *Scrooge*. Presented by Renown Pictures Corporation; George Minter Presents. Adaptation and screenplay by Noel Langley. Tulsa, OK: VCI Home Video, 1999. DVD.
Dickens, Charles. *The Annotated Christmas Carol: A Christmas Carol in Prose*. Edited with an introduction, notes, and bibliography by Michael Patrick Hearn. New York. Norton, 2004.
———. *Christmas Books*. London: Duckworth, 2005.
———. *A Christmas Carol*, illustrated by John Leech. A facsimile of the first edition. Introduction by Edgar Johnson. New York: Columbia University Press, 1956.
———. *A Christmas Carol*. Apple Classics. An Apple Paperback. New York: Scholastic, 1962.
———. *A Christmas Carol, The Chimes, and The Cricket on the Hearth*, introduced by Katherine Kroeber Wiley. Barnes & Noble Classics. New York: Barnes & Noble, 2004.
———. *The Life of Our Lord*. Nashville: Oliver-Nelson, 1991.
———. *Selected Letters of Charles Dickens*. Edited and arranged by David Paroissien. Boston: Twayne, 1985.
Glatzer, Richard, and John Raeburn, editors. *Frank Capra: The Man and His Films*. Ann Arbor Paperbacks. Ann Arbor: University of Michigan Press, 1975.
Guida, Fred. *A Christmas Carol and Its Adaptations: A Critical Examination of Dickens's Story and Its Productions on Screen and Television*. Jefferson, NC: McFarland, 2000.
Jordan, John O., editor. *The Cambridge Companion to Charles Dickens*. Cambridge Companions to Literature. Cambridge: Cambridge University Press, 2001.
Kaplan, Fred. *Dickens: A Biography*. Baltimore: Johns Hopkins University Press, 1998.
Maland, Charles J. *Frank Capra*. Twayne's Theatrical Arts Series. Boston: Twayne, 1995.
Pointer, Michael. *Charles Dickens on the Screen: The Film, Television, and Video Adaptations*. Metuchen, NJ: Scarecrow, 1996.

DAN OUELLETTE

Dylan, Bob. *Gotta Serve Somebody: The Gospel Songs of Bob Dylan*. New York: Columbia, © 2003. CK 89015 Columbia. CD.
Staples, Mavis. *Have a Little Faith*. Chicago: Alligator, © 2004. ALCD 4899 Alligator. CD.

EARL F. PALMER

Lewis, C. S. *The Horse and His Boy*, with illustrations by Pauline Baynes. The Chronicles of Narnia. New York: Macmillan, 1954.

———. *The Letters of C. S. Lewis*. Edited with a memoir by W. H. Lewis. Revised and enlarged edition by Walter Hooper. San Diego: Harcourt Brace, 1993.
———. *The Lion, the Witch and the Wardrobe: A Story for Children*, with illustrations by Pauline Baynes. The Chronicles of Narnia. New York: Macmillan, 1950.
———. *The Magician's Nephew*, with illustrations by Pauline Baynes. The Chronicles of Narnia. New York: Macmillan, 1966.
———. *The Screwtape Letters*. New York: Macmillan, 1943.
———. *The Silver Chair*, with illustrations by Pauline Baynes. The Chronicles of Narnia. New York: Macmillan, 1953.
———. *The Voyage of the Dawn Treader*; with illustrations by Pauline Baynes. The Chronicles of Narnia. New York: Macmillan, 1952.

SUSAN S. PHILLIPS

Aristotle. *Nicomachean Ethics*. Translated by David Ross. Revised with an introduction and notes by Lesley Brown. Oxford: Oxford University Press, 2009.
Baab, Lynne M. *Sabbath Keeping: Finding Freedom in the Rhythms of Rest*. Downers Grove, IL: InterVarsity, 2005.
Farrell, Edward. "Foreword." In *As Bread That Is Broken*, by Peter G. Van Breemen. Denville, NJ: Dimension, 1974.
Georgios, Archimandrite. "The Neptic And Hesychastic Character of Orthodox Athonite Monasticism." Online: http://www.greekorthodoxchurch.org/neptic_monasticism.html/.
Haidt, Jonathan. "Elevation and the Positive Psychology of Morality." In *Flourishing: Positive Psychology and the Life Well-Lived*, edited by Corey L. M. Keyes and Jonathan Haidt 275–89. Washington DC: American Psychological Association, 2003.
Heschel, Abraham Joshua. *The Sabbath: Its Meaning for Modern Man*. Boston: Shambhala, 2003.
Lawrence of the Resurrection, Brother. *The Practice of the Presence of God*. Translated by Mary David. The Spiritual Masters Series. New York: Paulist, 1978.
Peterson, Eugene H. *Christ Plays in Ten Thousand Places: A Conversation in Spiritual Theology*. London: Hodder & Stoughton, 2005.
Robinson, Marilynne. "Facing Reality." In *The Death of Adam: Essays on Modern Thought*, 76–86. Boston: Houghton Mifflin, 1998.

STEVE SCOTT

Berger, Peter L. *The Heretical Imperative: Contemporary Possibilities of Religious Affirmation*. Garden City, NY: Anchor, 1979.
Graham, Dom Aelred. *Contemplative Christianity: An Approach to the Realities of Religion*. New York: Seabury, 1974.
———. *Zen Catholicism*. New York: Crossroad, 1994.
Merton, Thomas. *Zen and the Birds of Appetite*. Shambhala Pocket Classics. Boston: Shambhala, 1993.
———, translator. *The Wisdom of the Desert: Sayings from the Desert Fathers of the Fourth Century*. Boston: Shambhala, 2004.
Needleman, Jacob. *Lost Christianity: A Journey of Rediscovery*. New York: Tarcher/Penguin, 2003.

Pennington, M. Basil. *Daily We Touch Him: Practical Religious Experiences*. Kansas City, MO: Sheed & Ward, 1997.

LUCI SHAW

Dickinson, Emily. *The Complete Poems of Emily Dickinson*. Edited by Thomas H. Johnson. Boston: Little, Brown, 1960.
Lewis, C. S. *Mere Christianity*. New York: Macmillan, 1952.
———. *The Pilgrim's Regress,* London: Bles, 1943.
Oliver, Mary. "Entering the Kingdom." In *Twelve Moons*, 21. New York: Little, Brown, 1979.
Shaw, Luci. *Polishing the Petoskey Stone: New & Selected Poems*. The Wheaton Literary Series. Wheaton, IL: Shaw, 1990.
———. *Writing the River: Poems*. Colorado Springs: Piñon, 1994.
Schultz, Jeffrey D., and John G. West Jr., editors. *The C. S. Lewis Readers' Encyclopedia*. Grand Rapids Zondervan, 1998.

Praise for *Radix* Magazine

"*Radix* magazine strikes such a welcome balance in this polarized world, as it always—like John Wesley—announces its text and then 'makes it cross-country to Christ as fast as it can'—; and this, in a way that does not require one to check one's mind at the door. We need more witnesses, like this, to an intelligent Christ-centered faith. I hope *Radix* finds an ever widening, and appreciative, audience."
—**Richard Bolles**, author of *What Color Is Your Parachute?*

"What a joy it is to have a Christian magazine with its own integrity—which has the courage boldly to seek the truth."
—**Madeleine L'Engle**, author of *A Wrinkle in Time*

"I read every word of the 'Jesus' issue. Superb! One of the best treatments of the whole controversy that I've ever seen. You do great work."
—**Philip Yancey**, author of *The Jesus I Never Knew*

"I love *Radix*. It's a wonderful, exciting, sweet, smart magazine. I really enjoy reading it."
—**Anne Lamott**, author of *Traveling Mercies*

"*Radix* has always challenged me to think clearly, to trust the Good News of Jesus Christ right at the center of everything, and to work out the meaning of that hope, faith, and love into the places where I live every day."
—**Earl F. Palmer**, pastor, author of *Love Has Its Reasons*

"*Radix* is increasingly meaty, and the substance of its meat is marvelously diverse and nourishing."
—**Luci Shaw**, poet and author of *Writing the River*

www.ingramcontent.com/pod-product-compliance
Lightning Source LLC
Chambersburg PA
CBHW032058230426
43662CB00035B/595